for Patrick
Noble true
words, fellow pilgrim, friend
GREEN
peace & joy!
Christopher Bamford
HERMETICISM

To Patrick
from
[signature] May '07

Die Alchemische Hochzeit von Christian Rosenkreuz,
JOHANN VALENTIN ANDREÄ, 1616

GREEN HERMETICISM

Alchemy & Ecology

Peter Lamborn Wilson, Christopher Bamford
Kevin Townley

Introduction by Pir Zia Inaya-Khan

Edited by Christopher Bamford

LINDISFARNE BOOKS
2007

ISBN 978-1-58420-049-9

Lindisfarne Books
610 Main Street, Great Barrington, MA 01230
www.lindisfarne.org

CONTENTS

Editor's Preface and Acknowledgments............................ VII

Introductory Words of Welcome.. 1
PIR ZIA INAYAT-KHAN

1. The Disciples at Saïs 9
PETER LAMBORN WILSON

2. One the All 29
CHRISTOPHER BAMFORD

3. Green Hermeticism 47
PETER LAMBORN WILSON

4. Quilting Green Hermeticism, "Texts and Tracings" 107
CHRISTOPHER BAMFORD

5. The Manufacture and Use of Planetary Tinctures 195
KEVIN TOWNLEY

Bibliography 203

About the authors.. 207

for all Green Hermeticists
everywhere

Editor's Preface and Acknowledgments

THIS IS AN "INSTANT BOOK." It is suggestive, rather than conclusive; fragmentary rather than comprehensive; impromptu rather than deliberate. Many important themes are only alluded to, and some, for instance, like the cosmos as a living spiritual Being, the work of innumerable spiritual Beings, have been barely touched on. Whole areas—like Islamic alchemy and connections with shamanism, Taoism, Hinduism, and Buddhism—though mentioned, have not been developed. At the same time, paradoxically contradicting the best of our intentions, the volume is preponderantly theoretical when it should, almost by definition, have been practical.

Despite such probable shortcomings, "Green Hermeticism"—the idea of re-imagining the traditional sacred sciences of nature, transmitted in the West under the rubric of alchemy or Hermetism—seemed, and seems still, too important and vital an impulse in the light of the contemporary ecological imperative to be lost in the ephemera of good conversation spread over a conference and a short summer course. The time is certainly ripe for a more spiritual interpretation of the "inconvenient truth" threatening our planet.

Then, too, there was the dawning realization of the idea's "ecumenical" potential: that the Hermetic and alchemical approach to nature was not limited to the West or to the Abrahamic religions, but was universal. This is obvious; perhaps its very obviousness has served to hide it. Not only is alchemy practiced worldwide—so that there is Indian alchemy, Tibetan alchemy, Chinese alchemy and so on—but the sheer reality that human beings live, and all religions, revelations, and philosophies necessarily occur, on earth and in nature, must mean that nature herself must be a common element uniting them.

The idea of recovering and re-imagining the sacred traditions of nature and cosmos is not of course new. Over the past half-century, beginning with the pioneering studies of Frances Yates (*Giordano Bruno and the Hermetic Tradition*, *The Rosicrucian Enlightenment*), scholars have slowly reconstructed the transmission and continuity of wisdom from the ancient world: through Islam into the medieval West and through the agency of the mysterious magus, Giorgio Gemistos Plethon, into the Renaissance. Well into the seventeenth century, as scholars such as Carolyn Marchant (in *The Death of Nature*) have shown, the hermetic-alchemical tradition provided a very real compassionate, cosmic, holistic, non-dualistic alternative to the fragmentation and alienation of modern science.

But with the ascendancy of the Cartesian-Newtonian paradigm (cemented by the chaos of the Thirty Years War, as Stephen Toulmin, the eminent philosopher of science demonstrated in his book *Cosmopolis*), mechanistic, dualistic science became dominant with all-too familiar consequences. Driven underground, the Hermetic and alchemical traditions then became part of what are now known as "esotericism." There they remained, except for the brief flowering we know as Romanticism. What we propose in fact (from one point of view) is none other than the fulfillment of the Romantic ideal—"Romanticism come of Age," as Owen Barfield said of Rudolf Steiner—of a new, universal, ecological, ecumenical holistic culture in which humanity, nature, and the divine renew their collaboration in the sacred work of the Earth.

The idea unfolded organically, beginning with a Conference on "The Sacred Theory of the Earth," held in New Paltz, New York, over the autumn equinox 2003. At this event, Peter Lamborn Wilson gave a talk (now Chapter One in this book) on the prophetic early German Romantic poet, philosopher, novelist, and proto-"Green Hermeticist" Friedrich von Hardenberg, better known under the pseudonym Novalis, which he assumed to avoid the censors. Peter focused his remarks on the *Disciples at Saïs*, Novalis' brilliant romanticizing of a new science, at once Pythagorean and alchemical and thoroughly postmodern. Oriented toward the future, Novalis, as Peter presented him, seemed to open the way to a truly holistic spiritual ecology. Deep and animated conversation followed. Pir Zia Inayat-Khan, an old friend of Peter's with a passionate interest in

Hermeticism and "Romantic Science," who had talked on "The Four Elements in Sufism," was particularly struck by the far-reaching implications of what Peter was implicitly proposing.

So arose the idea of "Green Hermeticism."

Peter and Pir Zia continued the conversation until, one early summer afternoon some eighteen months later, a first "official" Green Hermetic meeting was convened at the Sufi Community of Abode of the Message in New Lebanon, New York. In addition to Peter, Richard Grossinger (visiting from California) and Christopher Bamford participated. That meeting, in turn, proved sufficiently exciting to the presenters and participants alike that it was decided to extend the idea into a short course. Kevin Townley, a practicing alchemist and spagyrist, agreed to join Peter and Christopher in giving it. Thus, over three long weekends in 2006, the first course in Green Hermeticism unfolded with talks in the morning, spagyrical practice in the afternoon, and poetry, art, or sacred dance in the evening.

The present book can only begin to suggest the possibilities contained in the idea of "Green Hermeticism." It marks only a first halting and partial attempt to explore the riches contained in the magical confluence of our present time and consciousness with the divine gifts now available to all through Nature, understood and loved spiritually in the light of the sacred traditions of humankind. The task is enormous; and remains to be done.

At the same time, we hope that it will serve as a kind of "call" or manifesto in the spirit of the Rosicrucian Manifestos of the early seventeenth century.

These Manifestos—the "Announcement" (*Fama*) and "Confession" (*Confessio*) of the Fraternity of the Rose Cross—called for a "general reform" of science, art, and religion under the sign of the union of love and knowledge. On the basis of humanity's spiritual maturity and the new "Hermetic" understanding of nature now available, the author(s) of the Manifestos proclaimed the possibility of a new culture under the guidance of their Master, Christian Rosenkreutz, who had united the wisdom of East and West for the sake of world evolution. Thus they called for all those of like mind to join them in the research, study, and practice that would make their ideal a reality.

An "uproar" or *furore* ensued. From all the four corners of Europe, in tracts and volumes, Hermeticists, alchemists, and philosophers announced themselves and their willingness to participate in the "General Reform." But the author or authors of the original Manifestos never revealed themselves, causing great confusion; and then the Thirty Years War put an end to such ideals. Naturally, we do not seek to cause confusion or an uproar of any kind. But we do hope to plant an idea and a hope and to find like-minded others who wish to work together to incarnate the idea and make the hope a reality.

*

Many people worked hard to make our attempt possible. All must be thanked with a deep bow and a blessing for their being: above all, Pir Zia Inayat-Khan and all the dedicated, caring, and loving members of the Sufi Community of the Abode of the Message whose hard work made the meetings possible: especially Siddiqi Ferraro, Rahman English, Alia Wittman, Espahbad Yoshpa, Suhrawardi Giebel, Nur-Habib Tiven, Sarah Leila Manolson, Sarah Gilbert Miller, and all at the Abode Programs Office and the Operations Staff; then, too my colleagues at Steiner Books/ Lindisfarne Books, especially Gene Gollogly, Andrew Flaxman, Mary Giddens, Marsha Post, and Stephan O'Reilly, who entered into the project wholeheartedly without knowing too much about it; and of course my co-authors and co-conspirators, Peter Lamborn Wilson (who gave wise counsel and did yeoman work proofreading and copyediting) and Kevin Townley.

"The art of writing books has not yet been invented. But it is on the point of being invented. Fragments of this kind are literary seedlings. Many among them may indeed be sterile—still, if only some grow." (**Novalis**)

CHRISTOPHER BAMFORD

Introductory Words of Welcome

PIR ZIA INAYAT-KHAN

First, let me extend warm greetings to all of you.

It gives me great pleasure to welcome you here for the opening weekend of Green Hermeticism, which is an offering of the Suluk Academy. As many of you may know, the place where we are gathered today is the site of a former Shaker village, which was founded in the early nineteenth century. Some of you may know something about the Shakers. They were a mystical Christian sect who practiced ecstatic dance as a form of worship. They were also extraordinarily artistic craftspeople and sophisticated agriculturalists, who practiced herbalism and sold herbal remedies to support their communal ecology and economy. So we are the inheritors of an old tradition of sacred stewardship of the land.

My father Pir Vilayat Inayat-Khan established the present community, the Abode of the Message, as a Sufi community in 1975, but it was only recently, in 2002, that we established the Suluk Academy. *Suluk* means traveling toward the goal, journeying toward the One. *Suluk* also means fine conduct, an impeccable manner, which is what we strive to cultivate in ourselves here. "Green Hermeticism" marks the first time that the Suluk Academy has offered a course that is not just for Sufi initiates, but is open to all seekers.

Since it is my pleasure to welcome some first-time visitors, let me say a little about our community. As I say, it was founded in 1975, but its roots go much further back. Our Sufi Order was first brought to the West, to America and Europe, in 1910 by my grandfather, Hazrat Pir-o-Murshid Inayat-Khan, when he received the mandate from his *murshid* or spiritual teacher, Sayyid Abu Hashim

Madani, to bring the message of Sufism to the West: to unite East and West in the knowledge of the divinity within. Hazrat Inayat Khan traveled for many years in the West. But ultimately he returned in 1927 to India, where he lies buried in Delhi.

Hazrat Inayat-Khan was the inheritor of an ancient tradition. He traced his *silsila* or chain of transmission in unbroken succession through thirty-five teachers to the Prophet Muhammad. One of the teachers through whom the lineage of transmission passed was Shaykh al-Masha'ikh Hasan Muhammad Chishti. He lived in the western Indian city of Ahmedabad in the sixteenth century. None of his writings have ever been published, but they exist in manuscript, and these manuscripts have been preserved in a very old library in Ahmedabad. I have had several opportunities to consult this private esoteric library. One of the manuscripts deriving from this author is a volume of oral discourses. Here you find the extemporaneous conversations or "table talk" of a medieval Sufi master.

In one of these conversations, Shaykh Hasan Muhammad Chishti answers a very interesting question: "Who was the first Sufi?"

I know that some of you are familiar with the Sufi tradition, so perhaps before revealing the master's answer I will just ask you, who do you imagine was the first Sufi? Hazrat 'Ali? ... He is certainly the saint through whom our particular *silsila* is traced back to the Prophet Muhammad. The Prophet communicated to Hazrat 'Ali the esoteric teaching that was not given to the public. And so, in a true sense, Hazrat 'Ali is an originator, but that was not the answer Hasan Muhammad Chishti gave. He said the first Sufi was a son of Adam, namely, Shith 'alayhi as-salam or Seth, who was a sibling of Cain and Abel, one of the sons of Adam and Ma Hawwa in the Isra'iliyyat, that is, the lore of the Hebrews, which was absorbed into the Sufi tradition. Seth is remembered as a prophet among the children of Adam and Eve. But in a parallel body of traditional lore he has another significance and another name. He is called Agathadaemon.

Now, Agathadaemon is remembered in this parallel tradition as the teacher of Hermes Trismegistus. And Hermes Trismegistus is the prophet, king, sage of Egypt, above all of Memphis, who is remembered as the father of philosophy, and the eponymous founder of Hermeticism. So, in pointing to the figure of the Prophet

Seth, Shaykh Hasan Muhammad Chishti identifies the origin of Sufism with the origin of Hermeticism.

Through the ages the connection between Sufism and Hermeticism has been consistently reiterated. The Sufis often pointed to Egypt as their source, and some of the greatest alchemists were Sufis, including such figures as Dhu'n-Nun al-Misri, "He of the Fish," who was reputed to have the ability to read the hieroglyphs, and Jabir ibn Hayyan, the most famous Sufi alchemist. In more recent times, one of the very great spagyric alchemists of our own era was Manfred Junius, himself a Sufi initiate. So the relationship between Hermeticism and Sufism has continued down the ages.

Indeed, if one makes a comparative study of Hermeticism and Sufism one finds many points of doctrinal contact. Foremost among these, I would say, is the recognition that wisdom, called *hikmat* in Arabic, is an inherent property of the human soul that can never be circumscribed by the confessional boundaries of a particular religion. It is the heritage of all humanity, flowing in secret channels and crossing the boundaries of belief systems. This realization was and is shared by Hermeticists and Sufis, as well as by esotericists of all traditions. And so, Hermeticism was practiced by Pagans, Jews, Christians, and Muslims, and the esoteric work of the Sufis has likewise been opened at times to the followers of various religious communities. Sufis have consistently recognized the essence of their own faith reflected in the teachings and legacies of the prophets of other nations.

This is a very important realization, particularly in our time, when the world is so torn by the sectarian disputes and religious wars that follow from fundamentalist interpretations. The kind of interpretation practiced by Hermeticists and Sufis calls the reader of scripture to seek out the text's inner meaning and thereby to transcend the banal differences that form the substance of the meaningless squabbles constantly shedding blood across the globe.

Interestingly, this heritage of inter-confessional unity can also be traced to Egypt via the figure of the Prophet Moses, who personifies the exodus of the Israelites from Egypt. In the exoteric sphere, Moses stands for the transition from idolatry and tyranny to monotheism and justice, the dividing line between heresy and true belief. But precisely because Moses symbolizes the boundary between "self" and "other" in religion, among esotericists Moses becomes the figure who bridges the gap and reveals the hidden truth of unity, because we read in the book of Acts (7. 22) that Moses was trained in "all the wisdom of the Egyptians." In this view, Moses represents the golden thread that unites paganism and the "religions of the book" in the recognition of the inherent wisdom of the human soul, which is a dispensation of the Divine Guidance.

It is therefore no coincidence that alchemy is so closely associated with Egypt. As Christopher Bamford reminds us in his illuminating essay, the name "alchemy" comes from the Arabic *al-kimiya*, the place of black earth, which is an allusion to Egypt, the place of the ancient mystery school.

For these reasons and many more, it is a great pleasure and privilege to host this extraordinary program of study devoted to the exploration of the sacred and practical dimensions of spagyry, alchemy, and Hermeticism.

To conclude I would just like to share with you something about the background to this course. I owe a great debt of gratitude to Peter Lamborn Wilson, who invited me to a conference on the theme of "The Theory of the Sacred Earth" that he organized in New Paltz in 2004. That event was so inspiring that we decided to host a follow-up conversation here under the title "Green Hermeticism"—a wonderful term that coined to highlight our intent to bring the ancient and perennial wisdom of Hermeticism to bear upon the contemporary ecological task of caring for the Earth.

So our present meeting represents the fruition of a seed planted two years ago. We knew that between Peter Lamborn Wilson and Christopher Bamford we had the historical and metaphysical content of the Hermetic tradition thoroughly covered, but we still had to find a laboratory alchemist, specifically a spagyrist. And so the search was on. Now, it turned out that there was a *salika*, a "wayfarer" or student in the Suluk program, who had a friend in Boulder who was a real practicing alchemist! She directed us to Kevin Townley. Meeting him, we were sure that this was our man. We learned that he was the former President of the hermetic school of The Philosophers of Nature, and we also learned that he is a leader in the Dances of Universal Peace. This represents a point of contact with our own heritage, because the Dances of Universal Peace are occult dances formulated by Murshid Samuel Lewis, who was an original disciple of my grandfather Pir-o-Murshid Inayat-Khan.

The Dances first emerged when Samuel Lewis was traveling in India and visited Fatehpur Sikri, the capital city founded by Akbar, who was the Emperor of the Mughal Empire at the height of its glory. Akbar was also a devotee of the Sufi tradition of Ishraq, or Illuminationism. As Samuel Lewis was making a pilgrimage to the tomb of Shaykh Salim Chishti, Akbar's spiritual mentor, he was struck by an inspiration. He began to dance around the tomb. Subsequently, many dances were progressively revealed to him and he called them "Dances of Universal Peace."

The phrase "Universal Peace" is an English translation of the motto of Akbar's court, *salb-i kull*, "Peace With All." Under the motto of *salb-i kull*, Akbar was able to unite the many different castes and religions of India within a shared vision of the sacred. Akbar was also a patron of the alchemical arts as practiced in India under the name *rasayana*.

A work composed by Akbar's Prime Minister, entitled *A'in-i Akbari*, describes how alchemists produced two miraculous objects for the Emperor, one called the *surajkrant* and the other called the *chandrakrant*. The *surajkrant* was a kind of crystal. When it was held up to the sun at noon on a specific day, the rays of the sun passing through it would converge in a point of light that was used to kindle a candle. That candle would then be kept burning throughout the year as a sacred flame in the spirit of Ishraqi Illuminationism. The other object, the *chandrakrant*, was a stone which, when held up to the light of the moon, would exude water. So you see, examples of the cross-pollination of Sufi and alchemical ideas and practices crop up everywhere.

To attune ourselves for the work that lies before us, let us practice a very brief and simple form of meditation. To begin, please stand up. How do you take your stand in the world? Stand as you would stand before all that is true, closing your eyes, feeling the breath flowing in and out. With each inhalation, let the breath penetrate every cell of your body, right down into the tips of your toes. And as you exhale, empty yourself utterly, releasing every last portion of used gases. Filling yourself and emptying yourself, breathing in through the nose and out through the nose, notice how you are held aloft on the surface of the earth. Sense the weight of the earth pushing up and the weight of your body pushing down; be aware of the skin as the surface of contact where gravity, passionate attraction, is experienced physically. Survey your skeletal system rising up from the earth, your erect spine: congealed stardust, petrified light. Identify with the quality of embodiment in the density of bone. What is the experience of Spirit in bone? Not theoretically but proprioceptively. Feel it within you.

Now, let the breath shift and inhale through the nose and exhale through the mouth. No longer identify with the hard core of your body, but instead with its fluid circulation. Can you sense, first, the beating of your heart in your left breast? And if you can, can you sense the after-effect, the echo of the heartbeat in your hands, in your feet, in your neck, in your head? If you can, then your sense of self has been radically altered from the monolithic, homogenous sense of ourselves that we generally maintain. Now you feel the inner dynamism, fluidity, and rhythmic pulsation that is the constant state of the dark depths of the body. Just as water flows silently beneath the earth, beneath the skin seventy-five percent of the body flows as water. The ripples of the pulsing sense-field of one's fluid nature have no definite boundary, but radiate out in all directions, cascading into the environment at the level of subtle energy.

Now, let the breath shift again, inhaling through the mouth and exhaling through the nose, identifying with your metabolism, the process of digestion whereby calories are broken down, fuelling the furnace of the belly, producing heat and light. Sense viscerally the searing heat of the body and its bioluminescence, which can be seen with infrared vision. Remembering that as the body is transformed in its substance into photons, our spatial orientation is reconfigured as light travels at the speed of 186 thousand miles per second, utterly betraying the image we have of ourselves as situated exclusively in the space of our physical body.

Now, let the breath shift once again and this time inhale and exhale through the mouth, letting the breath become extremely light and deep and refined, breathing *prana*, the subtle essence of the air. Let this subtle essence pervade your body. Feel the reality of the invisible but ubiquitous medium that surrounds us, caresses our skin, flows through our pores, and fills our body with every inhalation and empties it with every exhalation. This is the medium that unites us with every breathing being, the medium in which we participate symbiotically with all green things in the equilibrium of an atmosphere that is a bubble in space wherein Spirit realizes its fulfillment in autopoietic manifestation. This atmospheric bubble comes from the "Breath from the All-Merciful"—the *Nafas ar-Rahman*—that flows ceaselessly from the solitude of eternity, the endless sigh of compassion.

When you are ready, return to your natural breath, feeling in yourself the balance and integration of earth, water, fire, and air, and recognizing your body as a microcosm of the cosmos in which all is contained.

Now let us open our eyes and close with a prayer:

> Beloved Lord, Almighty God,
> Through the rays of the sun,
> Through the waves of the air,
> Through the all-pervading life in space,
> Purify and revivify me, and I pray,
> Heal my body, heart and soul.
> Amen

Uraltes chymisches Werk, Abraham Eleazer, Leipzig, 1790

1

The Disciples at Saïs*

A Sacred Theory of Earth

PETER LAMBORN WILSON

Nature loves to hide (Becoming is a secret process).
　　　　　　　　—HERACLITUS (Guy Davenport Translation)

The sciences must all be made poetic. —NOVALIS[1]

If God can become man, he can also become element, stone, plant, animal. Perhaps there is a continual Redemption in nature. —Novalis

If the world is a tree, we are the blossoms. —NOVALIS[2]

Santos-Dumont, the Parisian-Brazilian aviation pioneer and inventor of the airplane, during a sojourn in his native land in 1934, saw federalist planes dropping bombs on rebel troops. He hanged himself later that day. His last words, as reported by an elevator operator: "I never thought that my invention would cause bloodshed between brothers. What have I done?"[3]

*An earlier version of this article was presented at a conference on "Sacred Theory of Earth" held at the Old French Church in New Paltz, New York, September 21, 2003. My thanks to all participants for their critiques and comments—Pir Zia Inayat-Khan, Rachel Pollack, Lady Vervaine, Robert Kelly, Bishop Mark Aelred, and especially David Levi Strauss, who responded to my paper and later gave me more quotes and references. Thanks also to Joel Kovel, Lorraine Perlman, Raymond Foye, Kate Manheim. Julia Manheim, for permission to use Ralph Manheim's translation of Sals, Bruce McPherson, Jack Collom, Christopher Bamford, Jim Fleming, Zoe Matoff, and the Huguenot Historical Society of New Paltz. An earlier version of this paper appeared in the journal *Capitalism Nature Socialism*.

FOR HISTORIANS TO SAY that A leads inevitably to Z—for example, that German Romanticism leads inevitably to Reaction, or that Marx leads directly to Stalin—is to mistake the bitter wisdom of hindsight for a principle of fatality. Such determinism also insults all revolutionary resistance with the implicit charge of stupid futility:—Since the real Totality is always perfectly inevitable, its enemies are always idiots. Global Capital was inevitable and now it's here to stay—ergo the entire movement of the Social amounts to sheer waste of time and energy. The ruination of nature was fated, hence all resistance is futile, whether by ignorant savages or perverse eco-terrorists. Nothing's worth doing except that which is done: there can be no "different world."

The "Ruination of Nature"

For Christianity nature is fallen, locus of sin and death, while heaven is a city of crystal and metal. For Capital nature is a resource, a pit of raw materials, a form of property. As nature begins to "disappear" in the late eighteenth century, it comes to seem more and more ruined. For some perhaps a Romantic, even a magical ruin (as in the dreams of Renaissance magi and their "love of ruins," grottos, the broken and "grotesque")—but by others felt simply as useless waste, a wrecked place where no one lives except monsters, vagabonds, animals: the uncanny haunt of ghouls and owls. "Second Nature" meaning culture, or even "Third Nature" meaning Allah knows what precisely, have usurped and erased all wilderness.[4] What remains but mere representation?—a nostalgia for lost Edens, Arcadias and Golden Ages?—a ludicrous sentimentality disguised as what?—as a sacred theory of earth?

The view of Nature as Ruin depends in part (or half-consciously) on the concept of a Cartesian EGO SUM alone in a universe where everything else is dead matter and "animals have no soul," mere meat machines. But if the human body remains part of nature or *in* nature, then even a consistent materialist would have to admit that nature is not quite yet dead.

Science, taking over the mythic task of religion, strives to "free" consciousness from all mortal taint. Soon we'll be posthuman enough for cloning, total prosthesis, machinic immortality. But somehow a

shred of nature may remain, a plague perhaps, or the ‹
"accident," blind Nature's revenge, meteors from outer
"you know the score," as William Burroughs used to say.

Taking the long view (and allowing for noble exceptions) science does precisely what State and Capital demand of it:—make
war, make money. "Pure" science is allowed only because it might
lead to technologies of death and profit—and this was just as true
for the old alchemists who mutated into Isaac Newton, as for the
new physicists who ripped open the structure of matter itself. Even
medicine (seemingly the most altruistic of sciences) advances and
progresses primarily in order to increase productivity of workers
and generate a world of healthy consumers.

Does Capital make death ultimately more profitable than life?
No, not exactly, although it might seem so to a citizen of Bhopal/
Love Canal/Chernobyl. In effect it might be said that profit *equals*
death, in the sense of Randolph Bourne's quip about war as the
health of the state (which incidentally means that "Green Capitalism" is an abject contradiction in terms).

Another science might have been possible. Indeed if we reject the
notion of fatality, another science might yet come to be. A new
paradigm is always conceivable, and theories now considered
defeated, lost, wrong, and absurd, might even (someday) be reconfigured into a paradigmatic pattern, a science for life rather than
death. Signs of emergence of such a science are always present—
because science itself wants to deal with truth, and life is true and
real. But the emergence is always—in the long run—crushed and
suppressed by the "inevitable" demands of technology and Capital.
It's our tragic fate to know and yet be unable to act.

Among those who do act, the scientists and warriors, many
believe (for the most part sincerely) that they're serving progress
and democracy. In their secret hearts perhaps some of them know
they serve Death, but they do it anyway because they're nihilists,
cynically greedy for big budgets and Nobel prizes. A few fanatics
actually hate the body, hate Earth, hate trees—and serve as shills
for politicians and corporations. In general most people find all this
normal. Only a few awake—but are blocked from action.

In the seventeenth and eighteenth centuries a sort of three-way
scientific paradigm war was waged in England and Europe. The

contenders were, first: Cartesianism - which denied *action at a distance* and tried to explain gravity by a corpuscular theory that reduced the universe to a clock-like mechanism set in motion by "God"; second, Hermeticism, the ancient science of the micro/macrocosm, which believed firmly in action at a distance but failed to explain gravity—and (even worse) failed to achieve the transmutation of lead into gold, which would at least have secured for it the enthusiastic support of State and capital; and, third, the school of Francis Bacon and Isaac Newton, culminating in the Royal Society—and the Industrial Revolution.

This scheme is vastly oversimplified of course. The actual history of "the triumph of modern science" is far more complex than the usual triumphalist version. We now know for example that some of the very founders of modern science were closet hermeticists. Bacon's *New Atlantis* exhibits strong Rosicrucian tendencies. Erasmus Darwin, Boyle, Priestly, Benjamin Franklin, and most notoriously, Isaac Newton, all immersed themselves in occult studies. Newton devoted millions of words to alchemy but never published a single one of them. William Blake, who skewered Newton's dead, "Urizenic" rationalism, had no idea that Newton was an alchemist. I've always suspected that Newton simply stole the idea of gravity as *action at a distance* (an invisible force) from Hermeticism. Amazingly, the math worked. The Royal Society suppressed its own hermetic origins and (especially after 1688) adhered to the new bourgeois monarchy, emergent capitalism, and Enlightenment rationalism. The spooky nature of Newtonian gravity still bothers some scientists, who persist in looking for corpuscular "gravitons." But the Newtonians won the paradigm war and "Newton's Sleep" (as Blake called it) still dims the eyes with which we perceive and experience reality, despite the new spookiness of relativity and quantum paradoxes.

Admittedly this historical sketch is very rough, and offered with some trepidation. The whole story of the paradigm war remains quite murky, in part because a great deal of research is still being written from a History of Science p.o.v. deeply infected with triumphalism. True, it's no longer fashionable to sneer at the alchemists or write as if everyone in the Past were stupid. But alchemy and hermeticism in general are still viewed in the light of modem science as failed precursors. The central hermetic doctrine ᴏ. "ensouled universe" receives no credence or even sympathy in aca demia—and very little grant money goes to magicians.

Therefore I offer only a tentative hypothesis. It appears that both the Cartesians and the Newtonians happily agreed in their eagerness to discard and deride the central thesis of the hermetic paradigm, the idea of the living Earth. Descartes envisioned only "dead matter," Newton used the concept of invisible but material forces; and their followers turned their backs on any "sacred theory of earth," banishing not only God from their clockwork oranges but even life itself. As Novalis put it, under the hands of these scientists "friendly nature died, leaving behind only dead, quivering remnants." These loveless scientists see nature as sick or even dead, and their search for truth leads only to "her sickroom, her charnel-house."[5]

Goethe, too, attacked the kind of science that bases itself on death—the butterfly pinned under glass or dissected rather than the butterfly living and moving. In his great work on the morphology of plants he founded a new branch of botany. Or rather, perhaps not quite "new." Brilliant as it was, it had predecessors. In some sense it was in fact based on hermeticism and especially on Paracelsus, the great sixteenth century alchemist.[6] German adherents of *Naturphilosophie*, and such independent thinkers as Goethe, or indeed Novalis (who was a trained scientist and professional mining engineer), might really be seen as "neo" hermeticists, steeped in Paracelsus, Jakob Boehme, and the Rosicrucian literature. We might call this whole complex or weltanschauung, "Romantic Science."

Erasmus Darwin (grandfather of Charles), a member of the Royal Society, doctor and inventor, comrade of Watt, Priestly and Wedgewood, wrote a strange epic poem based on the work of the Swedish botanist Linnaeus, in which the sex-life of the plants was expressed in hermetic terms deriving from Paracelsus, who wrote so beautifully of the "Elemental Spirits" of Earth, Air, Fire and Water: the gnomes, sylphs, salamanders and undines.[7] Darwin's marvelous *Botanic Garden* influenced P. B. Shelley (who also admired Darwin's political radicalism); thus Dr. Darwin could be considered a precursor of English Romanticism but also of Surrealism and the ecology movement. His poem has all the marks of the complex I've called neo-hermeticism or Romantic Science. It was published in England almost at the very time Novalis in Germany was writing his fragmentary "novel" *The Disciples at Saïs*, a neglected masterpiece of hermetic-Romantic science-theory (much admired by the Surrealists). Like *The Botanic Garden*, it is long out of print (at least in English).[8]

Early German Romanticism in general can be "read" as neo-hermeticism. Novalis, Tieck, Wackenroder, and Schlegel, as well as J. G. Haman, "the Magus of the North," have been vilified as "enemies of the Enlightenment,"[9] but one might prefer to see them rather as nineteenth century proponents of a seventeenth century "Rosicrucian Enlightenment" (as Frances Yates called it), now stripped of its medieval clumsiness:—a rectified hermeticism, refined by practical experience and dialectical precision. Hermeticism did not stop "evolving" with the failure of the Rosicrucian project. Romantic science was a direct continuation of it; and hermeticism has its scientific defenders even today (such as the well-known chaos scientist Ralph Abraham, a devotee of Dr. John Dee).

During the Second World War certain philosophers of both Capitalism and Communism decided to blame fascism on the German Romantic movement and its "final" theorist F. Nietzsche. Rationalism was defined as *good* and surrationalism as *evil*. Ecologists even today are often tarred with the brush of "irrationalism," especially when they're *activists*. A local real estate developer here in the Catskill Mountains of New York State recently called his environmentalist enemies, a group called "Save the Ridge," "Nazis" in an interview with *The New Paltz Times*. Everything that Capital wants is "rational" by definition and even by decree. Capital wins all the wars; ergo, Rationalism is "true," q.e.d.

But modern radicals such as the Frankfurt School (Benjamin, Bloch, Marcuse), the Surrealists, the Situationists, all decided to try to seize back Romanticism from the dustbin of History and to champion the surrealist and even hermetic program of left-wing anti-Enlightenment, anti-authoritarian and ecological resistance that a recent book has called *Revolutionary Romanticism*.[10]

I believe that today's ecological resistance cannot afford to ignore its own sources in a vain attempt to reconcile itself with the Totality and scientific apotheosis of Global Capital. Romantic Science is

FRIEDRICH VON HARDENBERG
(Painting by Franz Gareis, about 1798)

literally a *sine qua non* for the resistance to ecological disintegration. I would like to argue the case (tho' I'd be hard-put to *prove* it) that the "new" scientific paradigm we're looking for to replace the dead-matter/material-force scientific world-view of Enlightenment/ State/Capital, can best be found in the perennial but underground tradition of hermetic-Romantic science. Something very much like a manifesto for this movement can still be gleaned from the *Disciples at Saïs* by Novalis, a.k.a. Count Friedrich von Hardenberg.

An archetypal Romantic like Keats and Rimbaud, Novalis was born in a haunted house and died young and handsome on March 25, 1801, aged 29. Only the last three years of his life were seriously devoted to literature. In 1794 he met a twelve-year-old girl named Sophie von Kühn and fell in love with her; she died in 1797, as did the poet's beloved younger brother, aged fourteen. Both these ghosts haunted the rest of his life and work. In *The Disciples* they appear as the sophianic heroine Rosenblüte ("Rose-petal," probably a Rosicrucian reference), and the blue-eyed boy who inspires the disciples. This child has all-blue eyes like star sapphires, with no white or iris—an image that relates him to the famous symbol of the Imagination in Novalis's only completed novel, *Heinrich von Ofterdingen*: the elusive "blue flower" that became the emblem of German Romanticism.

The Disciples remained fragmentary, in part because the Romantics believed in fragments; Novalis called the text "fragments... all of them having reference to nature," although he'd hoped to expand it some day into a "symbolic novel." He worked on it while composing his best-known poems, *Hymns to Night*. The story's setting, the Temple of Isis at Saïs in Egypt, was doubtless inspired by Plato, who claimed that Solon of Athens learned the history of Atlantis there from the Egyptian priests. This Greco-Egyptian-Atlantaean nexus already suggests a precise hermetic intentionality, and Novalis makes it quite clear that the disciples at Saïs are to experience not merely an education but an initiation into nature, symbolized by *lifting the veil of Isis*—simultaneously an act of epistemology and of eroticism.

On the very first pages Novalis evokes hermetic science quite specifically:

> Various are the roads of man. He who follows and compares them will see strange figures emerge, figures which seem to belong to that great cipher which we discern written everywhere, in wings, eggshells, clouds and snow, in crystals and in stone formations, on ice-covered waters, on the inside and outside of mountains, of plants, beasts and men, in the lights of heaven, on scored disks of pitch or glass or in iron filings round a magnet, and in strange conjunctures of chance. In them we suspect a key to the magic writing, even a grammar, but our surmise takes on no definite forms and seems unwilling to become a higher key. It is as though an alkahest had been poured over the senses of man. (4-5)

The "scored discs of pitch or glass" probably refer to the Chladni Diagrams, patterns formed in resin or sand by sound, much admired by the Romantics.[11] "Alkahest" means universal solvent; the term was coined by the alchemist Paracelsus. The alkahest dissolves our vision, blurs it, renders it dreamlike. James Hillman once proposed that it doesn't matter much whether we remember our dreams or do anything about them, because the work that goes on in dreams happens irregardless of us. Might this be true of nature as well?

The "great cipher" (in the sense of "code") and "magic writing" suggest the occult interpretation of the Egyptian hieroglyphs, which had fascinated hermeticists since the Renaissance. The whole paragraph thus invites us to read everything that follows as up-dated Rosicrucian hermeticism.

On the subject of the hieroglyphs, Novalis later says this:

> They (the disciples) had been lured above all by that sacred language that had been the glittering bond between those kingly men and the inhabitants of the regions above the earth, and some precious words of which, according to countless legends, were known to a few fortunate sages among our ancestors. Their speech was a wondrous song, its irresistible tones penetrated deep into the inwardness of nature and split it apart. Each of their names seemed to be the key to the soul of each thing in nature. With creative power these vibrations called forth all images of the world's phenomena, and the life of the universe can rightly be said to have been an eternal dialogue of a thousand voices; for in the language of those men all forces, all modes of action seemed miraculously united. To seek out the ruins of this language, or at least all reports concerning it, had been one of the main purposes of their journey, and the call of antiquity had drawn them also to Saïs. Here from the learned clerks of the temple archives, they hoped to obtain important reports, and perhaps even to find indications in the great collections of every kind. (113-115)

Concerning the Veil of Isis Novalis says: "... and if, according to the inscription, no mortal can lift the veil, we must seek to become immortal; he who does not seek to lift it, is no true novice of Saïs" (17). At first this doctrine may sound promethean— the scientist "conquers" nature and ravishes her secrets—but in truth this is not the Enlightenment speaking here. The transgression, the violation of the paradox (you may not lift the veil but you must), can only be achieved by one who has already transcended the all-too-human—the Nietzschean hero who is none other than the hermetic sage.

Like all Romantics, Novalis believed in an earlier or more primordial humanity that lived closer to nature and more in harmony with it, as lovers rather than ravishers. In one sense he means tribal

peoples, "savages", peoples-without-government. But this "antiquity" also includes historical periods as well, such as that of the
Late Classical neo-platonic theurgists, or even the seventeenth century Rosicrucians, as the following passage suggests:

> To those earlier men, everything seemed human, familiar, and com-
> panionable, there was freshness and originality in all their percep-
> tions, each one of their utterances was a true product of nature,
> their ideas could not help but accord with the world around them
> and express it faithfully. We can therefore regard the ideas of our
> forefathers concerning the things of this world as a necessary prod-
> uct, a self-portrait of the state of earthly nature at that time, and
> from these ideas, considered as the most fitting instruments for
> observing the universe, we can assuredly take the main relation, the
> relation between the world and its inhabitants. We find that the
> noblest questions of all first occupied their attention and that they
> sought the key to the wondrous edifice, sometimes in a common
> measure of real things, and sometimes in the fancied object of an
> unknown sense. This key, it is known, was generally divined in the
> liquid, the vaporous, the shapeless. (21-23)

"The main relation ... between the world and its inhabitants:"—
in other words, ecology, the science of Earth's household oecon-
omie, the balance of a nature that includes the human: this is the
great subject of the little book, rising directly out of Novalis's hermetic vision of earth as a living being. This rather radical notion
does not really derive from Plato and the Platonists (as many
scholars carelessly maintain); the Platonists had an almost Gnostic
disdain for the mere shadows of material reality. Tribal and shamanic peoples almost always adhere to some view of nature as
alive, but the idea only re-enters "civilized" western thought with
the Renaissance magi, especially Giordano Bruno, Marsilio Ficino,
and Paracelsus.[12]

For Novalis the true language of science would be poetry:

> That is why poetry has been the favorite instrument of true friends
> of nature, and the spirit of nature has shone most radiantly in
> poems. When we read and hear true poems, we feel the movement

of nature's inner reason and like its celestial embodiment, we dwell
in it and hover over it at once. (25)

"To hover over and dwell in" simultaneously: the scientist like
the poet cannot objectively separate self from nature in order to
study it without also subjectively retaining an existential identity
with the "object." A split here would constitute an ecological disaster. In fact self and world must be experienced as reflections of each
other, as microcosm and macrocosm. "As Above So Below" as *The
Emerald Tablet of Hermes Trismegistus* puts it so succinctly.

> Those who would know her spirit truly must therefore seek it in the
> company of poets, where she is free and pours forth her wondrous
> heart. But those who do not love her from the bottom of their
> hearts, who only admire this and that in her and wish to learn this
> and that about her, must visit her sickroom, her charnel-house. (27)
>   Within us there lies a mysterious force that tends in all directions,
> spreading from a center hidden in infinite depths. If wondrous
> nature, the nature of the senses and the-nature that is not of the
> senses, surrounds us, we believe this force to be an attraction of
> nature, an effect of our sympathy with her.
>
> (...)
>
> A few stand calmly in this glorious abode, seeking only to embrace
> it in its plenitude and enchainment; no detail makes them forget the
> glittering thread that joins the links in rows to form the holy candelabrum, and they find beatitude in the contemplation of this living
> ornament hovering over the depths of night. The ways of contemplating nature are innumerable; at one extreme the sentiment of
> nature becomes a jocose fancy, a banquet, while at the other it
> develops into the most devout religion, giving to a whole life direction, principle, meaning. (29-31)

The image of nature as "holy candelabrum," contemplated by the
rapt adept, seems to derive from a Kabbalistic source, especially the
so-called "Christian Cabala" of Agrippa and the Rosicrucians such
as Knorr von Rosenroth.[13] The *religion of nature* here propounded by
Novalis strikes me as the single most radical idea of hermetic
Romanticism—the same idea that led Bruno to the stake in Rome in

1600. In nineteenth century America Thoreau was the great prophet of the faith, and the paintings of the Hudson River School its icons. In the twentieth century the American Indians re-emerged among the teachers of this path, giving it the sharp focus of shamanic vision. Hermeticism, like shamanism, cannot be defined exactly as a religion, nor exactly as a science. In a sense both religion and science have betrayed us;—and it is precisely in this sense that hermeticism offers us something else, something different. Romantic Science is also a spiritual path. Without this primary realization science is nothing but fatality, and religion nothing but a kind of anti-science.

The scientist poet

> never wearies of contemplating nature and conversing with her, follows all her beckonings, finds no journey too arduous if it is she who calls, even should it take him into the dank bowels of the earth: surely he will find ineffable treasures, in the end his candle will come to rest and then who knows into what heavenly mysteries a charming subterranean sprite may initiate him. Surely no one strays farther from the goal than he who imagines that he already knows the strange realm, that he can explain its structure in few words and everywhere find the right path. No one who tears himself loose and makes himself an island arrives at understanding without pains. (37)

The "subterranean sprite" refers directly to Paracelsus and the Elemental Spirits again: this is a gnome or kobold, Novalis's tutelary (and seductive) Elemental, inhabitant of the deep mines where the poet earned his living.

> Not one of the senses must slumber, and even if not all are equally awake, all must be stimulated and not repressed or neglected. (37-39)

Here Novalis sounds like Rimbaud; although he speaks of awakening the senses rather than deranging them, he hints at the possibility of a psychedelic path—or rather an *entheogenic* path—since the object and subject alike of the awakened senses is a goddess. "Entheogenic" means "giving birth to the divine within." It's a new

name for the hallucinatory experience of the *phantastica;* the term is
not liked or used by those who require no "divine hypothesis."

> Ultimately some who deny the divinity of nature will come uncon-
> sciously to hate that which denies them meaning. "Very well," say
> these scientists, let our race carry on a slow, well-conceived war of
> annihilation with nature! We must seek to lay her low with insidious
> poisons. The scientist is a noble hero, who leaps into the open
> abyss in order to save his fellow citizens.
>
> (...)
>
> Exploit her strife to bend her to your will, like the fire-spewing bull.
> She must be made to serve you. (43-45)

To this the Elementals themselves seem to reply:[14]

> "O, if only man," they said, "could understand the inner music of
> nature, if only he had a sense for outward harmonies. But he
> scarcely knows that we belong together and that none of us can
> exist without the others. He cannot leave anything in place, tyran-
> nically he parts us, and plucks at our dissonances. How happy he
> could be if he treated us amiably and entered into our great cove-
> nant, as he did in the good old days, rightly so named. In those days
> he understood us, as we understood him. His desire to Become God
> has separated him from us, he seeks what he cannot know or divine,
> and since then he has ceased to be a harmonizing voice, a compan-
> ion movement.
>
> (...)
>
> Will he ever learn to feel? This divine, this most natural of all senses
> is little known to him: feeling would bring back the old time, the
> time we yearn for; the element of feeling is an inward light that
> breaks into stronger, more beautiful colors. Then the stars would
> rise within him, he would learn to feel the whole world, and his
> feeling would be richer and clearer than the limits and surfaces that
> his eye now discloses. Master of an endless dance, he would forget
> all his insensate strivings in joy everlasting, nourishing itself and
> forever growing. Thought is only a dream of feeling, a dead feeling,
> a pale-gray feeble life." (69-73)

Contemporary environmentalists, caught up in the sharpened and swirling debates of what sometimes looks like an End Time, may feel disappointed that Novalis lacks vehemence in his denunciation of "evil scientists" (as Hollywood used to call them). But in the 1790s the full implications of Enlightenment science remained largely speculative. Satanic mills were only just beginning to appear, the concept of pollution scarcely existed. Novalis deserves credit for foreseeing so much so clearly—but nobody could have predicted what actually happened.

> Now speaking in yet another voice, Novalis explains that The epitome of what stirs our feelings is called nature, hence nature stands in an immediate relation to the functions of our body that we call senses. Unknown and mysterious relations within our body cause us to surmise unknown and mysterious states in nature; nature is a community of the marvelous, into which we are initiated by our body, and which we learn to know in the measure of our body's faculties and abilities. The question arises, whether we can learn to understand the nature of natures through this specific nature. (77-79)

This constitutes a perfect summing up of the ancient Romantic doctrine of microcosmic humanity and macrocosmic nature or existence itself.

> "It seems venturesome," said another, "to attempt to compose nature from its outward forces and manifestations, to represent it now as a gigantic fire, now as a wonderfully constructed waterfall, now as a duality or a triad, or as some other weird force. More conceivably, it is the product of an inscrutable harmony among infinitely various essences, a miraculous bond with the spirit world, the point at which innumerable worlds touch and are joined." (81)

> Everything divine has a history; can it be that nature, the one totality by which man can measure himself, should not be bound together in a history, or—and this is the same thing—that it should have no spirit? Nature would not be nature if it had no spirit, it would not be the unique counterpart to mankind, not the indispensable answer to this mysterious question, or the question to this never-ending answer. (85)

The Disciples at Saïs is a "novel" in that it uses a variety of voices—
but very few developed characters. The voices seem not to argue so
much as play out variations in the author's mind, thus allowing him
a typically Romantic freedom of inconsistency and self-contradic-
tion. For example it's not certain that Novalis himself believed that
"everything divine has a history;" but he seems to experience or feel
the idea as yet another variation on his great theme, the reconcilia-
tion of matter and spirit under the sign of nature.

> So inexhaustible is nature's fantasy, that no one will seek its com-
> pany in vain. It has power to beautify, animate, confirm, and even
> though an unconscious, unmeaning mechanism seems to govern the
> part, the eye that looks deeper discerns a wonderful sympathy with
> the human heart in concurrences and in the sequence of isolated
> accidents.[15] (87)

Novalis criticizes even the poets for not "exaggerating nearly
enough." The I–Thou relation between consciousness and nature
should lead to magic powers, so to speak, an ability to move nature
from within rather than as an alienated outsider.

> In order to understand nature, we must allow nature to be born
> inwardly in its full sequence. In this undertaking, we must be led
> entirely by the divine yearning for beings that are like us, we must
> seek out the conditions under which it is possible to question them,
> for truly, all nature is intelligible only as an instrument and medium
> for the communication of rational beings. (91-3)

(These "rational beings" of course include the Elementals, the
personae of nature.)

> The thinking man returns to the original function of his existence,
> to creative contemplation, to the point, where knowledge and
> creation were united in a wondrous mutual tie, to that creative
> moment of true enjoyment, of inward self-conception. If he
> immerses himself entirely in the contemplation of this primeval
> phenomenon, the history of the creation of nature unfolds before
> him in newly emerging times and spaces like a tale that never
> ends, and the fixed point that crystallizes in the infinite fluid
> becomes for him a new revelation of the genius of love, a new

bond between the Thou and the I. A meticulous account of this inward universal history is the true theory of nature. The relations within his thought world and its harmony with the universe will give rise to a philosophical system that will be the faithful picture and formula of the universe. (93)

The "art of pure contemplation" is also a *creative metaphysics*—that is, an art of the creation of value and meaning—and also "The Art" itself in a spagyric sense, the magical art of transmutation.

"Yes," says another voice, "nothing is so marvelous as the great simultaneity of nature. Everywhere nature seems wholly present." This hemetic thought leads on to a contemplation of the consciousness of nature as essentially erotic.

What is the flame that is manifested everywhere? A fervent embrace, whose sweet fruits fall like sensuous dew. Water, first-born child of airy fusions, cannot deny its voluptuous origin and reveals itself an element of love, and of its mixture with divine omnipotence on earth. Not without truth have ancient sages sought the origin of things in water, and indeed, they spoke of a water more exalted than sea and well water. A water in which only primal fluidity is manifested, as it is manifested in liquid metal; therefore should men revere it always as divine. How few up to now have immersed themselves in the mysteries of fluidity, and there are some in whose drunken soul this surmise of the highest enjoyment and the highest life has never wakened. In thirst this world soul is revealed, this immense longing for liquefaction. The intoxicated feel only too well the celestial delight of the liquid element, and ultimately all pleasant sensations are multiform flowings and stirrings of those primeval waters in us.[16] (103-105)

A man born blind cannot learn to see, though you may speak to him forever of colors and lights and distant shapes. No one will fathom nature, who does not, as though spontaneously, recognize and distinguish nature everywhere, who does not with an inborn creative joy, a rich and fervent kinship with all things, mingle with all of nature's creatures through the medium of feeling, who does not feel his way into them. (109)

Happy I call this son, this darling of nature, whom she permits to behold her in her duality, as a power that engenders and bears, and in her unity, as an endless, everlasting marriage. His life will be a plenitude of all pleasures, a voluptuous chain, and his religion will be the real, the true naturalism. (111)

*

The Disciples at Saïs is not a finished work. It ends with a passage on the figure of the "prophet of nature" that feels unfinished to me and even unrevised. Some commentators believe that it constitutes a character sketch of Professor Werner of Freyberg, his teacher of mineralogy, and apparently a true Romantic scientist. Undoubtedly Novalis meant to go on, to create a firmer narrative structure, perhaps to add more symbolic *märchen* like the Tale of Hyacinth and Rose-petal, perhaps to develop ideas about specific sciences such as mining. But the various and rather disorganized paragraphs of the book serve as aphorisms, complete little thoughts in themselves. Novalis gave up trying to combine his "fragments" with his narrative ideas. The latter went into his one complete novel *Heinrich von Ofterdingen*. The former went into his wonderful Aphorisms or Fragments, so admired by Nietzsche and indeed imitated by him in their blending of eighteenth century epigrammatic wit and nineteenth century ambiguity and Romantic fervor.

A complete exploration of Novalis as a conscious hermeticist and Romantic scientist would require a much longer work than this, in which for example a chapter would be devoted to the influence of Paracelsus, and also of the great Rosicrucian novel *The Chymical Wedding of Christian Rosycross*. Further chapters would compare ideas in *The Disciples* with parallel thoughts in Novalis's other works, his notebooks and letters, etc.—and then with the scientific ideas of his contemporaries such as Von Humbolt, Goethe, and the *Naturphilosophie* school.

Nevertheless *The Disciples at Saïs* by itself appears to provide a clear and concise summation—indeed a manifesto—for what we might now call *eco-spirituality*. If Novalis were writing today, two centuries later, no doubt he would have a great deal more to say about science as alienation, about the horrors of the industrial and "post-industrial" assault on nature, about pollution as the material manifestation of bad consciousness. He might be much more pessimistic now, less certain of the return of the Golden Age—that perennial goal of radical hermeticism and Rosicrucianism.

In 1968 German radicals like their French and American and Mexican counterparts re-discovered revolutionary Romanticism and seized back the *blue flower* of Novalis from the forces of reaction. "All power to the Imagination." Despite all vicissitudes and set-backs since the 1960s this paradigm is still emerging. It's exemplified in the almost-mystical ideas of certain quantum philosophers, chaos and complexity scientists and proponents of the Gaia Hypothesis: the idea that matter and consciousness are inter-connected—that the Earth is a living being—that science is an erotic relation. It persists in the ideas and actions of those few "defenders of the earth" brave enough to defy the greed/death/media-trance of the Totality and challenge the institutionalization of body-hatred, misery and boredom that constitutes our Imperium and drives our pollution of all time and space.

In the realm of science ideas can really be considered actions—and in this strange identity science retains an ancient and occult link with the magical hermetic tradition. But only a science freed from slavery to money and war (Capital and State) can ever hope to empower the ideas that would act as Novalis hoped his ideas would act: to save the world from the dark forces of Enlightenment, from "the cruel instrumentality of Reason"—not to fall into the opposite sin of irrational reaction—but to transcend all false dualities in a true "wedding," both alchemical and erotic, between consciousness and nature. That was the goal of the disciples, the lifting of the veil of Isis, the initiation into a lost language. If that still remains our goal today, does this prove that in 200 years we have been defeated?—or that we have not yet experienced the true dream of the sacred theory of earth that points the way to victory?

NOTES

1. Letter to A. W. Schlegel (IV, 229 in N's German Complete Works).

2. The other two Novalis quotes are from the "Notebook," translated by Thomas Frick in Frick and Richard Grossinger, eds., *The Sacred Theory of the Earth* (Berkeley: North Atlanic Books, 1986). Throughout this essay I will use the translation of *The Novices of Saïs* by Ralph Manheim (though I prefer the use of "Disciples" rather than "Novices"), in the 1949 edition published by Curt Valentin in New York, with a rather useless preface by Stephen Spender, and sixty exquisite drawings by Paul Klee. I can't think of a more appropriate illustrator—unless perhaps Joseph Beuys. See also C. V. Becker and R. Manstetter, "Novalis' Thought on Nature, Humankind and Economy: A New Perspective for Discussing Modern Environmental Problems," available on line from <cbecker@uni-hd.de>

3. Paul Hoffman, *Wings of Madness: Alberto Santos-Dumont and the Invention of Flight* (Hyperion, 2003); I saw the anecdote in a review.

4. In the lexicon of the US Parks Services, "wilderness" is defined as the areas most strictly controlled and regulated—a perversion of language possible only to a government bureaucracy.

5. Novalis, *The Disciples at Saïs*. See below.

6. A.k.a. Theophrastus Bombastus von Hohenheim, the most original thinker in alchemy since Jabir ibn Hayyan; died 1541 in Saltzberg.

7. Darwin's direct source was undoubtedly Pope's "Rape of the Lock," also based on Paracelsus via a strange little book called *Le Comte de Gabalis*, a treatise on the Elementals.

8. My copy of Darwin's great poem, with illustrations by Fuseli and William Blake, is a facsimile of the 1791 edition, by Scholar Press (London, 1973). Incidentally, Novalis was a reader of Darwin and refers to him as an authority in *Flower Pollen* (see *The Disciples at Saïs and Other Fragments*, translated by F.V.M.T. and U.C.B., with an introduction by Una Birch [later Pope-Hennessy]; London: Methuen, 1903). Novalis's beloved dead brother was named Erasmus. [later note: Thanks indirectly to our conference in New Paltz, a new edition of the Manheim translation of *The Novices of Saïs*, with the Klee illustrations, is now available from Archipelago Books of Brooklyn, NY (2005)]

9. By the Rationalist philosopher Isaiah Berlin, whose useful but polemical interpretation utterly fails to consider hermetic roots.

10. Max Blechman, ed., *Revolutionary Romanticism* (San Francisco: City Lights, 2000). See also Michael Lowy and Robert Sayre, *Romanticism Against the Tide of Modernity* (Durham: Duke University Press, 2001). Thanks to Joel Kovel for this reference.

11. E. E. F. Chladni (1756-1827) also invented a musical instrument called the euphonium.

12. The earliest version I've found is from Bishop Nicholas of Cusa (died 1464), who held that the Earth is a living "star," worthy of respect and even adulation. Needless to say Cusanus was accused of pantheism, and was greatly admired by the hermeticists.

13. "So-called" but not very accurately. Cornelius Agrippa was scarcely an apologist for any Christian orthodoxy. "Hermetic Cabala" might be a more precise term.

14. This speech is attributed by Novalis to certain of the novices, but strangely they speak of "man" as of an other. Such sentiments are attributed to the Elementals by Paracelsus. Perhaps some of the disciples at Sais *are* Elementals!

15. Among other things this passage could serve almost as a definition of Surrealism, especially in its hermetic phases, those that reveal it most clearly as a stage of the Romantic movement.

16. This passage reflects the seventeenth century scientific hypothesis of "Neptunism," now discredited but very popular with the Romantics.

Alchemie und Heilkunst, Von Bernus, Stuttgart, 1936

2

One the All
Alchemy as Sacred Ecology

CHRISTOPHER BAMFORD

THE HEALTH, and even future, of our Earth (which is not other than our humanity) seems under attack. Certainly, it is threatened. But our present scientific and philosophical approaches to nature, though noble and well intentioned in their aspirations, seem able to provide only short-term, band-aid responses that alleviate the symptoms, but provide no fundamental remedy. "Problems" addressed in one area become only more widespread and virulent elsewhere. Meanwhile, we persist in the behaviors and attitudes that caused the crises in the first place. The situation only worsens. Loss of topsoil, extinctions of species and habitats, wars, droughts, famines, oppressions and toxic pollutions proliferate. It is almost more than a heart can bear.

How much this actually affects Gaia-Sophia herself is of course unknown. She may even be waking up as some visionaries attest. Certainly many experience that nature appears more transcendentally beautiful with each passing year. Nevertheless, even if that is the case, and great evolutionary "earth changes" are underway, it is clear that we are being called to learn to think and be in another way, one more in harmony with our Mother, the beauty of the world, who is also cosmic nature, that Earth in the largest sense, which is for Christians the body of the Christ.

It is not hard to see how we have come to this point. Selfishness, greed, and the need for the illusion of dominion and control pervade our thinking. Though allegedly "value free" and "objective," all our actions, based as they are on the radical separation of self and other, subject and object, citizen and stranger, friend and enemy, humanity and nature, earth and cosmos, actually embody the dominant cultural paradigm or value of egotism, which we can call the disease of our times.

At one level, egotism appears as the double (or shadow) of our present "observer" consciousness that reifies the experiences of our psychological consciousness into objectification, reification: the illusion of *distance* and the fantasy of material causation. We experience ourselves as distant from one another, distant from nature, distant from the stars, distant even from the spiritual world. We find ourselves perpetually "elsewhere," rather than here. And distance in turn gives rise to the urge to separate, dominate, control, manipulate—and even lie—in the course of which hate becomes easier than love and prejudice than openness. In other words, we lack *intimacy*—with the world, the divine, and ourselves. At the same time and for the same reason, we lack a spiritual understanding of the fundamentals: space, time, light, causation, gravity and so on.

Above all, of course, we lack knowledge of Life—not just of biological life, but also of the indivisible, invisible Life that animates the cosmos: Cosmic Life. For all its effectiveness and technological range, modern science remains a science of what Rudolf Steiner calls "sub-nature," which is dead, and not of "Nature," which is whole, alive, and filled throughout with living beings: with Life. "Sub-nature"—the world of physics, chemistry and technologically applied mathematics—is cut off from nature. Sunk far below nature, it has descended into a virtually autonomous lifeless realm of its own. To redeem it requires that we move proportionately upward—toward Life, the right orientation for any true path of knowledge.

This has always been known. A sacred science of Nature or Life has existed from the beginning of humanity's spiritual journey. Selfless, dedicated to healing and harmony, and resting upon non-dual experience, it has accompanied, sustained, and underlain each religious epoch and every revelation.

Called alchemy or, loosely, in the West, Hermetism, it is the ancient, primordial, sacred science of Nature. Present in all historical cultures from India and China in the East to the Abrahamic West and always adapting its practice to its context, its origins are lost in the depths of prehistory. In a sense, it is the primal cosmological revelation. Nevertheless, in the great revival of mystical, esoteric traditions and practices during the last century, the tradition has—except for a few specialists—been largely ignored or simply read as a psychology.

In fact, not only alchemy, but also nature herself has been largely ignored. In the great revival of mystical, esoteric traditions and practices during the last century, the whole question of sacred or spiritual science has been left to one side. Although we have studied and practiced the teachings of the saints and sages of past ages assiduously, we have passed over their sciences of nature in silence. Perhaps, therefore, it is time to explore the relevance not only of our Masters' "inner" science, but also their science of Nature, which, because it is whole, includes, transcends, and erases all separations such as inner and outer.

This other science is vast. Its worldview is utterly different to our own, for it seeks to understand nature in itself, for itself, out of itself, as our sacred, holy, even divine source. It is therefore a path of praise, love, and adoration, of knowledge as a *donum dei*, a gift of God.

Contemporary science for its part, contrary to what we might assume, is not in any sense a path of knowledge. It does not know what it deals with. Indeed, in a way, it renounces knowledge. It is not concerned with truth, but only with what works and false theories, especially with a great deal of money behind them, can be extraordinarily fecund.

True knowledge, on the other hand, is a spiritual reality, a cognitive spiritual state of encounter.

From the perspective of *consciousness*, the shift from science to technology may thus be seen not only in terms of a movement from unity to multiplicity, but also, as, as has been said, *the degeneration of Love into utility*. To confuse utility with love is a fundamental loss of orientation, for love resides at the core of all as the tradition bears witness.

Pherecydes of Syros, for example, a teacher of Pythagoras, and "Hermetic" because learned in the Prophecies of Ham and the secret books of the Phoenicians, whose revelation is attributed to *Thoth* or *Hermes*, taught that:

> Zeus, when about to create, changed himself into Love; for in composing the order of the world out of the contraries he brought it to concord and friendship, and in all things he set the seed of identity and the unity which pervades everything.

Sacred science, then, works through love with the Mystery of the World or Nature.

*

In the beginning, according to one likely story, humanity was less physicalized, the world less dense, and the original Light still permeated all. Nature and grace were a single activity. Everything was a living symbol, the expression of spiritual reality. Nature resounded with meaning, and each human being was a prophet, able to hear and interpret the words of the gods reverberating through all phenomena. It was as if each person had his or her own religion. Yet there was complete harmony and wholeness. No distinction existed between interior and exterior, subject and object, friend and stranger. Heaven and Earth, the living and the dead, together with all the angels and elemental spirits, were one world, one cosmos. Human beings were still predominantly heavenly beings, woven into, and part of, the great symphonic stream of creation. The world, the cosmos, was light-filled music; and music was the world, the cosmos. Matter, too, was music: sounding light. Every plant and tree and rock, the sunlight on the water, the shape of the clouds, the dew, the wind, the flame, all feeling and intention, every smile and tear and burst of laughter, the dance of the synapses and the tremors of the inner organs—all sang the great hymn of cosmic evolution. It was a Golden Age.

Gradually, however, human beings fell out of cosmic unity toward self-consciousness. The world solidified. The light that sang in matter became veiled. Matter grew dark. Distinct states of consciousness—deep sleep, dream, and waking consciousness, as well as a fourth transcendent state—became differentiated. Waking sensory consciousness, an ever-narrowing range of awareness, began to dominate. Society became stratified. Functions and specialists arose. It was the time of the Ancient Mysteries, which sought to transmit and develop the primal understanding.

*

There were the primordial Earth Mysteries of the Great Mother, the Mother of the Gods and of all Living Things—above all, the Black Virgin Mother Goddess, the Universal Wisdom Substance, whose initiatory Mysteries of death and rebirth unfolded under many aspects and at many levels throughout the ancient world in caves and dark, damp places, hidden in creative folds of the Earth. Hers were the mysteries of life, death, and rebirth, continuity and transience: above all, the agricultural mysteries of fertility, germination, and growth, and the mysteries of food, of nourishment, fermentation, cooking, and healing.

Related—but who knows which arose first—were all the Mysteries connected with the sacrifice or transformation of earthly substances: stonework, metallurgy, mining, smith-craft, iron work, and pottery—all those "shamanic" crafts having to do with the Earth and with Fire, without which agricultural—settled—civilization would not have arisen.

Both of these—agriculture (cooking) and smith-craft—work with the mysteries of matter, but matter was then still understood to be alive, dynamic, and celestial. Earth was not yet separated from the cosmos, but took its place within the Unity of the Great Triad: Heaven, Earth, and Humanity.

As an ancient alchemical text states: "Above is the celestial. Below is the terrestrial. Thus the work is completed, masculine and feminine working together."

Above: Heaven is expansive, active, covering. Below: Earth is contractive, receptive, nourishing, supporting.

Bridging them is the progeny, the mediator, the pontiff: the human being, child of Earth and starry Heaven. The human being's task is circulation. Again, in the words of an ancient alchemical text; "It ascends from earth to heaven and descends again from heaven to earth, acquiring the power of realities above and below."

Rising, humanity spiritualizes matter; descending, it materializes spirit.

*

Nature, in this primal revelation, includes not only sublunary or earthly nature, but also planetary nature, as well as the world of the stars (cosmic or astral nature), and the world beyond the stars (divine nature). It is the whole creation, as in the saying or *hadith* attributed to the Prophet Mohammed, "I was a hidden treasure and I desired to be known and so I created the world."

The world in this sense—everything that is, true unity—is what ancient traditions called "Universal Man," the Cosmic Human or Anthropos, whose fruit human beings and the Earth are. In this tradition, humanity and the Earth are one: inseparable in origin and end. From this point of view, human beings are not so much little cosmoses, microcosms, as that the universe itself is a great Human, an "Anthropocosm."

*

As fruit, humanity and the Earth bear the spiritual seeds, which, if they germinate, will grow into the true universe—conscious, transfigured, and made light—so that God can know himself and be all in all.

Human beings are collaborators—co-laborers, co-workers, fellow farmers or celestial agriculturalists—with God in the great project of the transfiguration of all that is into unity and the living light of divinity. Call it "spiritual agriculture" or the "science of seeds," as Isis advises Horus in a text from the *Corpus Hermeticum* much quoted by the Masters:

> So go, then, my child, to a certain laborer and ask him what he has sown and what he has harvested, and you will learn from him that the one who sows wheat also harvests wheat, and the one who sows barley also harvests barley.... Learn to comprehend the whole fabrication, *demiourgia*, and generation of things and know that it is the

condition of man to sow a man, of a lion to sow a lion, of a dog to sow a dog.... See, there is the whole of the mystery.

From this point of view, alchemy, which is the science of matter, is also the science of seeds. For the ancients, matter was Light. It was sacred, holy, divine Fire from Heaven. Hence the taboos and curses often associated with those who worked with it. Everything, then, was Spirit, all was Light and Fire, came from the Spirit, and returned to it. Spirit alone was real. The sky, for instance, in some ancient traditions, was made of rock quartz or crystallized light. Metals—like plants and animals, and human themselves—were seen as cosmic seeds planted in the Earth. Ores were planted and grew in the Earth's belly, just as plants and animals were planted and grew on its surface. Seeds of both kinds came from the cosmos and were intimately related to, and remained united with, the heavens, giving rise to the science of signatures or affinities whereby the one was understood through the other. Agriculture, whether metallurgical or biological, was thus always a "celestial-earthly" activity. Under the action of Heaven, metals, like seeds, would naturally grow to perfection in the Earth, which was seen as the Heavens' womb. Left alone, any metal over aeons would thus become "gold." Mining and metallurgy were thus originally a kind of agricultural obstetrics. Working with the gods—the Heavens—humanity could enter into and enhance the subterranean embryology of the cosmos and collaborate with nature in God's work. Replacing nature's rhythms, the smith could bring to fruition what nature had begun.

*

As we know it today in the Abrahamic traditions, Hermetism or alchemy begins in Egypt.

Hermes from which the word "Hermeticism" derives is the Greek translation of the Egyptian Thoth, the patron god of science and knowledge, the judge and equilibrator of polarity, difference, and relation—spirit and matter, male and female, Heaven and Earth, Fire and Water, and so on.

The alchemist works with these relations in their processes: expanding and contracting, dissolving and coagulating, centripetal and centrifugal, dividing uniting. "Spagyrics," another name for alchemy, in fact, means, "dividing and uniting."

The word "Alchemy" itself derives in one interpretation from the Arabic Al-Kemiya, meaning "the black earth," most often taken to refer to Egypt, which was known as the Black Land after the fertility of the Nile flood plains. But it also connotes "black" as Black Virgins are black; and thus invokes the *material prima*, the prime substance of creation.

Egyptian Thoth-Hermes was called "the master of the heart and reason in all human beings," "the great, the only God, the Soul of Becoming." He was the mediator through whom the world was brought into manifestation. The master of creation, of every aspect and level of the formal world, he was Trismegistus, Thrice Great, the Master of the Three Worlds—sublunary, planetary, and cosmic. All knowledge was ascribed to him. He existed before the Flood, after the Flood, and still exists today as an initiatory state of knowing and being.

For Egypt, Thoth was the primordial culture-bringer, the institutor of all arts, crafts, and sciences—the healer, master architect, and founder of agriculture, smelting, and mining. His temple was called the "House of the Net," which indicates cosmology or the weaving of the world fabric or garment—each knot representing a conjunction of life and death, impulse and resistance, contraction and expansion.

Egyptian civilization of course was hierarchic, theocratic. At its center was the Temple, where the ancient arts, crafts, and sciences were ritualized as the initiatory embodiments of metaphysical and theological knowledge. Under priestly guidance, over four thousand years, Egypt achieved a unique level of perfection in which all functions and languages—myth, theology, hieroglyph, and geometry, for instance—were interconnected and realized in practical knowledge of the world and nature.

At the shift of the world ages—marked incrementally and historically first by the axial moment of Buddha, Pythagoras, Mahavira the Jain, Lao Tzu, and the Hebrew Prophets of the Exile, next by the conquests of Alexander the Great and the rise of Hellenism, which then prepared for the coming of Christ—the connections were broken. But the wisdom of Egypt was not lost. Texts were created—above all, the *Corpus Hermeticum*, a sort of Summa of Egyptian philosophy, and the *Emerald Tablet*. At the same time Hermetic elements of Greek culture—carried above all by the Presocratics (Pythagoras, Empedocles, and Heraclitus), but also Plato and Aristotle entered the mix, along with elements of Zoroastrian thought. The earliest alchemists—Ostanes, Pseudo-Democritus, Zozimos, Maria the Jewess, Kleopatra—all date from this Hellenistic period (300 BCE–300 CE). Thus Greco-Roman alchemy, at once craft, gnosis, philosophy, art and religion was born as the metamorphosis of the ancient Mystery Religions.

*

But the period of the political foundation of Christianity was not propitious for freedom of individual thought and research and, as this progressively diminished—was progressively repressed—the alchemical, philosophical, and hermetic thinking that was transmitting ancient mystery wisdom moved eastward, through Syria, into Persia. On the way, in an act of cultural transmission that has been compared to the transmission of Mahayana Buddhism from Sanskrit into Chinese, an enormous number of texts, the patrimony of the ancient world, were translated. The transfer was providential, for it meant that the fully flowering fruit of Hellenistic science and philosophy lay ready to be received by Islam. The result was that, within 150 years of its founding, Islamic alchemy reached its height with Jabir, whose immense oeuvre includes more than three thousand treatises.

From Islam, Hermetic alchemy traveled to the medieval West, the first work to be translated, *A Testament of Alchemy* of Morienus, arriving in 1144. Other translations followed. Franciscans took care of the transmission. Soon, too, original works began to be written and alchemy began a process of transformation. Figures like Artephius, Albert Magnus, Aquinas, Raymond Lull, Roger Bacon, and Arnold of Villanova, grasping the depth and range of the alchemical vision began to universalize into a complete divine-spiritual-physical path. Alchemy became *de facto* the sacred science of the West and laid the ground for the explosive influence of Marsilio Ficino's translations of original texts, beginning in 1463, with the *Corpus Hermeticum*. The rest is history. It remained only for great Renaissance Masters from Paracelsus, Basil Valentine, Bernard Trevisanus, Limojin de Saint-Didier and others up to Jakob Böhme, Van Helmont, and the Rosicrucians to complete the task.

Thus, at the time of the birth of modern science another participatory, gentle, compassionate science was available. It was the beginning of a new alternative culture. To understand the scope of this alternative, one need only contemplate the fact that, in the Christian West alone, catalogs of alchemical texts run to at least twenty to thirty thousand titles.

*

Besides the *Emerald Tablet*, the primary source for Hermetic philosophy is *The Corpus Hermeticum*. The many alchemical texts are really books of spiritual exercises or practice. (*The Emerald Tablet* is both).

Study of these texts reveals that the cosmos "is one mass of life, and there is not anything in the Cosmos that is not alive." But the cosmos is not itself the source of life. The source of life is the Good, which (or who) is "immortal life."

> The Cosmos is an instrument of God's will, and it was made by Him to this end, that, having received from God the seeds of all things that belong to it, and keeping these seeds within itself, it might bring all things into actual existence. The Cosmos produces life in all things by its movement; and decomposing them, it renews the things that have been decomposed; for, like a good husband-man, it gives them renewal by sowing seed. There is nothing in which the Cosmos does not generate life; and it is both the place in which life is contained and the maker of life.
>
> (*Corpus Hermeticum* IX)

The Hermetic universe is alive and is a unity. Both life and unity arise out of a conjunction or identity of complements. A manuscript of *The Goldmaking of Kleopatra* expresses the idea to perfection. A serpent with its tail in its mouth, the Ouroboros, encloses the motto "*En to Pan*," One the All. Another ancient text states: "One is the All, and thanks to it the All, and by it the All, and if the All did not contain the All, the All would be nothing." The circle is closed.

The universe is a uni-verse; there is nothing else. It is one-only, non-exteriorized, and recursive: everything is connected to everything else. The Corpus Hermeticum (XVI) says: "If any one attempts to separate all things from the One, taking the term 'all things' to signify a mere plurality of things, and not a whole made up of things, he will sever the All from the One, and will thereby bring to naught the All." Ostanes, too, in one of the earliest alchemical formulae, affirms: "Nature rejoices in Nature, Nature triumphs over Nature, Nature rules Nature."

What is involved is not a theory, but an experience—the experience of a state of consciousness in which the opposition between subject and object, inside and outside, observer and observed, is transcended to reveal the spiritual unity and creative interdependence of humanity and the cosmos. The Hermetic universe, the Hermetic work, and the human subject are one and the same. "Everything is the product of one universal creative effort," wrote Paracelsus. Hermes likewise teaches in the Asclepius, "The human being is all things; the human being is everywhere." To know this is gnosis. It is to be born again: begotten by God and conceived in silence in a womb that is wisdom. Reborn in this way, one comes to perceive, "not with bodily eyesight, but by the working of mind":

Father, now that I see in mind, I see myself to be the All. I am in Heaven and on Earth, in Water and in Air; I am in beasts and plants; I am a babe in the womb, and one that is not yet conceived, and one that has been born; I am present everywhere.

(Corpus Hermeticum XIII)

If one would know God, one must become like God, such is this science. Only like may know like. Becoming like God to know God, one comes to know like God. The knowing with which one comes to know God is only the knowing with which God knows. And as all things are in God, so they must also be in the human being and become conscious. But where? Since things are not in God as in a place, or space, corporeally, but rather invisibly, beyond space and time, the human being must withdraw from space and time, matter and motion, desire and memory. Outside space and time, consciousness is all. With each thought, we are there. There is only the present.

To realize this vision requires a radical transformation of consciousness or perception, a change in the way we know and perceive, "for all things which the eye can see are mere phantoms and unsubstantial outlines; but the things which the eye cannot see are the realities."

What is implied then is a schooling of the senses—a cleansing of "the doors of perception," so that, instead of being "stuffed up with the gross mass of matter" and "crammed with loathly pleasures," they may become active organs of true vision. Once this is achieved, one may "see with the heart Him whose will it is that with the heart alone He should be seen." Later students of the tradition like Paracelsus will term this faculty *Imaginatio Vera*: True Imagination, the Star in the Human Being.

"True imagination," writes Maurice Aniane in an extremely perceptive essay on alchemy, "actually 'sees' the 'subtle' processes of nature and their angelic prototypes. It is the capacity to reproduce in oneself the cosmogenic unfolding, the permanent creation of the world in the sense in which all creation, finally, is only a Divine Imagination."

To understand this, one must go beyond the idea of a single, unique act of creation and assume as well a "creative state" of continuous creation, metaphysical in nature, outside space and time. Creation is continuously unfolding, and consciousness may always know its states by virtue of the principle whereby "the One is the All." Hermetically, to know a god is to penetrate to a specific creative phase or relationship. As Hortulanus says, "Our Stone is made in the same way that the world is created." The world is not continuous as our senses present it to us. There are moments of eternity, gaps or openings in perception, which our senses conceal. For the Hermetist, it is by means of these "gaps" that causality—out of time—is effected by the gods who are themselves the "causes." Causality is vertical, for in the realm of phenomena—the horizontal plane—there are only connections without cause.

*

Alchemy is thus religion under the sign of cosmology. More than that, it is experimental religion—a path of the empirical realization. Simply put, it is the sacred science of the realization and enhancement of the subtle states of the human being and the universe, inner and outer, where these are seen as not-two/not-one—unified, reflecting each other, corresponding to each other at each point, perhaps distinguishable, but certainly not separable—just as subject and object, knower and known are inseparably one in the non-dual state which is the source of both. Thus, there is an axis of non-dual light that unites the universe and connects the human being and nature with the source of all.

Though there sometimes seem to be two alchemical or Hermetic paths—one mystical and inner, and the other practical, empirical, and laboratory-based—there is really only one, which is mystical and inner and practical, empirical and outer.

Uniting inner and outer, the alchemist becomes a universal priest celebrating a Eucharistic transubstantiation, whose species are not just bread and wine, but nature in its entirety.

To achieve this transubstantiation, the alchemist imposes nothing, but only "follows nature in her mode of operation." The rest is a gift of God, *a donum dei*: grace.

From this point of view, Alchemy is at once phenomenological or empirical *and* religious. Empirical, it is experimental and scientific. Religious, it is an initiatory path of prayer.

Phenomenologically, it starts with the unity of existence or matter and consciousness and with the unity of all phenomena of consciousness—consciousness always identifying consciousness.

If you would know the rose, become the rose. Become the rock. Become the plant. Become the metal.

From this point of view, nature or phenomena, through the commonplace, gives all the answers. Each event in identifying consciousness is its own answer. There is no beyond or outside.

What this means is that everything is a symbol.

All phenomena are symbols. They are the necessary representations of the knowledge they contain—the knowledge being that which makes them what they are, the principle according to which they function. Each thing in nature—bird, tree, and flower—is a question containing its own potential answer, meaning, and expla-

nation. All phenomena—light, color, sound—and all natural processes—germination, growth, digestion, and fermentation—
contain the power to evoke, in the prepared observer the true
response that is their meaning. This Hermetic doctrine of the reciprocity of human being and world is well represented by Goethe
when he writes:

> One knows oneself only insofar as one knows the world, becoming
> aware of it only within oneself, and of oneself only within it. Each
> new subject, well observed, opens up within us a new organ of
> thought.

In this philosophy lies the foundation of a true science of phenomena, a science of the commonplace, essentially dispensing with
all instrumentation and relying on consciousness alone—for consciousness is everything. Goethe says:

> The best of all would be to realize that every fact is already theory. The
> blue of the sky shows us the principles of color. We need not look for
> anything behind phenomena: they themselves are the doctrine.

Hermetic science is able to understand such phenomena as life,
light, space, time, matter—which modern science cannot fathom—
because it is able to experience phenomena as such, as God Himself knows them.

*

The symbol is what it symbolizes. It doesn't stand for anything,
but is the living presence of what it symbolizes. For the alchemist,
the universe, nature, every phenomenon is a concrete presence of
the powers that govern it. The Hermetic art of alchemy is then the
raising of the symbol into its living angelic archetype. But this is
not just an inner act; it is a reality. The alchemist sees with the eyes
of the Spirit—eyes of Fire—and confirms his theory through
higher perception or Imagination. Paracelsus calls it True Imagination, for it "sees," that is, confirms, verifies, and collaborates in the
"subtle" processes of nature, which are the continuous creation of
the world: the Divine Imagination.

Hermetic science is thus a discipline of mind and body. Rather than the objectification and control of the known by the knower, it seeks unification and identity—thereby transforming the knower and the known as perceived and experienced. The "object" is conceived of as a symbol. Everything observable is a symbol. Every symbol is observable. But note that a symbol or phenomenon, though observable, is not "repeatable" in the sense that ordinary science depends upon repeatability. Each observation or empirical confirmation is unique, single: an act of grace manifesting in the confluence of the right gesture at the right moment. Hermetic science strives for a qualitative, unifying exaltation of the relation of the knower to the known in the symbol through the act of knowing. Hermetically, knowledge and evolution are one, founded on the primacy of humanity as life and consciousness. Hermetists, finding themselves in a sense-based, psychological consciousness of multiplicity—that separates—and bearing within themselves the memory of original unity, are called upon to transform the one by the other.

Hermetic science is the way and contemplation of this process. Methodologically, it is a way of posing and articulating this unity, for unless each perception or act unifies, "things" (the consciousness that separates) cannot be seen as symbols.

The assumption of Hermetic science, then, is that the whole universe is sacramental, embodying and proclaiming the process of the revelation of unity—of unity as identity, however, rather than as non-duality. This unitary vision, subscribed to by all the great traditional men and women of "knowledge" is founded not upon a sensory material unity of nature, but on a spiritual unity.

This Unity was called the Prime Matter. It is not sensory matter, but is the water of life, the unmediated Divine Presence as the feminine element in nature, even the Holy Spirit.

*

Following the thinking of the twentieth century French alchemist, Henri Coton Alvart, let us briefly consider this Mystery.

First, there is the Mystery that the world is: the mystery of being.

Second, there is the Mystery of Movement, Metamorphosis, or Manifestation: not only "outwardly" in space and time (which movement creates), but also "inwardly," so that everything is born, grows, and dies, i.e. evolves, transforms. No thing, no form is permanent. How does movement arise? For the Hermetist movement arises as being encounters resistance, non-being. Between the two—between one and two—consciousness arises: a relationship.

Third, there is the Mystery of Intelligence. Movement is not disordered or chaotic. It is ordered metamorphosis. Everything moves, transforms, according to a rule—whether a falling body, the courses of the stars, or the growth of a plant. All follow a single rule or pattern of metamorphosis. This is the "pattern that connects" in Gregory Bateson's phrase: the thinking that is nature or the cosmos, which our ordinary consciousness granulates into bits and pieces in time and space. This third Mystery is the Mediator, the human function: Gnosis, which is life and light.

Thus the world is (1) substantial in its being; (2) consciousness in its movement or metamorphosis; (3) intelligent, knowable, by its organization. In other words, the macrocosmic world of nature and the universe—like the microcosmic world—is simultaneously body, soul, and spirit.

Corpus Mundi: the body of the world; the first matter of all things—which is the initial state of the cycle of modifications that metamorphosis will impose.

Anima Mundi: the soul of the world; the eternally active agent that makes things live and die, transforming all things without ceasing.

Spiritus Mundi: the intelligence at work in all things.

*

Working with these principles—which are the principles of creation as they are of the human being—the alchemist practices a spiritual discipline that allows him to participate in the world process. To do so is the Great Work. It is called the Great Work because it works to bring creation to its natural perfection, just as a gardener does in the garden or a cook in the kitchen. Thus the alchemist is a kind of gardener, or cook. He or she (or, often he and she) is also a kind of doctor. In other words, this is a very practical wisdom. It heals.

As doctor, the alchemist works to heal creation because, from the alchemical perspective, nature is "sick." It contains in it a principle hostile to it. This principle, the cause of the "fall," is still active, causing the dramatic mixture of life and death, wisdom and folly, renewal and decay that we see wherever we turn. One can neither deny the sickness that has penetrated creation, nor the marvelous solicitude that preserves it. All the natural kingdoms are sick; yet they perpetually renew themselves. Everywhere poison and remedy are in conflict—in our time, more so than ever.

The guiding principle of alchemy is the efficacious, curative, and omnipotent intervention of Unity—that is, Spirit—to overcome the pathology of the world, its death principle.

To do so, the alchemist works with the perpetual movement of the transformation of the Original Light of the world, which makes the seed germinate, grow, transmute food, and make new seeds. He works with the agent metamorphosis, which is the dance of spirit and substance, to enhance Life. As he studies the agent, he learns its rhythm.

This is a key, for rhythm, which is time, is metamorphosis and manifests the continually resurrecting power of the spirit.

The alchemist understands rhythm as the distance between seed and fruit. Such metamorphosis is not a simple succession of stages, or addition of parts, where you can see where one begins and another ends. It is the fulfillment of an end desired from the beginning: the end implied in the beginning. It is a whole. As such, it is outside ordinary time, which unfolds sequentially by placing one thing after another. Rhythmic metamorphosis is time as genesis. The phases of any such cycle of genesis constitute movement, life. The whole is Life itself. That is to say, the alchemist looks at all things as a cosmic biologist, for everything lives, which is from Heaven, a continuous and gratuitous gift of Spirit. Nothing is static. Everything forms a cycle of ordered spiritual metamorphosis: seven stages, four states, the cycle of the four elements—Earth, Air, Water, and Fire—applicable to all things.

Above all, the alchemist seeks in all things the healing, saving Ferment, the internal spiritualizing agent that underlines all transitory, discontinuous phenomena, the source of the metamorphosis of the four elements. This Ferment is a "fifth element." It is the

Quintessence, the permanent ferment in all things—in metals, minerals, plants, and animals, in the waters, the atmosphere, in cosmic light and space. Universally present, it would act unhindered according to its place or milieu—following the inspiration of the Spirit, which guides it—were it not for the "hostile" principle. The alchemist, God's right hand, seeks to overcome this pathology to enable the unrestricted flow of spirit through the world in all living things: minerals, plants, animals, and humans.

*

Much of alchemy can sound arcane, obscure to the point of incomprehensibility. The alchemical masters have their own language, which they use in a different way than we are used to. Our language, based as it is on a dualistic worldview, is denotative. Words have fixed meanings and appear to point to things. Alchemical language is connotative, contextual. It is its own reality. You have to understand the context to understand the meaning of individual words—whose meaning can vary considerably according to context. Double and triple meanings abound. The texts are full of wordplay and puns. Often the very obscurity can tempt us to give up. Yet we need this tradition. Our Earth and our humanity need it. For it teaches us the way to fulfill our human, earthly task as mediators, pontiffs, between Heaven and Earth. It is the path of ultimate service: to aid the divine powers in the task of true world evolution.

3

Green Hermeticism

PETER LAMBORN WLSON

I. GREEN HERMETICISM

HE GOD HERMES began life as a heap of stones marking the boundary of some Neolithic Greek farm field. He still incarnates (as Mercury) on dimes and pencils, and his Caduceus (two snakes in double helix coiled round a staff) has been misappropriated by the AMA.

As god of communication and silence, commerce and burglary (his first feat as a newborn babe is to rustle the cattle of Apollo), Hermes naturally becomes the patron of secret and dangerous arts such as writing. Thus he's identified with the Mesopotamian Nebo and the Egyptian Thoth, Ibis-headed baboon scribe of the gods, and eventually grows into Hermes Trismegistus ("Thrice-Great"), patron of alchemy, magic and the hermetic arts.

Worshipped from Celtic Gaul (as Lugh, inventor of all arts) to India (as Buddha, Wisdom, the planet Mercury), Hermes becomes the focus of a cult in Ptolemaic Alexandria that produced the Greek *Corpus Hermeticum*, a synthesis of ancient Egyptian and Indo-European wisdom traditions. Alchemy (the art of Khem, Egypt) takes on its classical form around the same time (say, 200 BC to 200 AD).

Hermeticism passed from its cradle-land onward in time and space to Judaism, Christianity and eventually Islam, as well as Hinduism and even Taoism. Since it's neither a religion nor a science in the narrow sense, but an *Art*, it can be reconciled with any religion—or with all religions. Modern science can be seen as the "suppression and realization" of Hermeticism, or perhaps as the *theft of its secrets* by such keen but closeted alchemists as Isaac Newton. If modern science's origins lie in Hermeticism then post-modern science now begins to sound like alchemy again, with its cyclotronic transmutation, mystical quantum leaps and chaotic attractors. Hermeticism seems relevant also in the ecological and environmental sciences—because Hermeticism has always been "green."

"As Above, So Below," the Hermetic doctrine of correspondences between micro- and macrocosm, derives from *The Emerald Tablet of Hermes Trismegistus*, a Greco-Egyptian text preserved only in Arabic.

Emerald green is the heraldic color of Prophetic Islam. In Sufi alchemy the "highest" color, that of the Philosopher's Stone, is gold-green. The Hidden Prophet Khezr is the Green man of Sufism, and immortal adept of vegetation and the water of life. Wherever he walks, flowers and herbs spring up in his footsteps, and he patronizes the hermetic arts.

The eighth century Iraqi Shiite (or possibly Manichaean) alchemist Jabir Ibn Hayyan (called Geber in the West) first developed the famous dyadic principles of *Sulphur* and *Mercury*. This occidental yang/yin symbolism spread as far as China and lies at the heart of alchemy's worldview.

The great sixteenth century Swiss alchemist-physician Paracelsus inherited the Sulphur/Mercury concept but realized that it required completion by a third term: *Salt*. Sulphur is soul, Mercury is spirit, and Salt is body. In one sense, this constitutes a Trinitarian solution to the problem of dualism. In another sense it represents a discovery of the dialectic. (The mystic Jacob Boehme picks this up from Paracelsus and passes it on to later German philosophers, eventually to Hegel and Marx—minus all magic.)

Paracelsus also shifts the focus of alchemy from transmutation of metals to the art of healing. Both plants and metals are used in this new medical alchemy, which he calls *Spagyria*, but the emphasis falls on herbal tinctures and distillates. The goal of spagyrics, an elixir of perfect health, is sometimes called the Vegetal Stone (as opposed to the Mineral Stone): the *Lapis philosophorum* seen as green, as a living emerald.

Paracelsus is remembered by academic historians of science as the weirdo who invented laudanum (tincture of opium) and the mercuric cure for syphilis. But he should be honored as the major source for Rosicrucianism, Northern Romanticism and its "Romantic Science" (including Swedenborg, German *Naturphilosophie*, Goethe, and Erasmus Darwin, neglected genius grandfather of Charles.) Spagyria is still practiced in Europe. Paracelsus also enjoyed vast influence in the Islamic world. Homeopathy and Biodynamics are basically neo-Paracelsian sciences.

In September 2003 a small conference on "Sacred Theory of Earth" was held in New Paltz, New York, where the idea of *Green Hermeticism* arose out of discussions amongst hermeticists, poets, Christians, Buddhists, neo-pagans, Sufis and assorted heretics. At this meeting, the obscure and little-read text *Novices of Saïs* by the German Romantic poet Novalis was presented as a virtual manifesto of Green Hermeticism, which might be defined as a *spagyric approach to the environmental sciences (and to their "crisis"), an approach both empirical and magical.*

II. GREEN HERMES

Protean, centrifugal, multiform, elusive, Hermeticism has long since accommodated and informed and encompassed many traditions. First it can be called shamanic. Shamanism is not a religion but an art; astrology and alchemy have clear Paleolithic and Neolithic shamanic roots (as Mircea Eliade makes clear), and the very structureless structure of Hermeticism reflects that of shamanism: the secret society or autonomous solitary practitioner, mystic and doctor, mediating the world of spirits (consciousness) and the world of Nature via an empiricism of the imagination. Moreover, historical Hermeticism met and mingled with shamanic traditions, for instance in seventeenth and eighteenth century Scandinavia and America.

Second, Hermeticism appears in its proper form as paganism, specifically the Greco-Egyptian synthesis of Antiquity. The inherent syncretism of paganism led in Late Antiquity to a delirium of interpretation (*"Interpretatio"*) wherein all forms of polytheism were conflated—the Celtic and Norse, Roman, Persian, Indian and even Chinese pantheons were identified with each other and exchanged memes across vast geographical expanses linked by Alexander, the Silk Road, the sea lanes from East to West and vice versa.

Third, Hermeticism is monotheist. Jewish: its present form cannot be understood without a grounding in Kabbalah and Angelology. Hermeticism is Christian (e.g., Rosicrucian); it is Islamic (the Ikhwan al-Safa, Jabir Ibn Hayyan, the Shiite gnostics, the guilds, magic, etc.). Then Hermeticism extends into yet more polytheisms: Hinduism shares its syncretisms, and even China adopts the sulphur-mercury theory of alchemy... or perhaps originated it. Who knows?

Hermeticism provides methods for direct initiations by angels and spirits. It has no need of authoritarian cults, but also no need to reject the traditional authentic on ideological or dogmatic grounds. It can be practiced alone, in groups (the Alexandrian or Rosicrucian model) or congregations (viz., the Swedenborgian New Church)—openly or in secret—as part of any religion or outside them all—without violating its traditional integrity. You can say that such initiation is orthodox within the tradition, which is not a religion but a movement of great complexity. It can be practiced without formal training (I knew an alchemist in Iran who learned what to do by dreaming), but not without direct experience.

Hermeticism also includes science. Alone of all faiths it can take an empirical approach to science—although not materialist. Many aspects of modern science work well within a hermetic paradigm, such as quantum mechanics, the Gaia hypothesis, Chaos theory, ecology, alt. tech and alt. energy, certain lines of consciousness (brain/mind) studies, etc. All good science is potentially hermetic; if true and elegant, then also necessarily symbolic. Hermeticism provides hermeneutic and heuristic devices for separating good science from bad results; for example, on one hand healing herbs, on the other hand the malignant technopathocracy and its "Obnoxious Machinery," as the Luddites called it.

Hermeticism has a *specifically* Green form of spirituality—a sacred theory of Earth—a defense of the body—and it gestates all these within its tradition, not as later add-ons. Where does the hermetic idea of the Living Earth come from? In the *Corpus Hermeticum* the concept is not too clear. Some parts of the *Corpus* seem imbued with a Gnostic Dualist hatred of the material world—and in fact parts of the text were found at Nag Hammadi. But other parts of the work (which is clearly not by one author) seem resolutely pantheist/monist, such as the *Asclepius* (which survived in Latin and was known to medieval Hermeticists). As a form of Neo-Platonism of course ultimately Hermeticism rejects radical Dualism; some sort of emanationist scheme must accommodate a view of the body as "low" and "dark," perhaps, but not separate from the soul, or from Spirit, which is metaphysical but not "alien" as in Gnosticism. Classical Hermeticism saves the sacred nature of Nature, but only barely. What a gloomy era! —Everyone denouncing crude old-fashioned paganism, the Earth, sexuality—in a contest to see which church, mystery cult or philosophy could most foully slander the body. (Christianity won.)

The Hermetic defense of Earth and (and of course by extension the body) really arises again from the Renaissance Neo-platonic project, which expressed a rectification of the Gnostic problem within Classical Hermeticism. Cusanus, Pico, Ficino and Bruno defended the living Earth against the world-despising aspects of Christianity. Body-hatred will return again and again to haunt the occultists and mystics—but the Renaissance rectification also remains alive within the tradition, and has always provided it with a dialectic opening toward some form of pantheist monism and nature religion.

Paganism no longer appeared to the Renaissance magi as a suffocating conservative force to be overcome, but rather as an exciting new (re) discovery and delightful perspective of liberation from certain repressive aspects of Christianity. For some a reform of the Universal Church was implied, whereas certain other radicals may have left the Church altogether.

Pantheist monism (or panentheist monism) describes the philosophical position of the pro-Earth tendency within Hermeticism. This is its answer to Gnostic remnants or revenants of body-hatred that still taint the tradition. The Hermetic position was sharpened in struggle against the Counter-Reformation, which burned Bruno at the stake, and eventually embraced Descartes and his vision of a dead universe ruled by the *cogito*—a kind of crypto-Augustinian dualism with dreadful implications for the Hermetic worldview.

In any case, Hermeticism can always and has always reformed itself, changed and yet remained the same, based as it is not on dogma but spirit. Here I believe the key figure is Paracelsus, both as a political radical (backing the peasants against Luther and the princes) and a medical/scientific radical, but also as a philosophical radical, a theosopher, an original and axial figure. Many of the seeds of later Rosicrucianism, Naturphilosophie, Romanticism and Green spirituality are first collected and sown by Paracelsus, who is also one of the earliest western Hermeticists to influence the Orient as well as be influenced by it. Islamic and Jewish alchemists adopted many Paracelsian ideas; Persian, Turkish and Arabic translations of his books can be found in old libraries in Istanbul. I see Bruno and Paracelsus as heroes in the eternal avant-garde of western culture, and Paracelsus especially as the "first" Romantic.

In his spirit contemporary Hermeticism can undertake yet another exorcism of its own spooks. Above all, it must be shaped into an active response to the disaster of Cartesian/Newtonian materialism, which (from the pro-Earth perspective) constitutes a worse enemy than the Gnostics or even the Inquisition. Hermeticism's complicity in some of the worst aspects of technology should be admitted and the errors rectified. (Most of them are not the fault of the Hermeticists but of those who stole their secrets and sold them to Power—people like Boyle and Newton.) The result of these reforms would be Green Hermeticism.

In this project of reform we also need to recall that there exists a very distinct "left wing" of Hermeticism; thus we can isolate *our* Art from that of the reactionaries and conservative neo-traditionalists. Enough to mention: Bruno, Paracelsus, Blake, Charles Fourier, or even the Surrealists. A secular Hermeticism is neither inconceivable nor *a priori* illegitimate. Thomas Paine's Druidic Freemasonry, or Fourier's Androgynous Masonry, provide precedents.

III. A MOSAIC OF HERMETIC IMAGES

The *Emerald Tablet* of Hermes Trismigistus is *green* and translucent. The heraldic color of Hermeticism becomes the highest color in alchemy (rather than red, as in the West). Luminous black and emerald green, the two Prophetic colors, are to be realized spagyrically; and perhaps the Philosopher's Stone in this view is both spagyric and vegetal, itself green, green from black like plant from soil, and thus organic rather than metallic. (Although of course for alchemy metals are also alive.)

Khezr, the Green Man; water spirit; herbs and flowers blossom in his footprints; he is patron of plants. He is certainly also patron of alchemists and hermetic artists (for example, of the marbled-paper makers of Turkey). He is also a patron saint of the ecological movement, like St. Francis. He dresses all in green (although with red shoes, or so I've heard).

The Ikhwan al-Safa pray to the Sun—just like the Alexandrian Hermeticists—just like Giordano Bruno, and Thomas Campanella, and Marsilio Ficino, and Charles Fourier. "Visible deity of the universe" they called it.

Christian Rosycross goes to Damascus and "Damcar" in the East, and to Fez in Morocco. Paracelsus is initiated in Constantinople and visits the Tatars and Moslems. The Rosicrucians advocate peace with Judaism and Islam.

Paracelsus, Swedenborg and Novalis were all professional mining engineers.

Eliphas Levi (*Ritual and Dogma of High Magic*) was a follower of Charles Fourier. The great demi-messiah also influenced Gérard de Nerval, Baudelaire, and Rimbaud. The nineteenth century Hermetic Left leads directly to Surrealism. Similarly a Romantic Left existed in Germany and England—think of Godwin, Shelley, Byron and Heine.

Influenced by vulgar materialist Marxism, the Left has sadly tended to repress the memory of its own spirituality. But many radicals now no longer believe in Progress and the technological fix. Now that the USSR is dead not even Marxists believe that the only important question about the means of production—technology—is "who owns it?" What's left of the Left returns now to other ancestors, ecologists like Kropotkin and Thoreau, or even the Marx who loved to read about American Indians.

We need to bury the myth that Magic and Romanticism are somehow inherently reactionary—a myth deliberately sponsored both by Stalinists and "democratic" cultural historians (like Isaiah Berlin) as a form of triumphalist absolutism.

Now that Marxism has crumbled, one victor holds the field: Enlightenment Rationalism's greatest victory: the Free Market as inexorable law of nature. The only possible dialectical negation of this thesis, I think, must come from the long-abandoned and even repressed Hermetic Left, and from Romantic Science, and from spirituality. *Green Hermeticism.*

This *assay* is not meant as more than a suggestion of a mood or taste; perhaps of possible directions for future hermetic projects. Certain modern scientists could have been mentioned, some of them conscious Hermeticists, or at least heavily influenced. The poetic and artistic realm is also not peripheral here but quite central. Only Hermeticism of all traditions recognizes art as praxis rather than as mere auxiliary "support for contemplation." Hermeticism defines itself as art—Our Art.

Green Hermeticism can be the basis for our approach to the coming revelation, the coherent spiritual movement that constitutes the only imaginable alternative to unending degradation of Earth and humanity.

IV. ORIENTALISMO OR HERMES CUTPURSE

Hermes appears at all crossroads as merchant, thief and linguist. His path has always involved appropriation. Syncretism. Theft.

The Taoist *Yellow Emperor's Scripture of the Hidden Talisman* describes "mutual burglary" as the founding principle of the universe. Earth, heaven and humanity all steal from each other. The clever thief (like a mouse in the granary) steals without seeming to steal; but the really great thief actually gives something in return, or *redistributes*, like Robin Hood or the heroes of *The Water Margin*. (See

"Mutual Stealing" by Zhang Jiyu, in *Taoism and Ecology*, Harvard, 2001.)

A branch of my family claims descent from an eighteenth century French highwayman-dandy named Claude Duval, who always enlisted a violinist on his expeditions so he could dance by moonlight with any fair ladies he chanced to rob. He was given to fits of ludicrous generosity and came to the usual Bad End. But as Lord Keynes said, in the long run we all do. Short lives can be dense with interest and satisfaction, a truism lost to today's timid struldbrugs and medicalized Methusalems. Duval was a *typos* of Hermes as "purse-snatcher" (to quote Giordano Bruno). Hermeticism itself appears as a path, or perhaps a musical tissue, of different burglaries. (A quote from jazz musician Rahsan Roland Kirk, who once told Steve Allen he got all his many horns from "different burglaries.")

Syncretistic Hermeticism is usually dismissed by modern historians as Late and Decadent. But as soon as anything like Hermeticism began to be heard of—its pre-echoes in Pythagoras and Plato—it had *already* absorbed Oriental wisdom from Babylon and Egypt—"always already"—and not just in Late Hellenism's days. In developmentalist historiography the "Late" is made to appear somehow spoiled and impure; "progress" belongs only to the Classical "origins of science" (or whatever), and to the Modern, its culmination.

Something of the same spirit seems to have infected the occasionally acrimonious "discourse" of recent Post-Colonialist and "Subaltern" Studies. "Appropriation" has assumed the status of a taboo and all attempts at "interpretation" are seen to uncover nothing but the *mauvaise conscience* of the interpreter. Translation itself falls under suspicion; "influence" and "diffusion" are denied. On the level of *Orientalism* of course these arguments have some merit—but perhaps the baby of the Orient is being thrown out with the bath water of Orientalism. A "mystic Orient" has always existed, even—perhaps especially—in the Orient itself. To differentiate this notion from Orientalism I call it Orientalismo.

A kind of Oriental Romanticism certainly existed for instance in Mughal India—a worldview (including a culture) rooted in comparative mysticism, the cults of love and art, and in a common vocabulary of images (rose, nightingale...).

Interestingly the Avicennan medical tradition adhered to by tra-
ditional Moslems in India and Iran is called "Greek" (*tibb-i Yunani*);
and Shakespeare would also have recognized it. The reformed
Paracelsian alchemical version of this medicine also reached the
East. Paracelsus and the Rosicrucians claimed they learned it in the
East in the first place, in Constantinople, Fez and "Damcar." So: is it
Occidental or Oriental?

Oriental Romanticism helped create Western Romanticism. It
introduced chivalric romance and romantic love into Western Literature. It introduced alchemy and the Hermetic sciences, the
whole Greco-Egyptian tradition, to the "Late Middle Ages." It
introduced certain key poets to certain key texts: the Latin translation of the Persian translation of the Upanishads in William Blake's
library, for example, or Goethe's Hafez imitations, or Schlegel's
reading of Sir William Jones. It influenced Western Romantic
poets such as Poe, Fitzgerald, Emerson and James Clarence Man-
gan.

Hermes controls communication: language itself as crossroad.
And crossroads are always haunted, sacred and forbidden at the
same time, dangerous but profitable for highwayman and merchant—and always the locus of transactions (X marks the spot)
between here and there, N / S / E / W, every intersection a compass
rose. You might say Western Romanticism realized itself in the
agony of its response to the Enlightenment and Industrial Revolution: in an *agon*, a dialectic. But Oriental Romanticism eventually
also realized itself in struggle against colonialism, modernism,
Westernism, neo-puritanism and other upheavals and catastrophes.
In fact the struggle culminates for both schools around the same
time, the end of the eighteenth century. The two movements thus
share an agonistic aspect (the same enemies) and common sources
(e.g. Hermeticism): the same ancestors and the same allies.

Syncretism never mixes this and that merely for one to conquer
or subdue the other. In syncretism mixture is erotic, a matter of
mutual attraction. Dara Shikoh the Mughal prince identified "our
Sufism" and "their Vedanta" as one in a spirit of love. He died for it,
martyred by his own brother Aurengzeb, crowned puritan bigot.

Under Akbar I syncretism resulted in a new semi-secret religion,
the Din Ilahi, an aristocratic and poetic version of the countless

Hindu-Moslem, Sufi-Tantra, universalist and syncretic popular cults of India, such as the Kabirpanth, the Sikhs, the Lingayat Sad-dhus, the Bengali Bauls, etc.

Long before the Hindu-Moslem mix, under the Greco-Bactrian and Kushan Dynasties, Greco-Roman paganism was syncretized with Buddhism, Hinduism, Zoroastrianism and Central Asian shamanism. Perhaps during this period Hermetic ideas from the West, already permeated with Oriental Mesopotamian and Egyptian influences, reached India "again" with alchemical and astrological trade goods—and even with a planetary divine Mercury, still recognizably Hermetic, still alive in Hinduism to this day. Contemporary Western Hermeticists should take note of this living initiatory source.

Syncretism in Eurasia may be even more ancient. The Scythian cannabis and ephedra cult spread from China to France (always outside "historical" notice, except by Herodotus). The Megalithic cult of big stones crops up everywhere, suggesting the unthinkable: Diffusion. The Bear Cult (in which a bear is worshipped and sacrificed as a messenger to the spirits) can be found—almost identically—in Japan (amongst the Ainu of Hokkaido) and the New World (e.g., the Algonquians). Celtic myth seems to preserve similar ritual remnants (Arthur the Bear); certain stars are called the BEAR in many supposedly unrelated cultures; evidence for the bear cult is even found in Neanderthal caves and burial sites. "Willendorf Venus" figurines are found from Spain to Siberia. Amber and ritual stone axes were traded all over Paleolithic Europe and Asia. The old pagan *Interpretatio* whereby one local deity is identified with another was not invented by Alexander but certainly goes back at least to the Neolithic ("the" Goddess), probably to the Paleolithic. In this view, the first image of Hermes would be the bird-headed shaman (like the ibis-headed Thoth) found in one of the caves of the Dordogne.

Such a list of examples threatens to get out of hand and exfoliate toward delirious proportions in true syncretic/hermetic style. Hinduism in its vividly exuberant popular forms can produce this same vertiginous sensation of a *too-much* that finally bestows coherence by overwhelming all "separative vision" with sheer baroque excess. Syncretism loves *difference*, not some melting pot Lowest Common

Denominator of flavorless theomonotony. Without difference there can be no orgy of *Interpretatio*, no plural marriage, no free love between religions and peoples. Harmony requires different tones, not monotones. Syncretism values the fortuitous mistranslation just as Hermeticism values certain false etymologies based on cabbalist wordplay. The whole Renaissance science/art of emblemology arose from the appropriation and mistranslation of Egyptian hieroglyphs.

For that matter, Fitzgerald *gave* Persian poetry to us by "mistranslating" it; Pound *gave* Chinese poetry to us by "mistranslating" it. Real translation occurs through the spirit not the letter, and not via any church of orthodoxy and scholarly purity. Translation is romance. Folktales are never translated, they simply appear *all at once* in the guise of yet another language. Hermes is the only translator: language itself in its divine aspect—admittedly always ambiguous and even devilish—because as Blake said, everything has its Form and its Spectre.

In the *Amphitheatrum sapientiae aeternae* of Heinrich Khunrath (1602) we see Hermes—who began his career as a shapeless rock or heap of stones in the corner of some Arcadian meadow—depicted in the form of an emerald mountain of words. Taoist sources mention a remote cliff face at which one must stare unceasingly for three years, whereupon a strange spirit-written script will finally be discerned in the very lithic sinuosities that mock and elude the act of reading. This text is/was/will be scripture unmediated by consciousness, an irruption of language in nature—text as miraculous initiatory force. Khunrath has imagined not only the very shape of the mystic peaks of Taoist landscape paintings, but also the very shape and function of the Rosetta Stone long before its discovery.

Sol as Hermetic godhead sparks emerald fires from the mountain (which, as rock, is a type of *sal*). These green sparkles are letters and words, metaphors that carry across some paralinguistic flash from the world of meaning to the world of expression. Green fire is Green Hermes, a link between nature as speechlessness and *Natursprache* as "spell," as mantric/semantic communication, the spark between you and me, or you and some tree.

Religious and magic writing—perhaps all writing—assumes the form of a mountain that never stops growing, that extends into

THE EMERALD TABLET, *Amphitheatrum sapientiae aeternae*, Heinrich Khunrath

vast Borgesian cosmo-libraries and overflows with words upon (or beneath) words, like the famous anagrams of de Saussure, which almost drove him insane. Tibetan experts in *Terma* and Taoist exegetes of spirit calligraphies find yet more writing in nature itself, inscribed in primordial rock or encased in trees or discernable in flows of cloud or water. Nature nature-ing (*natura naturans*) is mirrored by writing, as if human effort alone could never account for the infinitude of the mountain of words. Language languages; or as Chuang Tzu put it, language speaks without speaking. Pentecostal glossolalia and Taoist spirit-writing cults are still producing scripture even today; and Hermeticism still reveals similar dreamlike outpourings of inspired and anonymous text. The Emerald Tablet, the foundational script of Hermeticism, has neither human author nor original edition; it simply appears in Arabic and then Latin. It is a mountain that floats, like certain peaks in Taoist landscape paintings, on a sea of mist or magical erudition, a vagueness of wandering motifs, stolen words, misappropriation and re-appropriation, fortuitous mistranslations and apocrypha.

The presumed Greek original of the Emerald Tablet is "lost," so perhaps the original was in Egyptian hieroglyphs. It is not found in the *Corpus Hermeticum* but may well antedate that compendium. It belongs equally to Sufism, Kabbalah and alchemy. Hermes Trismegistus himself (the divine author) is a syncresis of Babylonian Nebu, Egyptian Thoth, Greek Mercury, and some deified Egyptian alchemist of school or series or family of Egyptian alchemists. In Renaissance pictures he appears as an oriental sage, robed and bearded.

What we wish to (e)valuate here is not the purity of some orthodoxy that was never really all that pure, but rather *theft*. Hermeticism is a magpie, a collector of spiritual brightnesses—and also the Aladdin's Cave where she makes her paradoxical subterranean nest.

As Michel Serres points out in his *Hermes*, the host, guest and parasite (or symbiote) are all one, all forms of Hermes, who is thrice-great. The host's hospitality consists of a dialectical or mutual theft that reveals itself as secret reciprocity. The Three Graces, who pass the gift amongst themselves in a continual round or potlatch, symbolize the original Golden Age *economy of the Gift* (as later defined by Marcel Mauss and K. Polanyi); the system's circularity can be discerned in the ritual trade of gifts amongst the "argonauts" of the Pacific Islands (see Malinowski).

Money—which Hermes also rules—parodies this circularity and reciprocity. The gift returns to the giver but the coin (circulating medium) does not return to the spender. The coin is a circle, but has two faces, like a hypocrite or cheat. Coins are exchanged but they ruin the Gift, which is *mutual theft*. Money is a zero-sum game, just as property is unmutual theft.

Hermeticism can be allegorized as a dinner party. Ficino's translation of the *Symposium* can be compared with the amazing magical banquet served by Queen Liberty in the *Hypnerotomachia Poliphili* (complete with recipes), or the Rosicrucian marriage feast in *The Chymical Wedding of Christian Rosycross*. Cookery itself is a form of alchemy, as the great contemporary Hermetico-Surrealist painter and cook Leonora Carrington realized when she inaugurated her magical dinner parties in Mexico City in the 1950s. For the cook as artist, the guest or even the hungry parasite has great value, because the gift has no existence without both giver and receiver, without reciprocity, the third thing, the synthesis. In potlatch the giver gains immense prestige or rather poetic status (songs are composed to insure the donor's immortality); like the famous Arab host Hatim al-Tayy, the giver bankrupts himself but is remembered as a hero by his people.

This is the spirit in which Hermeticism "appropriates" or even loots all traditions to make itself a meta-tradition, a grand syncresis or mountain of all textualities, translucent and green with life.

V. MYCOHERMETICS

On the level of technology Hermeticism should lay claim on an empirical basis to everything it can use—once it's been subjected to the basic Luddite test: whether or not it "harms the commonality." "Alternate technology" in other words. Huge advances have been made here since the 1960s and 70s, but the implications are always crushed by Capital (which simply cannot use any tech not conducive to perpetual economic growth). John and Nancy Todd call this alt. tech the "New Alchemy," and their own work in biofiltering systems for polluted water certainly deserves to be considered a perfect example of neo-Hermeticism. Here we arrive at real hard science, not only because it's elegant, but also because it works. It's not as "efficient" as power-driven sewage treatment because it doesn't waste resources nor make huge profits for corporations.

On the Big Theory level, Hermeticism should appropriate all the weirdest and most wonderful findings of quantum mechanics, chaos and complexity, mind and consciousness studies, biology, herbalism and ethnobotany, neurochemistry and psychedelic research, ecology and related sciences (geomorpholgy, etc.), the Gaia hypothesis, and so on. A coherent hermetic approach is needed, especially a framework for new categorizations of knowledge. A heavily funded think tank might help!

The soft sciences might also be taken over and reformulated: psychology, sociology and economics, for example. Mind-control technology, such as the new science of Transcranial Magnetic Stimulation (which has validated much of the work of Anton Mesmer, who was of course a Hermeticist), or the various "psychic discoveries behind the Iron Curtain," MKULTRA, remote viewing...all this belongs to a world that has always been half-hermetic, half-military/intelligence, ever since John Dee advised Queen Elizabeth and Walsingham her Spymaster on cyphers, propaganda, consciousness-management and image magic. Modern advertising, public education and other mass media emerge from a shadowy world of brainwashing, spin doctoring, opinion control and perception-distortion that Giordano Bruno would've recognized immediately as magical. The new Hermeticism is ideally sited to operate in this world, to turn it upside down, to use the *hieroglyphic critique* against it, to challenge all forms of consciousness-enslavement, to liberate *from* the image *through* the image, to teach the masses about image magic and take over the means of imaginal production—"the Gray Room," as William Burroughs called it.

"Magic doesn't work," whereas Newtonian/Einsteinian physics does work. But work is a curse, as even *Genesis* cheerfully admits— so perhaps that which doesn't work, or at least remains in the realm of ambiguity, might prove to contain a *mitzvah*.

In any case Hermeticism should at once re-form itself by stealing all the "holistic" aspects of science and technology useful to its cause. It can do this all the more easily because much classical/ modern science was in fact appropriated from Hermeticism in the first place (especially by Newton, Boyle and the Royal Society).

Mysticism and religion are constantly trying to recuperate whatever scientific paradigm is in fashion; the Big Bang equals creation *ex nihilo*, for instance. But the powerlessness of mysticism and even religion in relation to the power of capital and state (and the magic of money) often makes these claims seem pathetic rather than masterful, as if God needed approval from NASA or something. Even so, the work of popularizers—the Tao of Physics, Quantum Tantra, the New Alchemy, Chaos Magic, etc.—can play a cumulative role in chipping away at the monolith of "common sense" rationalism and official consensus reality. Perhaps we should prefer exuberant irrationality to dead Reason's death-grip on life. And in any case, real rationality, simple clear thinking, remains so rare a human experience we might as well call it psy-chedelic.

Can Freud be understood without the central underlying meta-phor of the steam engine? We are still *l'homme machine;* the sexist lan-guage may have been eliminated to include *femme,* but only as part of a grand project to recruit women into the Global paradise of pancapitalism (get 'em out of the house and garden and into real jobs!). The body loses its "moving parts," becomes a computer rather than a locomotive. *L'homme genome,* mechanism as Fate (and fate of course as character). "We can see... that the human body and not the steam engine, and not even the clock, was the first machine developed by capitalism." (Silvia Federici, *Caliban and the Witch*). And the last.

The point is not whether magic works or not—at least on the microcosmic level ascribed to it by its true believers. The point is that only the magical p.o.v., the Hermetic paradigm, can break the complicity between science and money, the ideological conspiracy or "breathing-together" of technology and wealth. In other words, Hermeticism wins or loses on the macrocosmic level of value and significance, not the level of utility and instrumentality. A science of biophilia, after all would possess higher values than mere mechanic efficiency.

Mycoremediation

Fungi are among nature's most powerful decomposers. Secreting strong enzymes, fungi can not only break down wood and organic matter but eliminate chemicals and bacteria as well.

Experiments conducted with oyster mushrooms have demon-strated their amazing ability to break down petroleum. Piles of earth contaminated with diesel fuel were inoculated with the fungi, which then grew through them. Later testing revealed a 90 percent reduc-tion in contaminant levels! The powerful enzymes in the fungi had effectively broken down the diesel's complex hydrocarbon chains into simpler, harmless parts of hydrogen and carbon. The mush-rooms that grew out of the toxic pile showed no residual traces of diesel, yet had green plants been grown in such soil, they might have become contaminated.

In coffee production, the coffee berry is the waste product. Rivers in coffee-producing regions are often polluted by caffeine that leaches from piles of discarded berries. Oyster mushrooms have been grown on these piles, successfully destroying the pollutant while creating a secondary crop. Oyster mushrooms have also been found to break down PCBs. Turkeytails, another common fungi, can degrade dioxin, pentachlorophenol and chromated copper arsenate.

(From "Low-tech Bioremediation" by Scott Kellog and Stacy Pettigrew, in *Earth First!*, Samhain/Yule, 2004; see www.rhizomecollective.org.)

Green plants can also be used to heal sick soil by cleansing it of heavy metals and pollutants, a process called phytoremediation. "In one study, two crops of Indian brassica grown on a test plot in Boston, Massachusetts, reduced lead levels in the soil by 63 percent. However, one problematic aspect of phytoremediation is the disposal of the harvested plants, which must be treated as hazardous waste due to their high levels of toxic metals." Incineration creates toxic ash, which must itself be disposed of at an expense probably well above the value of any precious metals like gold which might be recovered in the process.

This problem doesn't exist with mycoremediation because mushrooms break down metals into elements. You can eat mushrooms grown on poisoned soil, but not green plants. The authors don't seem amazed enough by this fact, which sounds almost like magic. Alchemists maintain that transmutation occurs regularly in nature. They say that chicken eggs contain more calcium than hens consume. In Iran an alchemist told me that gold can be scraped in tiny quantities from the teeth of dead sheep. Either grass contains gold or else the sheep transmute grass into gold, he suggested. Phytoremediation would seem to indicate the first hypothesis as more plausible (i.e., there's a bizarre but orthodox explanation for the phenomenon)—but what about honey? Honey has always been a favorite alchemical symbol not only for its amazing properties, but also because it "really is" a product of transmutation. Or so say the Hermeticists; biochemists would disagree. But can they make honey? Mycoremediation is of course a biochemical operation, not magic—but it certainly might be called spagyric.

Recently a fascinating controversy has arisen in taxonomic science. Are mushrooms "plants" or are they so different from green plants as to require their own "Third Kingdom?" I've read that mycology remains in its infancy and is still shrouded in mystery. A single fungal entity with all its underground mycelia can outweigh a whale, making the mushroom the largest living inhabitant of Earth. Spore invasions from outer space have been mooted, and not just by the epigones of Gordon Wasson and Robert Graves.

I've spent a good deal of time in a castle in County Cork, Ireland, which is not unlike our own Hudsonian bioregion, where a friend turned the former stables into a mushroom farm. He specialized in oyster mushrooms for the gourmet restaurant trade (great with scrambled eggs). Nearby and all over Ireland one finds "pookies" or Liberty Caps, a variety of psilocybin apparently native to the British Isles. Amanita muscaria is also found in Ireland. Oyster mushrooms transform poison into food; pookies transform the quotidian trance of inattentiveness into realization.

Green plants are also rich sources for psychoactives; mushrooms are not unique in this respect. Plants and mushrooms seem to possess distinct personalities or *personae;* experienced by the psychonaut as discarnate intelligences quite "outside" oneself, relatively autonomous, epistemologically active (they know things one doesn't know); in short, they appear to meet all the requirements of beings of the Mundus Imaginalis: they are subjectively objective.

Psilocybin mushrooms are famous for their "elves." Friends who've taken Amanita muscaria maintain that they shouldn't be called "hallucinogenic" or "psychedelic." The fly agaric, they say, is "something else"—perhaps, as Wasson claimed, Soma itself.

Could the mycoremedial power of fungi be related to the effect of certain species on the human immune system, known to Taoist doctors for millennia? Only the uneducated dupes of pharmocapitalism still believe that "modern medicine" is better than "herbs and potions;" the phamaceutical megacorporations themselves are roaming the jungles looking for witchcraft remedies and shaman brews to steal and copyright.

We needn't rake over all the work on ethnomycology, mushrooms and religion, carried out since Wasson's first expeditions to Mexico in the 1950s. I've contributed a few wild speculations myself in *Ploughing the Clouds: The Search for Irish Soma* (City Lights). The purpose here is simply to launch a neologism, *mychohermetics*. I suggest that ethnomycology and mycoremediation belong to a single category that could most usefully be studied under the general rubric of hermetic science or even alchemy. (The mycologist Paul Stamets has made brilliant contributions in both areas.) Many people believe that alchemists have always been interested in the *phantastica*, including mushrooms, thanks to their traditional respect for folk medicine and herbal magic. Historians have traced a continuous unwritten awareness of Amanita muscaria for instance in Austria and North Italy; how could Paracelsus have missed this? How did he obtain his direct visions of nature spirits and Elementals, the Gnomes, Salamanders, Sylphs and Undines? Why didn't he say so clearly? Ha-ha—when did alchemy ever speak clearly? Alchemy involves secrets. The true spagyrist flees all contact with kings and bankers; the Rosicrucian ideal is to heal all and remain unknown. The whole secret history of modern science concerns the theft of knowledge from Hermeticism. Technopathology is the result of evil alchemy, the "paradoxical counterproductivity" (Illich) of institutions monopolized by Capital. Alchemy's *materia prima* can be "found on any dung hill;" Hermeticism changes shit into gold. Modern science takes all the ancient dreams of magic and betrays them: the dream of flight becomes the nightmare of 9/11, the dream of transmutation becomes the reality of Hiroshima, etc. Technology turns gold into shit. Stealing from shamans usually involves taking a live complex organic plant or fungus and stepping on it till it becomes two-dimensional enough to synthesize. I'm not saying synthesis *per se* is evil or useless, but capitalism puts profit before health and therefore conspires to "medicalize consciousness," as Ivan Illich put it, to mediate between plants and humans, to suppress or flatten all psychoactive properties, and to monopolize the ownership of life itself. This is why spagyric medicine uses the *whole plant*, and not a synthesis of the "active ingredient."

Many mushrooms are coprophilic—that is, they're found on dung. You might say that fungi turn dung into consciousness, which can well be symbolized as gold. They turn poisonous metals into atoms of hydrogen and carbon; they transform death into life, literally, so you can scramble it with eggs and eat it. No wonder they've been worshipped as gods. The scholar John Allegro was thought to be insane when he identified Jesus as a mushroom—perhaps the same madness afflicts many shamans as well—and many hermeticists. It wouldn't be quite correct to include the fungal mysteries into "Green" Hermeticism, since mushrooms aren't green. But clearly they belong to the science we're proposing. Therefore I suggest a small but separate field within the science, and suggest the term mychohermetics as its name.

(Note: For a brief intro to artists working in bioremediation such as Mel Chin, see "The Alchemical Garden" by Amy Lipton, ecoartspace, at greenmuseum.org. For mycoremediation, see the magisterial and almost encyclopedic *Mycelium Running: How Mushrooms Can Help Save the World* by Paul Stamets; Berkeley: Ten Speed Press, 2005.)

VI. SHINING-THROUGH (*TAJALLI*)

The usual metaphors for the shining-through of the divine into matter (e.g., stained glass) smell a bit of Plato's Cave, as if the world constituted a scrim of dead but translucent matter *through which* light shines; that the glass stands for the archetypes; that colored shadows, "material things," are less real than the glass or the light. The spatial analogy seems clumsy. The unitarian p.o.v. stipulates that material things themselves (in, of and for themselves) are *per se* the shining-through. The glass metaphor unpacks (and tends to lose and forget) the original unity of light, archetype and object.

The Sufis are always hedging and shuffling around this point, lest they be accused of heresy (incarnationism, monistic pantheism, antinomianism). Almost any Sufi poem taken literally would land the reader in this dilemma. Hence all the endless apologetics and *pilpul* of the orthodox Islamic mystics; and the same is true, naturally, for all organized religions. Only animistic shamanism and certain kinds of paganism can deal openly with the scandal of *tajalli*. Within the monotheist religions only syncretism and heresy can accomplish, or at least attempt it, but only at the expense of outsider status and even persecution.

Hermeticism usually reaches us through the lens of Abrahamic Tradition—or the *filter*, perhaps, that separates us from the pagan original. But the pagan "original" is already filtered through Gnosticism and its world-denying extreme Dualism, or through Neo-Platonism and its modified dualism. The idea of *tajalli* and the "ensouled universe" or living Earth can be read into texts like the *Emerald Tablet* or certain sections of the *Corpus Hermeticum*. The idea is there *in nuce* but obscured by Gnostic distrust of life and Late Pagan world-weariness.

Cusanus, Bruno, Ficino, Pico *et al.* performed an esoteric hermeneutic or exegesis (*ta'wil*) on the hermetic material, de-turned or upended or collapsed the dualism and restored the idea of the living Earth, reading the old symbols in a new light (even making "fortuitous errors" regarding the Hieroglyphs for example): exegesis in the light of direct mystical experience and experiment rather than dead authority. Biophilia in the modern sense begins here. Old-time paganism simply worships "the world." Renaissance Hermeticism launches the *defense of Earth*.

Along one line of development this new *dignitas* of Earth (and the human) leads toward "early modern science," the Enlightenment, Rationalism, the de-souling and disenchantment of the universe, materialist reductionism—and at last to the treatment of Earth as dead matter, or something to be conquered. But on another line of development—the central but "forgotten" line—it leads to the Paracelsian/Rosicrucian counter-Enlightenment (or parallel Enlightenment, if you follow Frances Yates here), to Romantic Science (Swedenborg, Novalis, Goethe, *Naturphilosophie*, etc.)—the whole underground occult movement of the eighteenth and nineteenth centuries (including the "pseudo-sciences")—and paradoxically now to certain strange interpretations of post-Newtonian/Einsteinian science itself.

The antinomian implications of the *tajalli* experience persist and even increase in the context of the "orthodoxy" of capitalism and its neo-Enlightenment rationalistic program of reducing all relations to money relations. The fascinating proof of this is the literally incredible hysteria surrounding psychotropic plants. Consciousness itself, not various weeds and white powders, is clearly the *subject* of this panic and repression. No one cares anymore what you believe—it's no longer a matter of the Inquisition. The problem lies with what you see. Modern Democracy allows you any brand of pie-in-the-sky you like. The real *nomos* is no longer concerned with mere opinion, but with perception, and proprioception.

Unconsciously (or consciously, what difference would it make?), the power structure, the wielders of *nomos*, are convinced that widespread use of entheogens would cause a shift of perception away from the world of dead matter organized into commodities, and toward the world as alive, beautiful, sacred—and directly threatened by Money's inherent logic of greed and growth. Maybe this belief of the Drug Warriors is itself a hallucination? —Certainly they sometimes behave quite irrationally. But historical and anthropological data suggest otherwise. The Warriors have a valid point. Certain plants do seem to affect human consciousness.

Shamanism is the suppressed content of religion. That is, it provides all the stuff that *works*—which is then monopolized by the priests of the temples, then forbidden to the mere faithful, then suppressed, and finally forgotten. Religion is the suppressed content of ideology; even dialectical materialism is based on axioms of faith—and leads to the establishment of a Church. Ideology is the suppressed content of Post-Modernism (all that nostalgia for categories!). Russian dolls.

Only Hermeticism can overcome (or evade) this dreadful archaeology of the dialectic, because it has kept or rediscovered direct access to *stuff that works*, to shamanistic direct experience, to techniques (of "ecstasy" as Eliade said)—to an ecological science of consciousness—the *tajalli* of living Earth. Hermeticism, once rectified, reformulated, revivified and stripped of its failures (though not of its secrets) must appropriate, as a philosophy, the sciences and techniques of consciousness and re-contextualize them in a hermetic worldview with a militant Green ethics.

This vast work can only be carried out by many and over much time, but it could begin with theoretical work, with the hammering out of coherent theory. Not another orthodoxy, but also not spineless relativism nor mere academic futilitarianism. We need strategic theory.

Hermeticism will always be occult, but it can no longer afford to fail, to subsist pallidly in the shadows of charlantanry, New Age sewage and reaction. Politically Hermeticism should embrace its proud radical heritage—Paracelsus defending the Peasants' Rebellion, Bruno martyred at the stake, Blake the revolutionary Druid, Charles Fourier and Utopian Socialism, the Surrealists—the list could be endless.

Hermeticism is only partially the work of solitary visionaries and scientists; it also embraces both group work and social theory. The Alexandrian Hermeticists had a community, as did the Ikhwan al-Safa and the school of Jabir ibn Hayyan. Rosicrucianism may never have existed in the literal terms of the original manifestos as a secret society, but it certainly proposed a social program—based on tolerance and altruism—with revolutionary implications. Fourier as Utopian Socialist depicts a future in which Hermeticism might transform both nature and humanity. The point is not to resurrect one (or more) of these old social theories, but *to have a social theory*. The gist of it is already obvious: at a bare minimum it must be Green and anti-Capitalist. The details we can hash out later.

Obviously "neo-hermeticism" or whatever it will come to be called cannot achieve paradigmatic functionality without dialectic engagement; a clear sociology of science; a clear view of money (and its malign hermetic origins); a sharp critique of technology and repudiation of technocracy; a creative Green New Alchemy with clear results. None of this is possible under Capital; either because it threatens the bottom line of profit (or even Property itself), or else threatens the very perception of reality necessary to capital's totalitarian management of consciousness.

The ideal social group for Green Hermeticism *now*, perhaps, might be the "think tank"—equivalent of the Dark Age monastery. We can think of "tank" in the Hindustani sense of a cool shady pool of water with stone steps on all four sides, a few water lilies and lotuses, not as a military tank, or an aquarium or a gas tank. No doubt traditionalists would prefer a term such as "Invisible College." The whole point *this time* would be to keep it from turning into yet another Royal Society, selling out to the ruling paradigm. Funding must come from outside Capital—but outside Capital there is no funding. Catch 23.

A potent triumph for Hermeticism would be the discovery of an effective sacrament guaranteed (more or less) to induce the *tajalli* experience. But what am I saying? Many such sacraments already exist... and are forbidden. Even the harmless Haoma of the Zoroastrians (ephedra) has recently been banned by the Feds. To be effective in the hermetic sense the *phantastica* must be experienced in a structured "set and setting," or even ritualized in entheogenic ceremonialism, in order to bring out their full potential for consciousness transformation. In effect an entire culture needs to be created or "co-created" with and around the entheogenic experience. Again, a great deal of work has already been done on this, and we post-moderns are in an ideal position to use the past creatively. This cultural creation, itself a form of social magic in the Nolan (Brunoninan) sense, could be one subject of the Invisible College—one part of the subversive agenda.

Needless to say however that entheogenic ceremonialism alone is no solution to any problem. The very notion of problem-solving fails to serve the particular exercise in theoretical driftwork attempted here, theory in the etymological sense of vision, looking-at, see-search. The semi-or roughly secret society, think tank or Invisible College we hypothesize would have to concern itself with the entirety of Romantic Science and Green Hermeticism, not just with the question of *tajalli.* But where consciousness itself (or "sweet love") is deemed a crime, the College must be prepared to think like a nest of heresy. "Heretics Unite!," as Henry Corbin used to say. (Actually, anarcho-federation might be better.) Anyway, there's nothing to lose but chains of false consciousness –and everything to gain: the Sacred Earth.

VII. CONCRETE AND CEMENT

The Roman Empire invented concrete to "solidify with the minimum of voids" a world all too porous and fluid, to make space itself more dense and compacted in heavy auras that still hover around Roman ruins. Concrete may even warp time by altering gravitational fields. The secret was lost and not rediscovered till the nineteenth century, needless to say. Paradoxically concrete time speeds up not down. Then it collapses.

Natural cement was discovered in Rosendale, New York, circa mid-1820s, and used to build much of New York City including the Brooklyn Bridge, that first thought best thought of Modernism. The Rosendale biome was pierced and scored with canals and mines. Kilns smoldered in the hills, a nightly Bosch-scape of satanic mills. Progress uncovered a nest of Rip van Winkles lost in the backwoods since the seventeenth century: Dutch drop-outs, Hessian deserters, runaway slaves, rogue Algonquians, all mixed and known to Eugenic Theory as "the Jukes."

After Rosendale's boom came the sudden ascendancy of artificial Portland cement. The D&H Canal dried up. Time collapsed around the village. Portland cement is weaker than the natural stuff, but faster drying, making it ideal for twentieth century capitalism with its illusory lightness and airiness, secretly deploying malign alchemical forces to ideologize consumerism, concretize the imaginal and use it to oppress the masses with the heavy hard time of rationalized labor.

Not to say concrete's bad in itself. Blake insists everything has its Form and its Spectre. Blakean geniuses use cement's bounding line to depict visionary space: Simon Rodia's Watts Towers, for instance, or the concrete fantasy gardens of crazy Wisconsin and Iowa, or Gaudi's incomplete cathedral: form without function except on psychic levels symbolizing matter's attempt to merge with imagination and vice versa. Grotesque Concrete. Surreal Cement.

Roman concrete must have been invented by Hermeticists. Its recipe expresses all four Elements—fire in the form of *pozzuolana* or volcanic earth; water as the lime slurry; earth in the gravel and crushed brick; air in the volcanic tuff. Thus it can be seen as alchemical artificial "perfect" stone, an improvement or refining of Nature, a quickening of her slow movements, like instant stalagmites. This would explain its resonance (both positive and negative) with Imagination. Hence also its use in the Pantheon in Rome—the dome as heaven—the syncretism of "all the gods" as memory theater—magic used to empower Imperium.

Modern ferroconcrete incorporates the metal of Mars or Nergal, the god who presides over war and the emergence of the Iron Age—Civilization as hegemony—again: the idea of empire. It is perhaps no coincidence that cement and iron expand and contract under temperature change at the same rate. "Compressive stresses are sustained by the concrete and the tensile stresses resisted by the steel" (*Columbia Desk Encyclopedia*): an expression of the Hermetic dialectic. Hermetic secrets that fall into the hands of Power (whether church, state or corporation) have their value reversed, form to spectre, gold to feces. Instead of Watts Towers or buildings in the shapes of ducks and elephants (once so popular in the United States) we get the titanic prometheanism of post-Bauhaus XXIst century neo-Brutalism, building as machine to re-shape human consciousness not toward autonomy, pleasure or wonderment, but uniformity and work (with a bit of PoMo frou-frou thrown in to distract the attention of viewers from the Same Old Big Box). Civilization as hegemony again, Imperium again and again, the Roman triumphalism of the Global Empire of Pure Kapital, first in its stalinoid "International" form, then as "Irony." (Marx might say, "second time as farce.") Surely DisneyLand would not be possible without ferroconcrete... nor the World Trade Center Towers. Pure Image Magic.

Now Rosendale slipped imperceptibly back into the slough of Jukish timelessness for half a century during which the cement mines and furnaces fell into picturesque ruin—a whole decline and fall in miniature. Progress took itself off elsewhere. Cement/concrete moved up the river to Greene County, to Cementon-on-the-Hudson. Today there's a very heavy psychic aura up there; last vestiges of XXth century titano-industrial spaces bend the light over the valley into gray zones.

But even in this New Cyber Age, capital has still not outgrown its need for cement and other remnants of the Old Economy. Far from it. If heavy industry has almost vanished from our privileged region it's not because the whole world is growing Greener. The demise of small industry and small farming in New York has allowed forest to spread; real estate has become more important than production, so the verdant "viewshed" must be preserved. I confess to conflicting emotions: I don't want to live near any cement factories. I'm glad I can afford (barely) to stay in an area where sprawl is resisted—if not always successfully—and environmental concerns are politically hot. But I know it's a luxury. I know that the cement factories will simply be shunted off to Mexico.

Moreover, a subtle miasma hangs over the whole concept of "preservation," the transformation of nature into spectacle, the museumization of the past, green tourism, heritage tourism, the picturesque as "resource," view as commodity. Are we the colonizers of our own Washington Irving Xmas card? Tourists-in-place? Passive scopophiliacs? If we add nothing beautiful to the landscape, does what we *preserve* turn into mere inauthenticity and parodic self-representation?

Blake says Imagination *is* the world we live in, not some abstract realm of ideas. Those who refuse this knowledge are condemned to live in *someone else's* idea, concretized in concrete.

Actually we now live inside the idea of money, i.e., inside money's own image of itself—which accounts for the eerie "post-human" look of the new globalism. The tools with which this idea is expressed have been cyberized in an attempt to achieve the machine's own image of itself as pure money. Concrete is flexile enough to be shaped into these abstractions, these buildings without organs. So concrete still rules our destinies. Civilization would've been impossible in Sumeria without clay, "the first plastic." Concrete is an alchemical preparation of this clay. The Roman Empire which perfected this plastic "never died," as the lunatic SciFi Gnostic illuminatus P.K. Dick used to insist. It went into remission during the "dark" ages: Chartres uses no concrete. But it survives and always takes new forms. In a sense the Church tried to suppress it, but eventually became it (as in the churches of Corbusier). Capitalism, based on Roman laws of property, inherits the lost secret of concrete.

Who was that John Smeaton who invented hydraulic concrete in 1756? Maker of navigational instruments, he rebuilt the Eddystone Lighthouse with his amazing new stuff. Was he the "keeper of the Light" who "married a mermaid one fine night?" Was he a Royal Society Freemason? Was he a thief of Hermetic secrets in the service of Power?

The trick to living such a life would be to evade all the major technologies based on theft of Hermetic secrets. Ben Franklin stole electricity, that Freemason and member of the Hellfire Club and the Royal Society. Internal combustion was filched by Christian Huygens (d.1695), another scientific instrument maker who discovered Saturn's rings, opposed Newton's corpuscular theory of light with a wave theory—and designed an engine to run on gunpowder explosions. Gunpowder was attributed to the alchemists Roger Bacon and Berthold Schwarz, but they learned it from Arab hermeticists who learned it from the Chinese, who used it to exorcize demons (and still do). Too bad the Jukes got mixed up with cement. They tried to evade civilization by living like Indians up in the Binnewaters, but found themselves stuck in the way of Progress. The Eugenicists discovered them and made up the name Juke and made it a byword for backwardness, rural petty crime, incest, zero-work mentality, mixed blood, bad blood. Other dropout "isolate" communities around here went unnoticed, like Pang Yang or the Eagle's Nest, because they weren't sitting on such valuable real estate. A few such strange hamlets persist today—I could name names. But I prefer to keep them roughly secret; in fact, I rather aspire to such status myself. I'd like to get out from under the sign of concrete and degenerate back into the true American way of life: "Gone to Croatan."

Having learned to live without these technologies, it might then prove possible to re-appropriate them and liberate them in the sense that Gaudi liberated concrete. But even metallurgy was once an alchemical secret (see Eliade's *Forgerons et alchemistes*) and it was used to create the very basis for the emergence of hegemonic Civilization. (Hence the uncanniness of mines, miners and smiths, and the abhorrence of all "primitives" for the "rape of the Earth" involved in mining metals.) Reversion to Stone Age tech and its non-authoritarian *communitas* seems impossible, short of an "End" of Civilization itself.

But at least we can try to cultivate an hermetic critique of substances and techniques. The concept of the "sick building," now discussed as a matter of bad lighting or ventilation, should be enlarged to include an alchemical analysis of the structure (the shape) of the building and its materials. Living space becomes antibiotic under certain conditions, just as other aspects of environment are polluted by poisonous airs, lights and noises. Local premodern vernacular building is always trustworthy and always in good taste (e.g. the wigwam, Dutch stone house, English barn). Vast concentrations of steel and concrete cause negative energy basins to accrete. In such a context architecture must go on the occult defensive: perhaps blood sacrifices on the cornerstones, or horse skulls buried under floors! Reich's theory about the orgone accumulator or "box" as a composite of organic and inorganic materials might reveal that ferro-concrete actually attracts and traps negative or "deadly" orgone rays.

In theory one could design a spagyric house. Joseph Beuys, himself an alchemist, Anthroposophist and anarchist, might call this "social sculpture." Note his use of stone, copper and living trees in his "7000 Oaks" project of urban renewal.

One of the earliest uses of concrete in American architecture was the Octagon House of Orson Fowler, you guessed it, an occultist anarchist (and phrenologist). It was the buckyfuller dome of the mid-nineteenth century "first" New Age of Reform and spiritualism, a house for the People, eccentric and jewel-like, but actually quite livable and cheap to build. Concrete as shaped by visionary and self-taught architects may prove to be possible in alchemical building, if used with full consciousness of its occult significance.

VIII. LYCANTHROPY

No surprise that opium is touted in old pharmacopeias as both cause and cure of lycanthropy. To take a drug is already to turn into an animal: to rise above or sink beneath merely all-too-human consciousness, which, as Bataille points out, consists largely of consciousness of death.

Shamanism makes a science of such botanical shapeshifting. Religions then crystallize these kinetic discoveries into static images; for instance, the Egyptian beast-deities. All help comes from outside human ken. Even monotheists envision bird-people as semi-divine.

Werewolf ointment was rich in atropine and datura. DMT convinces you you've experienced reptilian or plant awareness and in expert brews like ayahuasca it can open up protean relations with jaguars or jungle vines. Chinese alchemy developed exercises and drugs to mimic archaic shamanic transformations into cranes, tortoises, even trees. The *männerbunden* did it in ecstatic assemblies; the wolves, eagles and imaginal beasts that inspired these secret societies later populate European heraldry, commemorating "marriages" between barbarian ancestors and various beasts or were-beasts. Or— as with American Indian clans—the ancestors themselves were animals once upon a time. Or adopted by animals, wolves perhaps, like the founders of ROMA (AMOR backwards); wolfchildren, *enfants sauvages*, who constitute a kind of erotic subset of such legendry.

Children, even infants, seem to know about these beast–identities instinctively, even now in a world where real wild beasts are nearly never seen and even domesticated animals have become rare. Possibly this "instinct" actually results from instructions transmitted non-verbally (and "unconsciously") over thousands of generations of mothers and children—gestures, skin temperatures, pheromones, facial expressions, "auras"—teaching children how to "think with animals"—and even more secretly (hermetically) think as animals. Consciousness is not from the brain alone but the whole body in relation to total environment; so also with communication, the sharing of consciousness.

The first images were images of animals. Once I stood on a random street corner in Manhattan and counted six or seven animal images within my immediate sight, mostly being used to sell products. The walls of our caves are still adorned with adored and remembered beasts.

Extinction of a species would then mean—really and not just metaphorically—extinction of an aspect of humanity. The earliest (Neanderthal) evidence for religion reveals Cave Bear worship—a religion still practiced today, or in the "ethnographic present" (e.g., amongst the Ainu of Hokkaido, or the Algonquians of my region, who sacrificed their last sacred bear in 1876). Or put another way: wipe out a species and we're forced to become it somehow, to go on suffering in its place... the dodo... the passenger pigeon.... And the sudden rediscovery of a "lost" species, like the ivory-billed woodpecker, feels like partial resurrection, temporary salvation.

Are vegetarians and vegans refusing to act like animals by not killing and eating other animals? Perhaps there is a kind of Cartesianism at work here, a split between the Cogito and the soulless beasts? " I don't like animals and I don't want them in my mouth," as a veggie friend once told me. Gnostic Dualists practiced vegetarianism not because they loved animals or considered fleshly animality too sacred, but because they attributed it to cosmic evil. They longed to "rise above the flesh" as pure spirit; their Perfecti stopped eating altogether, yearning for the "Consolation" of a slow holy suicide.

Disdain and even hatred for hunters has become a class thing in modern America. "Hunters are all rednecks and reactionaries," as a loud local Green politico recently proclaimed. Soi-disant enviro's often seem secretly motivated by mere NIMBYism and real estate values; their "enemies" are often farmers and hunters. Is this sick or what? Is "Nature" a theme park? Is Nature a hobby, a sport, an educational resource? Doesn't a subconscious strain of covert fear, misunderstanding and even hatred often appear to lurk beneath such pious sentiments?

Capitalism exacerbates this split; Communism (as the highest form of Kapital) merely re-enforced the notion of nature as raw material for exploitation. A healthy society would have no need for Environmentalism—and Environmentalism is itself a symptom of sickness, not of health. Reification of nature as something separable from human consciousness—whether in order to exploit it or fetishize it—always tends toward false consciousness, and a bad conscience.

To paraphrase Rimbaud, one must be absolutely Green. Of course. But "one must" be green not as triumphalist but as penitent, realizing always that one can act only from sickness, not from health. Fatuous optimism loses every battle. Pessimism never even fights. One is obliged to act as an *anti-pessimist*, if one is to act at all.

The sole medicine that might still heal the split between nature as object of knowledge and nature *as knowledge*—or so we think—was concocted by Hermeticism, which itself is neither religion nor science but ART, and therefore compatible with all sciences and religions, or with none. Each stage of alchemy "is" (among other things) an animal: crow, peacock, lion, phoenix, unicorn, mermaid or other heraldic-mythic shapeshifter or beast/god; Hermeticism always found animals good to think with. Sumer and Egypt appropriated their divine or demonic hybrids from earliest Paleo-and Neolithic shamanisms (like the bird-headed man of Lascaux).

This ancient relation sometimes manifests darkly, as in the witch's toad and cat-familiars; sometimes lightly, as in the companionable ravens and lions of certain saints, Sufis and Zen hermits. Although derived from different roots (maybe), the words *venery* and *venery*, meaning the art of love and the art of hunting, remain identical—with the very sense of identity urged by Novalis in *The Disciples at Saïs* between consciousness and nature.

For Paracelsus the alchemical dyad of Sulphur and Mercury failed to solve the problem of the Philosopher's Stone. There must exist a third principle: Salt, the body, the necessary resolution of the dialectic. The body is also the animal. Only this triplicity (or "trialectic") can "redeem fallen nature" precisely by re-integrating it into the divine and the human, not just as an epiphenomenon but as essence. This is—or would be—*the re-paganization of monotheism*—or more precisely, its hermeticization.

In Classical Hermetism the dialectic appears as Mercury's Caduceus—the stick with two snakes. By a stupid twentieth century error this symbol was appropriated by the medical establishment in place of its proper symbol, the staff of Asclepius, which has *one* snake, animal patron of the incubation of healing dreams. The AMA should either give back the Caduceus to Hermeticism, or else earn it by renouncing allopathic rigidity and embracing hermetic pluralism. But I digress.

The Caduceus makes Hermes Heaven's Herald, able to communicate rapidly (even instantaneously) at a distance. Hence Hermes or Thoth invents writing, which narrows the scope of speech into a far less subtle form but makes it act at a distance in space and time—like magic. Thoth is an ibis-headed man or else a purple-assed baboon. Herald as messenger is also the herald of heraldry with its language of beasts and werebeasts; for example, a crane with a stone in its claw stands for the Cranston family. Rebus is the essence of writing. In alchemy the Rebus designates the Hermaphrodite, itself the resolution of a dyad. As. M. Serres pointed out Hermes always appears as "the Third," the parasite at the dinner table, the "cutpurse" as Giordano Bruno called him: language as theft.

Hermes of the *Homeric Hymns* steals Apollo's cattle on the very day he's born, meanwhile (for extra fun) inventing the lyre from a tortoise shell. To mollify Apollo he gives him the lyre; the god of the Muses later bestows it on Orpheus, who uses it to charm animals and even trees. This lyre is Harmonia Mundi, the sound of the cosmos that rests on Turtle's back. (And everyone knows "it's turtles all the way down," as the old shamaness told the missionary who asked, if the world stands on a tortoise, what does the tortoise stand on?)

The charming of animals and trees implies something other than the conquest of nature. Orpheus does not exploit the animals as "resources" and so they mourn his martyrdom sincerely. Could animals ever be insincere? And the werewolf—as we know from old movies—is the most painfully sincere of all monsters.

Neo-shamanism has popularized the archaic notion of "animal helpers" or personal totems. If the practice sometimes veers toward vulgar make-believe savagism or sentimental Bambiism, nevertheless, in the long run, it has positive and even poetic aspects—and perhaps real validity. After all, it's difficult to cultivate relations with nature without relatives, specific kinships and modes of identity. In this context even heraldry appears no longer dry snobbery but potent animal magic.

Take Crane-Stone again—the blazon of one branch of my family. Is it merely a "punning crest?" Scottish (and German) heraldry is rife with Masonic/Rosicrucian symbols and alchemical references. Generally, serious historians disdain it for these very fancies (it's "late and decadent"). The crane is the European ibis; or rather the ibis is the Egyptian crane in modern taxonomy. All cranes seem a bit uncanny. Their nests are "lucky." Ancient Celts and Taoist Immortals sometimes became or rode on cranes, or kept their magic medicine in "crane bags." The Cranstons were neighbors of Sir Walter Scott, and he depicts them in *The Lay of the Last Minstrel* as haunted by a "goblin butler." We're also related to that wizard Earl of Bothwell executed for practicing witchcraft against James I and VI of Scotland. I presume that we descend from some druidic werecrane, just as other Scots clans claim descent from silkies (wereseals), or certain French families from Melusine, the famous werewater-snake or fresh-water mermaid.

Such connections are useful to Hermeticists as once to Paleolithic dreamers of venery. Art is possession by animal spirits. If consciousness itself arises from an awareness of death unknown to animals, then all human culture must begin with the magic of becoming animal to defeat death.

IX. PROTECT YOURSELF FROM IMAGE MAGIC

Most of the time we scarcely wake up past the minimum of awareness needed for work, school, or the myriad distractions of media and entertainment. This is not honest sleep, but a kind of low-grade semi-trance state of sub-awareness in which senses are dulled and mind is lulled.

The active imagination—in all its forms from dreaming to active creativity—shuts down and almost suffocates in this airless atmosphere of crypto-trance.

Every once in a while we wake suddenly. Perhaps we experience little epiphanies or intense emotions, deep aesthetic shock/pleasure, love, sublime awe, visions, strange coincidences or adventures—"peak experiences" (to quote Colin Wilson's use of that term). But it's difficult to sustain these waking moments—and sometimes very painful. Not all wake-up calls are nice.

In our quasi-trance condition of "everyday" consciousness we are bombarded by images. As a culture we suffer image overload and approach a crisis or catastrophe of imagic saturation. Advertising, PR, spin doctoring, infotainment, reality management, political and economic brainwashing ("education"), propaganda, sheer media sickness: we whirl in a vortex of imagery, most of it aimed at manipulating our responses in some way.

Image magic (the two words are related of course) can be defined as the bringing-about of change in the real world through manipulation of consciousness by images.

How for example does an advertisement work? Whatever may be said about psychological behaviorism and subliminality, etc., the actual effect of an effective ad is akin to magic. It causes action at a distance by manipulating images—and words, which "fixate" the images and activate them, like spells.

The hermetic science of image magic was revived during the Renaissance and especially richly by three magi: Marsilio Ficino, Giordano Bruno and Cornelius Agrippa. Many of their works appear in modern translations and will repay the reader's close attention. What follows is merely an application to our modern condition of their theories. If I use their prescriptive language of "should" and "must," I do so without any intention of dogmatism. There's always more than one way out of a labyrinth.

Protection from images, resistance against representation and alienation, constitutes only half the work. It's not just a simple matter of auto-deprogramming or psychic self-defense. As in certain martial arts there is no good defense without attack.

It's as if both eye and image are simultaneously emanating "rays." The magi believed this literally, but it still works as metaphor. The question is: who's to be master, I or image? In order to *win*, eye must not only stop the flow but reverse it. Not just protection but *projection* is required.

Iconoclasm has its attractions but it's not the hermetic solution. One frees oneself from the image *through* the image. Application of hermetic critique and hieroglyphic theory demands not just denial but deployment: mastery of the image.

Nevertheless the first step consists of stopping the flow. The term "media fast" was coined (by the Dutch anarchist collective Adilkno) to indicate the need for temporary drastic cold-turkey cutting-out of all images.

During such a retreat the imagination will reactivate itself. Entheogenic phantastica (many still legal) may prove useful, or vigorous physical action—"cutting wood, drawing water"—or walking in forests or mountains, or tantric sex... whatever breaks the trance: a traditional spiritual retreat, or a mad love affair. But in any event, one should make it a pleasure; convince one's body as well as one's mind.

The next step is *hermetic critique.* The "chains" of images must be broken, as Bruno says; deep analyses of image complexes must be carried out to exorcize and erase their power. Ideally we should concentrate on complexes that have obsessed and controlled us without our permission, or even conscious awareness. This is the iconoclastic stage, and may prove very painful.

Next, or simultaneously, one develops "ritual protection." Here aspirants may attempt empirical validation of traditional hermetic methods of psychic self-defense to protect wakefulness against dulling or even attack from malignant forces. The idea of the vivifying of idols, from the *Corpus Hermeticum,* provides a key to this work: we enliven our own imaginal power as defense against falling victim to someone (or something) else's.

This leads logically to the next step; but again, these "steps" may be simultaneous rather than sequential; namely, to the hermetic science of projection: "speaking in hieroglyphs." Here the experimenter reverses the flow and sends images *out*, projects them like rays, in attempts to transform consciousness and bring about change.

In effect this sounds like art. And it is. Not simply art in the modern sense but Art in the old hermetic sense. In our society the artist is considered a special kind of person, but in a normal society (as A.K. Coomaraswamy insisted) every person would be a special kind of artist. Any activity in life can be that life's creative expression and can change the world, however subtly, however small the scale.

However, *projection* is also a form of resistance against the forces of consciousness management, perhaps in a small way even an attack on them. Other people are now involved. This social dimension implies a politique of image magic.

Eventually we must hope for the emergence of major projects involving many people at once in social change through the suppression of image magic as oppressive consciousness manipulation; and its realization as social art, or the hermetic art of life. New magical media (some extremely ancient) will allow new forms of resistance against the malignant counter-hermeticism of money itself, which is pure imagination and yet all-powerful as "God:" against death of creative imagination, death of biosphere, death of utopian hope. We would like to envision a *movement*, a widespread reversal of the image flow, its deturnment from death to life and to spirit.

Because of course the practice of image magic in this sense is a spiritual path. The seeker who began with magic as metaphor now realizes that it's real, real as it needs to be. That the Earth is a living being, that the universe is ensouled, now appears as a necessary hypothesis or axiom. Something like an existential leap of faith is required.

But if image magic involves other states of consciousness in which such leaps can be contemplated without vertigo, it is also a science, a knowledge, an Art. It demands no religious affiliation and can be pursued outside all organizations and dogmatic structures. It requires no gurus, although it needs teachers and activists, even militant activists.

But it begins with the individual. It bestows immediate benefits, not just distant aspirations for social change. The realization that one has been manipulated may be painful. But the goal—mental wakefulness and imaginal freedom—seems well worth the risk.

X. AROMAL BAPTISM

Life *per se* has a certain smell to it, a light and vibrant perfume, such as that which emanates from a far-off meadow of flowering weeds on a vagrant breeze, or from the nape of a beloved neck. This scent can outlast death, losing only its individuality into a general "odor of sanctity" sometimes noticed in tombs of saints or in association with certain psychic states. This scent of preservation-of-life provides a clue to the mysterious nature of that "spiritual mumia" mentioned by Paracelsus.

Ordinary mumia (if genuine) consisted of actual powdered mummies from Egypt. Untold hecatombs of wrapped corpses were harvested; it's a wonder anything was left for archaeologists and museums. Both Christians and Muslims valued the stuff as a cure-all, and the alchemists were fascinated by it. Never having seen any, I conjecture that the aromatic gums used in mummification (described by Herodotus) must still have retained some scent even after thousands of years.

In alchemy scent constitutes a kind of soul of a substance. Just as mummification was thought to preserve soul (or an aspect of soul) and grant it immortality, so the perfume of the drug mumia indicated its potency for life, its medicinal virtue. Ficino speaks of the health-giving properties of certain odors, whether simple, as in living nature, or compound, as in hermetic incenses and perfumes. The very existence of "gas" (*chaos*) was first propounded by an alchemist, Van Helmont; J. Priestly discovered "dephlogisticated air" (oxygen) by alchemic research.

When I pour hot water over good Chinese tea, such as the Phoenix Bird Oolong (competition grade) that sparked these thoughts, its perfume almost exactly duplicates the breeze that blows through my kitchen window half the year permeated with a melange or bouquet of all wildflowers, crops and trees to the West, a kind of generalized bouillabaisse of whatever's in bloom. In other words, the tea comes back to life; or rather, was never entirely dead, like some pharaoh, or Zanoni, or Comte de St Germain.

Ultimately Paracelsus identifies spiritual mumia with the Imagination, or more precisely with the subtle but operant efficacy of the imaginal, its "shakti" so to speak, its power. For Charles Fourier smell was the *axial* sense, the most direct and central and yet most esoteric. He spoke of *aromal rays* emitted by living beings including stars and planets. "Astral rays" and "planetary influences" are here conceived as aromas. That which orchestrates the sense of smell is simultaneously the most sensual and most spiritual of organs, conveying meaning beyond words or images, as well as the *élan vital* itself.

Fourier believed that the wretched condition of our present Civilization resulted in part from the blockage of cosmic aromal rays, which he called the sex organs of planets and stars. The universe was meant for an aromal jouissance now denied it by false consciousness and oppression, exemplified nowhere so clearly as in the atrophy of smell amongst the civilized, and especially the bourgeoisie.

But worse was to come. The twentieth century city eliminated even the vestiges of the organic (horseshit, garbage, wood smoke, body odors, sewage, abattoir and charnel house…) in favor of the odor of that which never had life, the machine.

Of course even petrol was once alive; even metals have life; even plastics and industrial chemicals have living analogues or remote links with some vanished form of life—but the machine itself has a "smell," perhaps largely psychic, that never existed in nature. It has nothing to do with either life or death. By comparison life and death constitute one entity, the machine another, almost an opposite. You may say the machine smells of nothing, but the alchemical nose (or gnose) knows that certain kinds of "nothing" stink of negative mumia. They smell of the denial of the imagination.

When modern people say they have no sense of smell they mean that they have no awareness of odors, that they allow stinks to govern their subconscious states. They give no true attentiveness to odors because smell seems atavistic and meaningless in our culture. The residual astringent stench of the laundry detergents most of us use for example creates a dismal miasma around us, a fence against (other) odors, and a defense against the shameful smells of the social body. Body odor is considered grotesque (perhaps "carnivalesque"), and so are certain heavy organic perfumes. Our ideal state, shut in car or engaged with TV or PC, involves no odors whatsoever.

The circus stinks. Underneath its effluvia lurks an animal musk no longer pleasurable to our hygienic and narrow little self-awarenesses. Smell is perversion. The bazaar stinks—of spices—but also of dung, filthy leather, foul dyes. Wal-Mart smells like nothing on earth. The commodity itself may be given an odor, like cars that are sprayed with "new car" aerosols based on such obsolete features as leather and rubber. Capital designs odors to activate unconscious urges to shop. But nothing is allowed an odor of its own, even food.

Our religions have largely eliminated incense and the ones that still use it are suspected of perversion or terrorism. In my memory India represents the paradise of smells—sewage, death, spices, perfumes, sanctity galore—the place where strong smells go when they die. And childhood is a kind of India.

Now that I've left the City I find my nose sharpened, I realize that certain odors (some of which are not recognized as such) were distorting my "astral" perceptions either by suppression or misdirection.

The ancient Chaldaeans "opened the mouth" of a magic idol by directing toward it certain stellar and planetary rays and burning before it certain aromatics. The soul can be awakened to and awakened by scents because scents act as magic to the subconscious—invisible, impalpable yet potent. According to the Latin *Asclepius* this is the way humans "make" gods, a process analogous to the divinization or transmutation of the self. In effect a (re) vivification occurs which is also a (re) membrance or (re) assemblage and evocation of the numinous. The numen itself becomes a perfume or mumia.

XI. ALCHEMICAL GEOREMEDIATION
OR THE ASTRAL GARDEN

Erasmus Darwin (1731-1802), grandfather of the more famous Charles, wrote an immense and astonishing epic poem—*The Botanic Garden*—describing the "loves of the plants," personified as nymphs and fairies, but based with scientific rigor on Linnaeus's taxonomic system of classifying plants by their sex organs. (Darwin was the first English translator of Linnaeus.) The various spirit characters were derived from the great alchemist Paracelsus, just as Dr. Darwin's favorite poet Alexander Pope used Paracelsian Elementals (gnomes, sylphs, undines, salamanders) in his "Rape of the Lock."[1]

The Botanic Garden, much admired by Shelley and other Romantics, shocked the London of 1795 with its orgiastic botany, its radical pro-French politics, and its unbridled Hermeticism. Modern historians of science are equally shocked. They want to see Erasmus as Charles's ancestor, Galton's ancestor, a precursor of modern science, an eighteenth-century "Improver," inventor and tinkerer of genius, friend of Watt, Priestly, Wedgewood. They want to save Darwin from his old reputation as libertine anarchist (friend of Godwin) and crackpot Hermeticist. But Darwin and his fellow natural philosophers were members of a "Lunar Society;" they were readers of alchemy, like Newton and Boyle. And *The Botanical Garden* was illustrated by William Blake and Henry Fuseli. Linnaeus himself was a mystic and relative of Swedenborg. The historians of science are simply wrong. Darwin was a hermeticist, a Romantic Scientist.

We still use a version of Linnaean taxonomy in modern botany. We see it as a typical encyclopedic Enlightenment-inspired work of reductionist science, a matter of dead flowers and butterflies pinned to boards, a kind of *cutting up* of Nature's unity—in fact a denial of it. Goethe criticized this kind of science of death rather than life: one cannot understand the morphology of plants and animals only by studying lab specimens, but by observing living beings.

For Darwin however the value of Linnaeus lay precisely in the life (sexual life) that defined his original system. It reflected the life of Nature as a whole—the living Earth. Erasmus Darwin's theory of evolution visualized all life as descended from one original primordial protozoan cell. Rather than "survival of the fittest" it depended on *survival of the happiest*, for life is love, sexuality, desire. Darwin describes England's ancient limestone hills (vast heaps of diluvian marine shells) as "monuments of past delight." His own botanic garden in Litchfield was built for his ladylove and future wife.

Clearly the Enlightenment and Modern Science have misused Linnaeus—a man who had his portrait painted as a Lapland shaman and speculated about the locale of the Garden of Eden. He too should be rescued for Romantic Science—for Green Hermeticism.

After reading Darwin's terrific poem I started to wonder about earlier hermetic systems of classification. What if we supplemented Linnaean taxonomy with other parallel systems based on good hermetic principles of Signatures and Correspondences? Perhaps we could breathe life back into taxonomy, give it some secret magical annexes, re-sexualize it, re-alchemize it.

Anyone who's looked at Culpepper's *Herball* knows that all plants are "ruled" by planets and zodiacal signs. These Signatures are useful to herbalists, spagyrists, farmers, magicians and poets. However this system offers only 7 x 12 = 84 possible categories of genera. It seemed to me that more complexity was called for.

The purpose of hermetic categories is not to cut up in order to kill or control, but to cut up and re-assemble in magical and creative ways, to re-unify. *Solve et Coagula*, the spagyric dogma: dissolve and re-combine. Occult systems always proliferate entities uncontrollably because they tap the infinite reservoir of correspondences rather than the box that holds Occam's Razor. Let 1000 flowers bloom!

At this point *The Art of Memory* by the late Dame Frances Yates must be consulted. Inspired by Lull, Fludd and Bruno, Renaissance magi memorized the floor plans and details of real or imaginary palaces, gardens, theaters and cabinets of curiosities. Every fact they learned could then be saved by storing it mentally in some hallway or niche, under the sign of some detail in fresco or tapestry or flowerbed, filed away for future mnemonic retrieval and use. But the memory palace is a *magical* encyclopedia: it gives rise to new combinations. We might say: new synapses are formed spontaneously. Genius happens.

Having already inherited an astral taxonomy for plants, our ideal source for constructing a more complex botanical memory theater or garden should also come from the stars, and especially the Moon, Soma, Ruler of All Plants. As it happens, a perfect architectural set of such asterisms already exists: the Lunar Mansions. Our memory palace will be a portion of the very heavens.

As an astrological system or "zodiac" of sorts, the Lunar Mansions may belong to untold depths of prehistory. Alexander Marshak (in *The Roots of Civilization*) demonstrated that our Cro-Magnon ancestors already practiced a counting system (using sticks and stones and bones) based on lunar cycles of 7, 14, 28 and variations. The Moon was our first clock, first calendar.

Arguments have been made for a Mesopotamian—an Indian—a Chinese—and an Arab origin of the Mansions. The arguments all have merits and demerits. My best guess is that the system emerged in its present form somewhere along the time/space axis between Sumer and the Indus Valley Civilization. This would explain its easy transmission to "the Arabs" (and thence to the West) and also its obvious antiquity in Vedic India. Still very early (perhaps pre-Buddhism) the system reached China, where it was adapted to even earlier autochthonous lunar calendars and symbol-sets. (This theory could well be wrong... so, beware.) The Lunar Mansions are called *Manzilat* in Arabic, *Nakshatras* in Sanskrit, and *Hsiu* in Chinese.

Lunar Mansions[2] divide the sky's ecliptic belt into arcs of 12 degrees 51 minutes, corresponding approximately to the daily mean motion of the Moon through the ecliptic, resulting in 28 (or 27) mansions of asterisms—constellations or parts thereof—which remain more-or-less the same in China, India and the West. Nowadays the Mansions play a big divinatory role in Chinese and Indian astrology, but have grown dim in the West, where only occultists like Cornelius Agrippa ever took them seriously.

As Agrippa says, the Moon acts as a lens that focuses the rays or influences of the asterisms (and the planets that pass through them as well) onto the living plants, animals and minerals of Earth; As Above, So Below. Each Mansion thus "rules" a series of correspondences: animals, plants, aromatics, gems, colors, occult forces, etc.

Comparing the different Signature-series in Chinese, Indian and Arabo-Western versions we find very few exact matches. Obviously different cultures and bioregions find different series of symbols and resonances. But the principle behind the various symbologies remains the same, just as the belt of stars remains the same, in all the variants.

Moreover, there do indeed exist a *few* similarities amongst the systems, enough to prove the transfusion theory (but shedding no light on origins).

In order to test the usefulness of the Mansions as a classificatory system I decided to investigate one of the few examples of similarity across the variants: Mansion 28, which is number 27 in the Indian system, and number 15 in the Chinese. (This Mansion's stars comprise parts of Andromeda and Pisces.)

Occulted under this sign I discovered none other than the Green Man himself: Khizr, the Hidden Prophet and master of Sufis with no masters—the ancient spirit of vegetation become patron saint of Islamic ecology—and of Green Hermeticism—the immortal Ziusudra.

Who is Khizr?

According to Hugh Talat Halman,[3] "The Koran relates that Moses journeyed with a companion and guide named al-Khizr, 'the Green'. Asked by his companions why his name was 'the Green,' the Prophet Muhammad explained that barren places where Khizr had sat turned green with vegetation."

While reading the archeological work *Looking for Dilmun* by Geoffrey Bibby, I noted that many old shrines of Khizr are found in the area that was once ancient Dilmun, especially the island of Bahrain. Utnapishtim, the immortal who meets Gilgamesh in the epic, lived in Dilmun. Obviously the immortal Utnapishtim is the immortal Khizr. This would explain a line in the Qur'an that still baffles many commentators. When Moses meets the unnamed Hidden Prophet (identified as Khizr by all the tafsirs) in Sura XVIII, they meet at *majma'al-bahrayn*, the "meeting place of two seas." This trope refers to the two prophets of course ("oceans of wisdom"), but also to a specific place. The Sumerians spoke of a mysterious ocean of fresh water under the salt water of the Gulf; the god Ea or Enki of Eridu presided over the occult space where the waters met. Its earthly manifestation was the island of Bahrain. This fact was already known to certain scholars but I'd missed it. The medieval Alexander Romances in which Khizr appears as Alexander's cook or guide; in which Khizr and Alexander search for the Fountain of

Youth in the Land of Darkness; in which Khizr succeeds but Alexander fails, and so on—all this is clearly based on the Gilgamesh epic. Alexander is Gilgamesh.

The *Gilgamesh* version of the immortal prophet's origin has an even earlier source in Sumerian material concerning the Flood. Here the hero's name is Ziusudra, which may be etymologically related to the name Khizr. Ziusudra already possesses many Khizrian characteristics. He receives messages direct from the gods; similarly, Khizr is the master of 'ilm laduni, unmediated direct knowledge from God. As he does so he stands by a wall, which will reappear in one of the Qur'anic stories. When the gods reward Ziusudra for building the Ark and saving life on Earth from the Flood, by making him immortal ("life like a god...breath eternal...") and appointing him king of Dilmun, they also appoint him "preserver of the name of vegetation and of the seed of mankind." In *Gilgamesh* this vegetation motif joins the immortality motif and becomes *a plant of immortality* owned by Utnapishtim. Gilgamesh loses the plant and thus his chance of cheating death.

Is this the earliest written reference to such a plant? If so, light might be thrown on the Indo-Iranian cult of Soma/Haoma, the entheogenic plant of immortality celebrated in the *Rig Veda* and the *Yashts*. Sumer and the Indo-Aryans could have "met each other" through Harappan culture. Much Sumerian literature dates from around 2000 BCE or earlier, while the *Rig Veda* is dated somewhere between 1800 and 1500 BCE.

The original Vedic patron of Soma is Indra, the thunder god, although other deities are also involved. In the Puranic period, the "ownership" of Soma is said to pass to Shiva, who therefore wears the Moon (Soma) in his tangled locks. No one now knows exactly what Soma was, but contemporary Shaivites use *ganja* (cannabis), often prepared as a drink (*bhang*) in much the same manner as Soma was prepared (pressed, strained, etc.). The Ganges River flows from the Moon on Shiva's brow; *ganga* equals *ganja*. According to *The Indian Hemp Drugs Commission Report of* 1893–4, Khizr or Khadir is a very popular figure amongst both Muslims and Hindus, and is considered the patron saint of bhang.

Khizr himself is not a Shiva-type. Of all the Vedic deities associated with Soma, he most resembles Pushan, the Nourisher, and protector of travelers. In any case, the entire complex undoubtedly reveals much about the origins of alchemy and the concept of the Philosopher's Stone as a vegetal *elixir vitae*.

Green is perhaps the most sacred color in Islam, although black as well is sacred for Shit'ites. These are heraldic colors in the strict sense, both symbolizing and "blazoning" the Prophet's household. The Prophet praised three things "of this world": water, greenness or greenery, and a beautiful face. Libyan revolutionary theory has already made explicit the link between Islamic greenness and the Green ecological movement. Khizr represents and dispenses the Water of Life, both figuratively as initiation on the Imaginal Plane, and literally, to save lost wanderers in the desert. He is the vegetation spirit *par excellence*, the Green Man of Celtic myth, perhaps indeed a manplant, like the portraits of Arcimboldo. The *Emerald Tablet* of Hermes Trismegistus reached Europe via an Arabic version, and the hermetic truth of the living earth or "ensouled universe" was absorbed by Sufism. On the mystical level this realization relates to the experience of *wahdat al-wujud*, the unity of being. On the level of science it gives rise not only to alchemy but also to ecology, the knowledge of the interconnectedness of all things, including consciousness. On the level of ethics, it implies the necessity for an activist and even militant Green praxis, illuminated by the vision of nature as *tajalli* or "shining through" of the divine in material things, "Allah's Waymarks." Khizr is the perfect patron for such a movement.

In the Chinese *Hsiu* system we find no mention of fish under number 15, *K'uei* (meaning "Astride"), the image of which shows a star-spirit riding a wolf.[4] But number 14 immediately preceding it includes the image of a *fish's mouth*. Fish "stands for" Khizr because he brings a dried fish to life by washing it in the ocean (in the Koran) and because he witnesses two fish disporting like the sign of Pisces in the Fountain of Immortality in the Land of Darkness (in the *Alexander Romances*). In one version of the Romance, Alexander is so jealous of Khizr for attaining immortality he throws the cook into the ocean—but Khizr becomes a fish monster or merman and swims away. (See Henry Corbin's book on Ibn 'Arabi for a reproduction and explication of the famous Persian miniature showing Khizr and Alexander contemplating the fish in the Fountain.)

Here are the relevant texts on Mansion 28:

The twenty-eighth and last Albotham or Alchalcy... that is Pisces.... Increaseth harvests... secureth travelers through danger-ous places. A seal of copper, being the image of a fish, and they per-fumed it with the skin of a sea fish, and did cast it into the water, wheresoever they would have the fish to gather together."

AGRIPPA, *Three Books of Occult Philosophy*, Trans. D. Tyson
(St. Paul, MN: Llewellyn Publications, 1993.)

Note that the Angel Raphael, who protects the boy Tobit on his travels, is also involved with the fish; no doubt another manifesta-tion of this mytheme.

Ban al-hut: ... two bright stars from the head of Andromeda, near to which is a group of small stars in a curved line, out of which the Arabs make a fish, and these stars are falling into the wide-open mouth of the fish, whence the name belly.

ABU RAYHAN AL-BIRUNI, *The Book of Instruction in the Elements of the
Art of Astrology* (London: Luzac & Co., 1934, 164:28)

...Thirty-two faint stars in the southern tail of Pisces... Its symbol the fish or the double-headed drum... Revati means the Wealthy... moksha, spiritual liberation... Presiding deity Pushan, the "nurturer" of the Rig Veda, protector of flocks and of travelers. Kshiradyapani shakti: the power of nourishment (milk). Female elephant.

D.M. HARNESS, *The Nakshatras* (WI: Lotus Press, 1999.)

... Pusan is associated with semen, that is, the offering (Soma), and its chalice, the moon.... Pusan is toothless, and feeds upon a kind of gruel...

A. DANIELOU, *The Myths and Gods of India* (Rochester, NY: Inner Traditions, 1985)

Nota bene: Ziusudra is the "preserver of the seed of mankind"—i.e., semen. As far as I know no historian of religions has hitherto identi-fied Khizr and Pushan. The historical figure Uways al-Qarani of Yemen is considered, like Khizr, the patron of all Sufis who have no living master. Uways met the Prophet Mohammad, his contemporary, only in dreams. In Sufism, those who are "disciples of Khizr" are also called Uwaysiyya. Interestingly Uways, like Pushan, has no teeth (knocked out in a battle). Paracelsus maintained that whoever drinks the Elixir of Youth would first lose and then regenerate all hair and teeth. The loss—but not the regrowth—is in fact a symptom of mercury poisoning, the alchemist's typical job-related disease. Some of these connexions may be fanciful—and why not? —inspired as they are by the XXVIIIth Mansion of the Moon.

And by the way, *Utnapishtim* and *Pushan* seem to have a lot of letters in common; and anyway, false etymologies are the salt of hermetic exegesis!

To summarize: the Lunar Mansions worked quite well for me as a magical memory system or series of correspondences: —they created a new fact (new to me anyway): that Khizr "is" Pushan, old man, patron of travelers, bringer of nourishment, toothless and immortal. I concluded that the Lunar Mansions had functioned here as a potent heuristic device and had set up a new synapse: an *Aha!* moment. I felt that the Hsiu/Nakshatra/Manzilat/Lunar Mansions could undoubtedly be added (or multiplied) with the Seven Planets and Twelve Zodiacal signs to create a new astro-botanical taxonomy with potentially 7 x 12 x 28 = 2362 genera or categories. But unfortunately, since I'm not a botanist, someone else would have to work out all the details and implications. I thought my thought-experiment was over.

But no. The Lunar Messenger Service had more to add.

One day, between two sessions of teaching the inaugural course in Green Hermeticism at the Abode of the Message in New Lebanon, New York, I happened to pick up an old magazine from the trash, in a moment of utter vacuity, and scanned it for no particular reason. The following "strange news" item caught my eye.

Tree Therapy

When some residents of Bombay, India, are looking for an antidote to stress or illness—or even for a prospective mate—they want to go sit under a tree. A tree that corresponds to their astrological constellation, that is, in one of the city's existing or proposed *Nakshatra Udyans*, or astral gardens.

"In our astral gardens, you could sit under a tree and feel less stressed and more perked up—even get cured of an ailment," says K.L. Velodi, Bombay's garden superintendent, who is excited at the prospect of creating astral-themed parks. While the Mahim Nature Park already has a space devoted to a twenty-seven-tree astral garden (to match the twenty-seven constellations), other such gardens are in the works. One, at Juhu, will include sculptures of the zodiac signs, models of the constellations, explanations, and perhaps even a resident astrologer.

And according to Sharadini Dahanukar, M.D., head of the department of Pharmacology and Therapeutics at Bombay's K.E.M. Hospital, astral gardens offer health benefits. "There's a definite correlation between the health-related predispositions described under each constellation and the recorded medicinal properties of the tree linked to that constellation," she explains.

But it's not just the curative aspects of the trees that makes Babubhai Bhawanji, a local municipal corporator, eager to set up an astral garden in his constituency in Dadar. "It will bring about national integration as people of all religious affiliations will sit together under such trees, and young people looking for partners will be able to spot a prospective mate under a tree of a compatible constellation," he says.

Even if the gardens don't have their intended cosmic benefits, Dr. Dahanukar points out that there are more down-to-earth reasons to set them up. "If we can bring native trees to the city and teach people to value, nurture and plant more trees, it would be a valuable initiative."

SAMEERA KHAN

I clipped the piece and threw the magazine away, so I can't tell you its name. I was annoyed that its readers were being asked to share a hip snicker at the expense of silly superstition-ridden Indians. I however was struck by wonder and amazement. What a brilliant idea! The Nakshatras are indeed shared by many religions and cultures, as I had learned. The Udyan really does symbolize the kind of Universalism that is India's glory, and is propagated at the Abode of the Message according to the teachings of its founder, Hazrat Inayat-Khan. How dare this journalist sneer at such ideals?

To date the only other interesting fact I've learned about the Nakshatra Udyan is that it was built on formerly polluted land, which was cured by bioremediation techniques, in the midst of a terrible slum neighborhood far from the center of Bombay.

A first comparison springs to mind: —the "social sculpture" of German modern artist Joseph Beuys (d. 1985). Greatly influenced by Hermeticism, Anthroposophy and anarchism, in 1982 Beuys decided to rescue the drab polluted German city of Cassel by planting 7000 oak trees in and around it, accompanied by his own enigmatic basalt monoliths and buried copper wires. A great deal of "magic" went into the work, but Beuys emphasized its social and artistic aspects—hence, "social sculpture." Even so, his esoteric intentions are not difficult to discern.

Beuys had fallen in love with Celtic culture; the oaks and stones constituted a druid grove. After the successful completion of the planting in Cassel, he intended to move to Ireland, found an experimental university, and repeat the 7000 Oaks project. But he died too soon.

On Samhain (Halloween) 2000 I was invited to Ireland (along with my friend David Levi Strauss the Beuys scholar and poet) by Gordon Campbell and the Academy of Everything Is Possible, to take part in a Beuysian installation or preliminary planting of 7000 oaks (and monoliths) at Uisnach, the ancient ritual center of Celtic Ireland. Our tree ceremony (in the rain) went beautifully, as did the several parties in nearby decaying Georgian mansions with champagne that preceded and followed. Since then however the project has fallen on hard times: corruption of agencies, greed of farmers, insensitivity of state-run archaeological authorities, etc. We're now hoping a few oaks will survive at Uisnach—maybe only seven—as a druid grove for modern times.

The Nakshatra Udyan in Mahin Nature Park appears to me—at least in theory—a perfect realization of Beuysian Hermetic Social Sculpture. The land was seized back from psychic and actual pollution—transformed by bioremediation *and* magic into a social good—and inspired by the Lunar Mansions. Suddenly I realized that the "memory garden" I'd been tinkering with in theory could exist in actuality as a real garden (with "real toads," to quote Marianne Moore), synthesizing in one artistic/scientific/magical experiment all the themes of Green Hermeticism: —the *Astral Garden*.

Ideally this garden would exist as an experiment in *alchemical georemediation*. Since I just invented this slogan or rubric, let me try to explain what I mean.

Imagine a small meadow or field, a piece of land, perhaps somewhere near New Lebanon. Once upon a time this place had a life. It
had "forests... Indians..." (as Thoreau said, his last dying words). It
had farms; later perhaps a sawmill or some other form of now-van-
ished small "renewable energy" industry. It had history: perhaps an
incident of the Anti-Rent War occurred here; perhaps the Shakers
once farmed this field.

Now however this place is nearly dead. Forests, Indians, farms,
mills, magical stories—all now extinct, gone and forgotten. Even
worse: it's become an abandoned parking lot—or dump—or rub-
ble-strewn waste—a mere symptom of America's technopathocracy—drained of productivity and health—drained of meaning—a
no-place place.

But "No-place Place" is precisely the meaning of the word utopia
(in Sufism, *Na-Koja-abad*, "NowhereLand"), which can also become
eutopia, the "good place." Here is the perfect spot for our astral garden. We want to re-vivify this bit of land on every level: body, soul,
and spirit. When we're done with our work we want this place alive
and healthy again—but not just that. We want to use astro-alchem-
ical means of healing, as well as conventional bioremediation, not
only to cure this land but also to restore its authentic significance.
To re-enchant it.

Hence, not just bioremediation is required but the *georemediation* of
a specific topos or geome. If it were prairie, we'd attempt prairie res-
toration; if forest, we'd attempt re-wilding. But since it's a field, we'll
use "celestial agriculture" as our goal. It will be done *alchemically*,
meaning that the "redeeming of matter" on all three levels (body,
soul, spirit) will constitute our method. We want to do this for the
common wealth and we want to do it in *communitas*. But we also want
to do it as spiritual exercise, as alchemy in which the lab/oratory is
found outdoors as well as within ourselves; as an action in what Novalis called the necessary poeticization of science: alchemy as an art
form with ramifications on both individual and social levels.

Thus the re-vivification would have three aspects or parts:

1) The Soul or psychic level, symbolized in alchemy by "Sulphur."
This constitutes the realm of astrology, ceremonial magic, religio-
shamanic ritual, art and social sculpture, land art, poetry, image

magic, hieroglyphics, music and dance, etc. The goal here would consist of maximizing the *imaginal* means of georemediation.

2) The Spagyric level, or Green Hermeticism in the strict sense, brings us to the Spirit level: quicksilver of course, the alchemic "Mercury." What would constitute a specifically alchemical form of bioremediation? To discover this is our goal. Perhaps—if the land in question is not totally lifeless—all the "weeds" growing there could be harvested and purified spagyrically to produce a spray or "fertilizer" to return to the land and its next crop.[5] A great deal of thought—conferences, think tanks—could be devoted to the planning of a protocol in detail.

3) The third level is "Salt," the *body*. Here I would categorize conventional and non-spagyric methods of bioremediation such as Paul Stamets's mycoremediation or the water purification systems designed by "New Alchemists" John and Nancy Todd—systems involving no machinic energy, no non-renewable resources. Needless to say there's a lot of soul and spirit in such systems (and a good deal of body in our first and second categories), but I include them here because they're material and empirical. Also here we would deal with non-allopathic means of bioremediation such as Biodynamic composting. (Rudolf Steiner based his theories on folk-herbalist and hermetic sources such as Paracelsus, Basil Valentine, and homeopathy, but biodynamic agriculture does not use Spagyria *per se*.) Here we also need advice from Native American healers, organic gardeners and farmers, local herbalists and wildcrafters.

Are we interested in *comparing* all these various methods in a scientific spirit of experiment—or do we want to *combine* them all in the cause of an immediate and total praxis? The good alchemist would do both—*solve et coagula*—analyze and synthesize. Our astral garden will be an educational experience, not a guaranteed done deal. How much can we learn and discover?

For now the Astral Garden remains just another thought experiment. So it would be pointless to speculate on the exact form of this real world manifestation. The area around New Lebanon includes many polluted and distressed locales and many poor communities eager to help themselves (and especially their youth) by helping each other. Moreover, grant money is available for bioremediation and for art projects—and combinations of the two. Not many grants are awarded to self-professed alchemists in contemporary America, but "bioremediation art" is already a recognized hot new field. Given the real commitment of even a small group, the astral garden could become solid reality.

In that speculative spirit I'll end with a purely notional or conceptual grid design for an astral garden, one that could be applied to almost any actual physical space. Our garden would emphasize the Seven Planets and the 12-sign Zodiac, because these are the best known astral symbols in our culture. The Lunar Mansions will be present as an esoteric dimension such as they occupy in al-Biruni's Sufi Astrology or the Image Magic of Cornelius Agrippa. In China and India the Lunar Mansions play a huge role in romance and marriage; compatabilities and clashes are determined by elaborate systems of lunar divination. We want this romantic erotic aspect of our garden to flourish in a "Language of Flowers," herbs and trees. So we must emphasize the Western Zodiac, which plays precisely this role in our occidental astrology—as any hometown newspaper horoscope column will readily confirm.

The four corners of the garden will be "protected" by *Herms*. The original form of Hermes was a heap of stones marking the boundary of a farm field—and here we return him to his most primordial function.[6] The points on my "map" occupied by asterisms can be marked with stones, perhaps carved with appropriate sijils and symbols. Appropriate plants will grow around these symbols. Obviously we can't use Indian Nakshatra Signature-trees like the mango, the neem or the sacred fig.[7] But local equivalents will be found, either in traditional sources like Culpepper and Agrippa, or by means of psychic empirical research.

The "squared circle" plan includes the traditional garden design of a) the Quincunx (center and four points) and also b) the four-square or "Paradise" plan of Koranic heaven and Persian gardens:

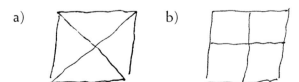

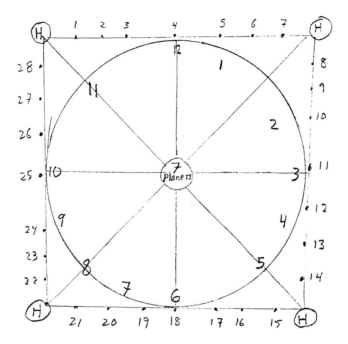

The Quincunx is marked by the four Herms and the central temple. The foursquare division by watercourses with central fountain also marks the four directions, N/S/E/W, and the Four Elements. The circle of 12 represents the Zodiac, and the square of 28 the Lunar Mansions. The exact relation between Zodiac and Mansions can be adjusted on the basis of a chart from Bepin Behari, *Myths & Symbols of Vedic Astrology* (N. Delhi, 2003), p. 168.

Here the center is usually seen as a fountain or tank, and the cross-arms as irrigation channels, like the rivers of Eden. Sir Thomas Browne praised the Quincunx design in his weird treatise on horticulture, *The Garden of Cyrus*. In the center of the Quincunx will be found a "temple" to the Seven Planets. The center of the four-square plan (which coincides with the center of the quincunx) will contain a pool or fountain, reminding us of the Prophet's words: "Three things of this world I love: water, greenery, and a beautiful face; and the coolness of my eyes, which is prayer." As the inscription on a Mughal garden gate put it:

If there be a paradise on earth
Surely it is here, it is here.

Symbols of the Zodiac and Nakshatras

NOTES

1. Pope picked up his information from a strange little "novel" called *Le Comte de Gabalis;* the name is perhaps a corruption of "Kabbalah," or else belongs to one Philip à Gabela, a shadowy seventeenth-century Rosicrucian (see F. Yates, *The Rosicrucian Enlightenment*, 45-6).

2. The English word is directly related to the Arabic *manzil*, mansion or house; also to Mesopotamian *manzalti* and Hebrew *mazzaloth*, "stations," places where the gods have stopped.

3. For articles on Khizr by Halman and myself, see *Elixir* no. 2, spring, 2006.

4. Derek Walters, *The Complete Guide to Chinese Astrology*, 108.

5. I owe aspects of this notion to discussions with the Green Hermeticism group at the Abode of the Message, and with Kevin Townley, fellow teacher and practical spagyrist.

6. The Herm is of course also phallic; hence it wards off the evil eye and baleful witchcraft. In Arcadia and later in Italy the phallic Herm becomes the god Priapus, scarecrow-with-a-dildo, obscene guardian garden gnome; Latin poets composed dirty jokes in his name, collected as the *Priapeia*.

7. Thanks to Thomas Meyer for these and other details of Jyotish, Vedic Astrology, mantras and yantras, etc.

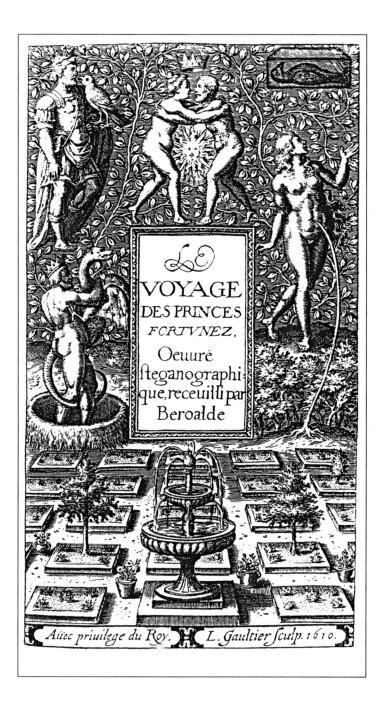

VOYAGE
DES PRINCES
FORTVNEZ,
Oeuuré
steganographi-
que, receuilli par
Beroalde

Auec priuilege du Roy. L. Gaultier sculp. 1610.

Appendix to the Alchemical Garden

FRANÇOIS BÉROALDE DE VERVILLE
LE VOYAGE DES PRINCES FORTUNEZ
1610

L'Histoire veritable ou le Voyage des princes fortunez divisee en IIII entreprises. Par Beroalde de Verville. A Paris, chez Pierre Chevalier, au mont Saint Hilaire. M.D.C.X. Avec Privilege du Roy. "The True History or the Journey of the Fortunate Princes, divided into four undertakings. By Béroalde de Verville. Paris, published by Pierre Chevalier, at Mont Saint-Hilaire. 1610. With Royal Privilege."

François Beroalde de Verville, Canon of the Cathedral Church of St. Gatien at Tours, published this immense novel (800 pages) in 1610, a few years before the Rosicrucian manifestos appeared. In 1600 (the year of Giordano Bruno's martyrdom by the Church in Rome) he had published a French version of the famous *Hypneroto-machia Poliphili*, the vast romance attributed to Francesco Colonna (Venice, 1499), and added to it his own "Steganographic Preface," in which he gave an alchemical-hermetic reading of the text.

In a preface to *The Fortunate Princes* Beroalde gives this definition of his exegetical method:

"Steganography," writes Beroald (f.2), "is the art of representing plainly [*naivement*] that which is easily conceived but which under the coarsened features of its appearance hides subjects quite other than that which seems to be presented; this is practiced in painting when some landscape or harbor scene or portrait is shown which conceals within itself some other figure which can be discerned by looking from a certain viewpoint determined by the artist. This is done also in writing, when an author discourses at large on plausible subjects which enfold some other excellencies which are known only when read from the secret angle which uncovers splendors concealed from common appearance."

Beroalde's claims to hermetic depth seem to have annoyed the art historians, who, like historians of science, have an aversion to the esoteric. Speaking of the *Hypnerotomachia*, Anthony Blunt says the Steganagraphic Note and Frontispiece "seem to have very little to do with the *Songe* and are... not in themselves important." He calls Beroalde a libertine, and associates him with a group of similar minor writers: "Socially this group was a relic of the chaos, material and moral, of the end of the Wars of Religion. Its members typified the Bohemian escape from the unpleasantness of the world into a doctrine which denied that there could be any positive standards for the conduct of life."

They "degenerated into anarchy" and were "attacked by the progressive writers of the period," an attack carried out " in the name of reason and common sense on the fantastic and affected culture" of writers like Beroalde.

Edgar Wind calls Beroald's edition "debased," and accuses him of bringing the argument "down" to a (merely) alchemical level. He attacks Jung for the same kind of flattening of interpretation, which he calls "an erosion of categories." This criticism might be justly applied to Jungianism, but I find the scolding of Beroalde rather puzzling. The alchemical level of the *Hypnerotomachia* will strike anyone as obvious, provided they've already read a few alchemical texts or even modern studies on alchemy.

That Beroalde was a "libertine" however is quite true. Like his literary master Rabelais he admired the *Hypnerotomachia's* mystical agenda of equating love with god rather than God with Love, so to speak—in other words, its crypto-paganism.

Another novel by Beroalde, *Le Moyen de Parvenir (Fantastic Tales, or The Way to Attain)* was translated by the great horror-story writer Arthur Machen (privately printed, Carbonnek, London?, 1923), who himself had links to the hermetic tradition via the Golden Dawn. Machen justly called it "A Book Full of Pantagruelism"—bawdy, obscene, grotesque, carnivalesque and downright dirty. Clearly Beroalde lacked Rabelais's genius, but shared his philosophy of *Do What Thou Wilt*. Still it's surprising to hear Machen declare that Beroalde was "merely whimsical" and that "there are no hidden, royal secrets; only an infinite oddity" to be found in the *Tales*. In fact the book is another exercise in steganography and is packed with hermetic references. To take one example almost at random:

There was the friar who preached at Dampierre, while we were seeking the philosopher's stone with all the barons of Normandy, and drinking good wine, which the fool Nabot had made my lord de Chansegre to bring there, in order that we might discover the power of projection. There was white wine and red wine; the one was to make silver and the other potable gold. (p.185)

Beroalde was a practitioner of the *lusus seriosus* or "serious joke," a specialty of hermeticism. His edition of the *Hypnerotomachia* was dedicated:

Aux beaux Esprits Qui
Arresteront Leurs Yeux
Sur ce projets de plaisir Serieux

(See *Le Tableau des riches inventions couvertes du voile des feintes Amoureuses, qui sont representees dans le Songe de Poliphile*. Desvoilées des ombres du Songe & subtilement exposées par Béroald. P. ii.)

When Béroald jokes repeatedly that the Philosopher's Stone "is" wine, women and song, he does not do so to debase alchemy but to elevate pleasure. Rabelaisian hermeticism can be usefully compared to Hindu Tantra in which "matter is redeemed" and pleasure therefore a sign (or means) of *attainment* or quasi-auto-divinization.

Béroald himself designed the frontispieces for the French *Hypneroto-machia* and *The Fortunate Princes* as emblematic keys to his steganographic exegesis of the texts. From an alchemical perspective they make perfect sense. Klossowski describes the action in our picture thus:

On the frontispiece, the conjunction of the opposing Principles is shown as a royal embrace, ultimately resulting in the Solar Perfec-tion of the Philosopher's Stone. The volatilization of the Fixed, in Dissolution, is represented by a mortal combat between the King and the winged Dragon. (The nudity of the King indicates the pre-liminary purification of the Matter). The result of the fight is Death and ensuing Putrefaction, symbolized by the Raven in the coffin. The King holding the Eagle demonstrates the Fixation of the Volatile. The naked Eve is the *Albedo*, Whiteness or First Perfection, which eventually emerges from the Night of Death.

Below, in reconquered Eden, flows the Fountain of Life.

The tree which grows through Eve's body occupies the whole background of the upper register of the picture, but it springs from the alchemical Eden below; it is the Tree of Life, plant of immortality, the Vegetal Stone itself. The gods, goddesses and animals in the upper "sky" might also be seen as planets and asterisms shedding their influences on the plants of the Garden below.

Renaissance and Hermetic Emblems often set their "infinitely odd" scenes against backgrounds of idyllic landscapes or formal gardens:

But in emblematic art everything is emblematic, including the *backgrounds*. Hermeticism includes a vision of the Golden Age to be restored through rectification of humanity's relation with Nature. The emblematic landscape or garden *stands for* this attainment.

ATLANTA FUGIENS, M. Maier, Oppenheim, 1618

4

Quilting Green Hermeticism

A Tissue of Texts and Tracings

CHRISTOPHER BAMFORD

NATURE

WE NO LONGER UNDERSTAND NATURE. We speak of nature as what environs us, of human nature, of cosmic nature, and even of divine nature: as if nature were not one, but many. We also speak of the "nature" of a thing or being as that by which it is or becomes what it is— as if nature were what contains all possibilities. But we ignore—in both senses of avoiding and not knowing—how these are related.

In other words, when we speak of nature it is as if we are invoking something we know we ought to know, of which perhaps we dimly remember some scraps, but which is now largely a forgotten knowledge. Any real sense of the experience or meaning of nature is lacking. What remains is only a fragmentary memory carried by words, which, for the most part, we use automatically and without thinking.

We look at a stone, a plant, an animal, a planet, a star, or even another human being—and perhaps we have a name for it—but what it *means*, what it *is*, and what it *does*, and how in the depths of being we are *related* to it, escapes us completely. The world around us has become essentially meaningless. We may know what we can do with it but, in the deepest sense, we no longer understand it.

At the same time, vaguely and without really knowing what we are talking about, we have grown used to dichotomizing or splitting nature. Just as we oppose consciousness and matter, we contrast nature and humanity, nature and grace, nature and art, nature and spirit, nature and history, and so on. We say "and" but actually understand "or," as if there were two different realities at play. Yet the "and" tells us, if we listen to it, that our dichotomies are really one: two sides of a single coin, distinguishable perhaps, but not divisible. How odd, then, to separate them—to imagine humanity and nature, for instance, as independent entities— when our experience tells us that they are, if not one, then so intimately related as to be so potentially and ideally. After all, there is nothing outside that is not simultaneously inside. There is nothing outside that is not the precise counterpart of something inside. Every star, mineral, plant, and animal finds its place and function within us and "magically" works its effect. In fact, there is nothing that we can eat, breathe, see, smell, hear, touch—or think, imagine, or intuit— that does not find its place within us in one way or another. When we eat spinach or burdock, stand rapt before a flower or rock, bathe in the difference between sunrise and sunset in wonder at the colors, or walk barefoot through the green shoots of a meadow still wet with spring dew—if we attend selflessly to the union then occurring—we can begin to sense our magic identity (or approximation) with the world. The poet Samuel Taylor Coleridge must have experienced something of this when he wrote in his Notebook:

> In looking at objects of nature while I am thinking, as at yonder moon dim-glimmering through the dewy window-pane, I seem rather to be seeking, as it were *asking* for, a symbolical language for something within me that already, and forever exists, than observing anything new. Even when that latter is the case yet still I have always an obscure feeling as if that new phenomenon were the dim awakening of a forgotten and hidden truth of my inner nature.

Goethe called it the "holy, open secret:"

When contemplating nature
Always attend to the one and to the all:
Nothing is within and nothing is without,
What is inside is outside.
Grasp then without delay
The holy, open secret.

In another version, Goethe mysteriously notes that there is always both identity and *something more*: "Nature contains all that is in the subject *and something more;* the subject contains all that is in nature *and some thing more.*" Whatever "more" means, it is certainly important (no system here) always to leave the situation *open* to the grace—the *donum Dei*—of the unknown and unknowable infinite on both sides, thus safeguarding the primacy of the mystery.

This qualification aside, we might say then that we are in some way "symbolized" with nature. Symbol comes from the Greek, *bolein,* meaning to "throw or bring" and *sym* (as in "sympathy" or "symphony"), meaning "together." *Symbolein,* therefore, means, "to throw or bring together." A symbol is a two-in-one: a unity. Legend has it that the first use of the word was by the Pythagoreans of ancient Greece to describe their way of recognizing each other. Each Pythagorean was given the half of some figure such that when he or she met another Pythagorean who had the other half, they could put together (*symbolein*) the two halves to make a whole and in this way recognize each other as Pythagoreans. Special handshakes serve the same function. Nature *and* humanity and nature *and* grace are two halves of one whole in this sense. But today, instead of being symbolic, the relationship has become diabolic, which comes from *diabolein* and is the opposite of "*symbolein,*" meaning to "throw apart."

Meanwhile, nature is apparently disappearing, dying, being destroyed; and since we are "symbolized" with it, our humanity and our connection to the divine is likewise diminishing. We are losing her and ourselves. Increasingly, she seems to epitomize only the same change, transience, and decay that we experience in ourselves. She is beginning to seem more and more like history, which is also losing its meaning. In fact, all we have therefore are ruins, vestiges, and traces—whether of divine nature, cosmic nature, or human nature. Fragments of a long-forgotten alphabet surround us and we have become fragments to ourselves. We have forgotten the natural language that is our birthright and, speaking the artificial language of our psychological, ego-based consciousness, wreak havoc wherever we go.

This is not to say that nature—Gaia—is perhaps not herself also awakening. Certainly, she seems more intensely beautiful every year. In that sense, if we can awaken our sleeping conscience, her destruction at our hands is perhaps our wake-up call to recognize *her* awakening power. But even if this is so, as she is generally understood today, nature—once the source of all meaning and existence—has become contingent, accidental: a token for what we seek to control and dominate. Yet the reality remains that nature is the common context of every human manifestation. She is what connects all times and places in their spiritual being and aspirations. Every earthly manifestation, every revelation, unfolds in nature where we live and in and with which we have our being. But our religions seem to tell us little of the place of nature in our redemption, salvation, or enlightenment.

Nor should we ever forget that nature is above all a *spiritual* reality. What we witness through our senses and experience imaginally in what have now become exceptional states (but were once universally accessible) is always the work, the traces, the revelation or manifestation of spiritual (non-physical) beings. In this sense, the study of nature is always, whatever else it is, also angelological. Of course, from the Hermetic point of view, ecology and biology are not different in this from psychology and astronomy: in the end, all are angelological.

As Green Hermeticists, then, we must ask: What is our spiritual responsibility with regard to Nature? What is our relationship to Her? At the end, when the divine is become all in all, "the hidden treasure known," what will happen to Her? What is Nature's role in our journey?

To ask such questions is to confess that we have forgotten what the ancients knew—that nature is human nature; and that if we destroy her we destroy ourselves. We have forgotten what they knew: that she is the only guide and must be followed prayerfully, patiently, and humbly "in her mode of operation." Certainly, it is all very well to love nature. Our physical and emotional wellbeing—

and certainly our survival—seem to be tied to her. But—beyond ensuring our physical survival—does she not also have a fundamental role to play in our "spiritual" evolution, our continuing evolution into the Godhead? Does she have a role in our redemption or enlightenment? And, if so, do we have a role to play in her final assumption into the spiritual world?

No wonder, she is the overriding mystery. She surrounds and permeates us. She is our context, the common ground of all human experience. At once, stellar, cosmic, planetary, mineral, plant, animal, and human, she is rightly called the womb of all things, our All-Mother. The word "nature," from the Latin *natura* deriving from *nascire*, to be born, tells us as much. Nature is she who gives birth, unfolding, and producing all becoming: the producer, the one who pushes forth. "Nature" in this sense is the same as we find in the Greek root *"gen,"* from which we get *genesis* (becoming), itself but another word for nature. *Natura* in fact translates the Greek *physis*, which also means, "that which is moved," emerges, moves forth, flowers, and produces beings. Rarely do so many roots coincide.

As the root of all becoming, our All-Mother calls us today. To help ourselves we must help her and so we must seek her aid to aid ourselves in every way we can. No better place to start exists than the sacred sciences of Nature as these reach us in the traditions of alchemy and Hermeticism. But to understand them, we must learn to think differently.

*

GOETHE ON NATURE

"This essay was sent to me a short time ago from amongst the papers of the ever-honored Duchess Anna Amelia; it is written by a well-known hand, of which I was accustomed to avail myself in my affairs, in the year 1780, or thereabouts. I do not exactly remember having written these reflections, but they very well agree with the ideas, which had at that time become developed in my mind...."

(JOHANN WOLFGANG VON GOETHE, May 26th, 1828)

Nature! We are surrounded and embraced by her—power-less to leave her and powerless to enter her more deeply. Unasked and without warning, she sweeps us away in the round of her dance and dances on until we fall exhausted from her arms.

Endlessly, she creates new forms: what is there never was; what was will never return. All is new, yet forever the old.

We live within her, and are strangers to her. She speaks with us unceasingly, but does not betray her secret. We work on her constantly, yet have no power over her.

She seems to base everything on individuality, yet to care nothing for individuals. She is always building, always destroying, but her workshop is unreachable.

She lives in countless children, but where is the mother? She is the sole artist, creating the greatest contrasts out of the simplest material, the greatest perfection seemingly without effort, the most exact certainty always veiled with a touch of softness. Each of her works has its own being, each of her phenomena the most isolated idea, yet all create a single whole.

She plays out a drama: we do not know whether she herself sees it, yet she plays it for us, who stand in the corner.

She is eternal life, growth, and movement, yet she does not move on. She transforms herself endlessly but there is not a single moment's pause in her. She has no concept for stopping and she has set her curse upon standing still. She is firm. Her tread is measured, her exceptions rare, her laws immutable.

She has thought and ponders still, but not as humans do, but as nature does. She keeps to herself her own all-embrac-ing meaning, which no one may discover from her.

All human beings are in her and she is in all. With all, she plays a friendly game and rejoices if ever one wins something from her. With many, she plays so secretly that she ends her game before they know it.

Even what is most unnatural is nature. Even the coarsest, most narrow-minded person has something of her genius. Whoever does not see her everywhere sees her clearly nowhere.

She loves herself and clings to herself eternally with innumerable eyes and hearts. She has divided herself to enjoy herself. Insatiable, she always brings forth beings to enjoy her, to communicate herself to.

She delights in illusion. Whoever destroys this illusion in themselves or others, she punishes like the sternest tyrant. But those who follow her trustingly she takes to her heart like a child.

Her children are innumerable. With none is she sparing, but she has her favorites, those on and for whom she lavishes much and sacrifices much. Greatness, she protects.

She flings her creatures out of the nothingness and tells them nothing of where they come from or where they are going. They must only run; she knows the course.

Few springs drive her, but these never wind down, but are always effective, always manifold.

Her drama is always new because always she creates new spectators. Life is her most beautiful discovery and death is her device to have much life.

She wraps us in dullness and forever spurs us on to the light. She makes us dependent upon the earth, sluggish and heavy, yet always shakes and wakes us up.

She gives us needs, because she loves movement. It is a wonder how little she uses to achieve all this movement. Every need is a favor, soon satisfied, soon roused again. When she gives us another, it is a source of new pleasure. But soon she comes into balance.

At every moment she prepares the longest race and at every moment she has reached the goal.

She is vanity itself, but not for us, for whom she has given herself the greatest importance.

She lets every child practice its arts on her, every fool judge her and thousands to pass over her dully, without seeing her. In all she takes joy. From all she draws her profit.

We obey her laws even in resisting them; we work with her even in working against her.

She makes all she gives a blessing, for she begins by making it indispensable. She delays so that we long for her; she hurries so that we never have our fill of her.

She has no language or speech, but she makes tongues and hearts through which she feels and speaks.

Her crown is love. Only through love do we come to her. She opens chasms between all beings, and each seeks to devour the other. She has separated all to draw all together. With a few draughts from the cup of love she makes good a life full of toil.

She is all. She rewards herself and punishes herself, delights and torments herself. She is rough and gentle, charming and terrifying, impotent and all-powerful. All is eternally present in her. She knows nothing of past and future. The present is her eternity. She is kind. I praise her with all her works. She is wise and still. We can force no explanation from her body, nor tear any gift from her that she does not give freely. She is full of tricks, but to a good end, and it is best not to notice her tricks.

She is whole and yet always unfinished. As she does now, she may do forever.

To each she appears in a unique form. She hides herself in a thousand names and terms, and is always the same.

She has placed me here; she will lead me away. I trust myself to her. She may do with me. She will not hate her work. I have not spoken of her. No, whatever is true or false, she has spoken it. All fault, all merit, is hers.

*

A FORMATIVE METAPHYSICAL POWER

There is a gift of the gods—so at least it seems evident to me — which they let fall from their abode, and it was through Prometheus, or one like him, that it reached humankind together with a fire exceeding bright. The human beings of old, who were better than us and dwelt nearer the gods, passed on this gift in the form of a saying. "All things," so it ran, "that are ever said to be consist of a one and a many, and have in their nature a conjunction of limit and unlimited." (PLATO, *Philebus*)

For Hermeticism, nature or creation is a living, spiritual, conscious, fourfold unfolding unity: a "formative metaphysical power." Titus Burckhart confirms this when he writes: "The expression 'nature' has a very precise meaning. It does not simply mean the involuntary becoming of things, but rather a unitary power or cause whose essence may be known by perceiving its all embracing rhythm—a rhythm which rules both the outward and the inward world."

In the words of a founding mother of Hellenistic alchemy, Maria the Jewess, also called Maria Prophetessa, the legendary sister of Moses: "*One becomes two, two becomes three, and by means of the third and fourth, realizes unity: thus two are but one.*"

The unity of four-in-one that Maria invokes in her saying, which was called by Jung the most important in alchemy, is what the ancient Pythagoreans called the holy Tetraktys, which is in a sense none other than the four states of consciousness common to all traditions: the waking state, the dream state, the state of dreamless sleep, and the fourth state.

I

I I

I I I

I I I I

In other words: in order to "create," One must become Two—it must look at itself. It must divide. The unique, irreducible, indivisible cause-source One must become Two. This cut or scission is the mystery of polarization or separation. It reveals that the One must contain its own opposition: the capacity to resist itself. With the self-gaze of the One, is born the process of unity's becoming multiplicity. With the primal self-gaze, difference, relationship, and specification begin.

In that sense, the whole process of creation occurs between One and Two. What occurs is a deed, an action: a primal function. In Goethe's words: "In the beginning was the deed." The first deed or function is the primal creative scission or relationship that creates consciousness, whose prolongations of gift and reception will unfold as the entire sequence of the generative beings and powers (or functions) that work throughout the becoming and transformations of universal nature. Consequently, the universe or nature is in fact nothing but consciousness and in its unfolding nothing but an evolution of consciousness from its beginning to its end, which is its return to unity in conscious knowing. Evolution and involution, creation and redemption, is nothing but consciousness knowing, realizing, itself. As the hadith says, "I was a hidden treasure and I desired to be known..."

Nature, from this point of view, is consciousness. Consciousness is the seed-cause, the primal causal energy, containing within it source, fruit, and end, the unity of which as we shall see is time as genesis. Consciousness seeks itself through all its metamorphoses and its path is the path of nature, which is an unvarying rhythm.

"Nature is a succession, an expanded succession, in the spirit of the unique genesis," writes Schwaller de Lubicz, spelling out succinctly the consequences of this view:

> The origin of the universe being a single and unique source of energy there is, because of this, a communion between all things. There is a kinship between a certain mineral, a plant, and animal, and a human. They are linked because they are of the same nature, because in the final analysis there is only a simple series of basic characteristics whence, by combinations, innumerable possibilities emerge..."

Note that the "origin," which makes possible such communion and affinity, sympathy and signature, is in no sense remote from us or primeval. Present and constant, unity is always there, out of time. Creation is "continuous." It is the very "mystery" of every moment—of the every day—available to all of us to the extent that we can extract ourselves from the confines of psychological space and time in which we imprison nature and ourselves through our concepts.

According to this view, the cycle of creation unfolds through four functions:

I.   Polarization or separation

II. Affinity or choice, selection

III. Harmony, that is the consonance of attraction and repulsion, which leads to: fecundation

IV. Determination/specification/individuation: the innate intelligence that is the characteristic quality of an entity.

This cycle is true for the universe, as for every living thing in it. It is, in fact, what places us in a relation of potentially conscious identity with the universe, because—as all the traditions teach in one way or another—we are potentially its final term ("the image and the likeness".) The whole universe thus seethes with Life by virtue of the unfolding cosmic functions or spiritual beings to which our innate consciousness is intimately related because, as the mean term between the beginning and the end, we unite the whole. This is why every natural object is for us a hieroglyph of sacred Hermetic science, a symbol. Each animal each species of plant, each mineral group is a stage in the process of the Creator's becoming aware.

The universe then is a language that expresses itself ceaselessly in its living function in the language of our innate "intelligence"— the intelligence of the heart.

Humanity's realization of all the living divine-spiritual functional orders of nature in this sense is what the tradition calls: the Temple. To build the Temple, we must go beyond objectification to identification, which is the simultaneous realization of the functions of nature and our innate potential. This is a difficult task because it calls upon us to enter a different world than we are used to: a non-dualistic world, in which everything is different: matter, spirit, nature, cosmos, humanity—and even language, which is the way our understanding of these is reflected and communicated. In alchemy, all of these are spiritual—oriented toward the spirit, calling the spirit, praising the spirit: which is ONE—one cause, one life, one light, one universe, one existence: a single genesis taking multiple analogous forms.

Thus the source becomes mineral; the mineral becomes plant; the plant becomes animal; the animal becomes human; the human becomes divine. The mineral suffers for the initial sacrifice or scission, which gives consciousness its path of evolution, seed and fruit. The plant by this metaphor then suffers for the mineral; the animal for the plant; the human for the animal; humanity for the cosmic human being; and the free cosmic spiritual-divine human for the unknown, unknowable Cause. Suffering and dying are thus that through which consciousness—one Being—evolves. Suffering, scission, the painful rack of paradox experienced right to the bone is what inscribes consciousness. Alchemically, the role of suffering (affliction, pain, crucifixion,) is a "salt" process. It is the "Cross in nature," as the Christian Hermeticist Douzetemps called the alchemical chapter of his mystical work, "The Mysteries of the Cross." In the words of Dhu l'Nun, an early Egyptian Sufi alchemist: "It is the salt of the faithful and when the salt lacks, the faithful become rotten." Truly we are called to be "the salt of the Earth." More generally, Rumi puts it so:

> I died as a mineral and became a plant,
> I died as a plant and became an animal
> I died as an animal and became a Human.
> Why should I fear? When was I less by dying?
> Yet once more I shall die: I shall die as a Human
> To soar with the Angels; but even from angelhood
> I shall have to pass on: all except God perishes.
> When I have sacrificed my angel soul,
> I shall become what no mind can conceive.
> Let me not exist! For non-existence
> Proclaims in organ tones: "To him we shall return."

Time is the key to this unfolding, but not time as duration or extent, but time as genesis or the painful distance between seed and fruit. This law of genesis—the distance and stages between seed and fruit—is identical for each thing. Psychological consciousness separates these but in fact they constitute a single movement. Schwaller de Lubicz writes:

> Taking the seed or grain as example we see that plant and final fruit actually exist potentially in the seed where no tangible form exists for a cerebral or psychological consciousness. From this potentiality to final effect, time marks the stages or phases that may be classified (into four or seven or nine etc.). None of these is qualitatively separate; one engenders and is found vitally in the other. When, following the initial putrefaction, the seed divides into root and germ, and the germ grows up as the root grows down, the potential fruit cannot be situated: it is as much in root as in germ. This "occult"

power—in conformity with cosmic power—decides when leaves, branches, sexualized flowers, and new seeds and ovules for proliferation will appear from the trunk.

*

AS ABOVE, SO BELOW

1. THE EMERALD TABLET OF HERMES TRISMEGISTUS

It is true, no lie (without falsehood), certain, and without doubt most true: that which is below is like that which is above, and that which is above is like that which is below, to accomplish the miracles of the one thing.

As all things are and proceed from one by contemplation (meditation) of one, so all things are born from one by adaptation (adoption).

The Sun is its father. The Moon is its mother. The wind carried it in its belly. The Earth received and nourished it.

The father of all works of wonder (*Telesma*) in the whole world is here.

Its force or power is whole if it is turned into Earth.

Separate Earth from Fire, subtle from gross, gently, with great prudence.

It ascends from Earth to Heaven and descends again from Heaven to Earth, acquiring the power of realities above and below. Thus you will re ceive the glory of the whole world and because of this all darkness will flee from you.

This is the power of powers, for it overcomes all subtle things and penetrates all solid things.

Thus the world is created: the little world according to the prototype of the Great World.

From this and in this way marvelous adaptations are made of which the means are given here.

Therefore I am called Hermes Trismegistus for I possess the three parts of the philosophy of the whole world.

Finished and perfect is what I have said of the work of the Sun.

2. HORTULANUS' COMMENTARY ON THE EMERALD TABLET

Preface.

I, Hortulanus, that is to say, a Gardener, so called because of maritime gardens bordering on the seacoast, unworthy to be called a Disciple of Philosophy, yet being moved with love for those I love, wish to make a true declaration and explanation of the words of Hermes, Father of Philosophers, whose words, though dark and obscure, sincerely declare the whole operation and practice of the true Work. Where the Holy Spirit is working, philosophers, who try to conceal knowledge in their writings, assuredly do so in vain.

Chapter I.
The Art of Alchemy is True and Certain.

The Philosopher says: *It is true,* namely, that the Art of Alchemy is given unto us, *without falsehood.* He says this to convince those that affirm this Science to be deceitful, that is, false. It is *certain,* that is, it is proved, experienced. For whatever is proved, is most certain. And most true, without doubt, because the most true Sun (gold) is engendered by Art. He says most true in the superlative, because the Sun (gold) engendered by this Art, excels all natural Sun (gold) in all proprieties, medicinal and others.

Chapter II.
The Stone must be Divided into Two Parts.

Next, he touches the operation of the stone, saying: *That which is below is like that which is above.* He says this because the stone is divided into two principal parts by Art: namely, into the upper part, which rises up, and into the lower part, which remains below fixed and clear. Yet these two parts agree in virtue. Therefore he says: "that which is above is like that which is below." Certainly, this division is necessary: *to accomplish the miracles of one thing.* That is to say, of the Stone: because the lower part is the Earth, which is called the Nurse and the Ferment and the upper part is the Soul, which quickens the whole Stone, and resuscitates it up. That is why separation and conjunction being accomplished, many miracles are effected in the secret work of nature.

Chapter III.
The Stone Contains the Four Elements.

As all things are and proceed from one by meditation of one. Here he gives an example, saying, as all things came from one, that is, a confused Globe, or a confused mass, by meditation, that is, by the thinking and creation *of one*, that is to say, of omnipotent God, so all things are born, that is, come forth from this single thing, that is, one confused mass, by *adaptation*, that is by the sole commandment of God, and are a miracle of God. Thus our Stone is born, and comes forth from one confused mass, containing in it all the (four) Elements, which are created by God, and by His miracle our stone is born and comes forth.

Chapter IV.
The Stone has a Father and a Mother, namely, the Sun and Moon.

As we see that one living creature naturally begets more living creatures like itself: so the Sun (gold) engenders the Sun (gold) artificially, by virtue of the multiplication of the Stone. That is why it follows that *the Sun is its father*, that is, the Philosophers' Gold. And just as in every natural generation, there must be a fit and convenient womb, a proper place to receive the seeds with a certain consonance of resemblance to the father, so likewise in this artificial generation, the Sun must have a matter which is a fit and consonant womb to receive his seed and tincture: and this is Philosopher's silver. Hence it follows that *the Moon is its mother.*

Chapter V.
The Conjunction of the Parts is the Conception and Generation of the Stone.

When these two receive each other in the conjunction of the Stone, the Stone develops in the belly of the wind and that is why he says afterward: *The wind carried it in his belly.* It is well known that the wind is air, and air is life, and life is the

Soul. I have already said of the soul that it quickens the whole stone. Hence the wind must carry the Stone and carry it again, and bring forth the magistery. That is why it follows that it must receive nourishment from its nurse, the earth. Therefore the Philosopher says: *The earth is its Nurse.* Because just as the infant without receiving food from his nurse would never grow up and reach maturity, so likewise our stone would not become mature without the fermentation of the earth, which is called nourishment. So: of a father conjoined with its mother, the *thing* is engendered, that is to say, children who are like their parents—children, who, if they do not have a long decoction will be like the mother, and retain the father's weight.

Chapter VI.
The Stone is Perfect if the Soul is Fixed in the Body.

Next he says, "The father of all works of wonder (*Telesma*) in the whole world is here," that is, there is in the work of the Stone a final way. And note that the Philosopher calls the operation, "the Father of all the Telesma" or works of wonder, that is to say, of the whole secret or treasure *of the whole world*: that is, of every Stone that may be found in the world. It is *here*. It is as if he is saying: Behold I show it you. Then the Philosopher says, Do you want me to teach you to know when the virtue of the Stone is perfect and complete? It is when it is converted and changed into his earth. Therefore he says, *Its force or power is whole*, that is, complete and perfect, *if it is turned into earth.* That is, if the soul of the Stone (which we have mentioned before may be called wind or air and in which the whole life and virtue of the stone consists) be converted into earth—the earth of the stone— and fixed, so that the whole substance of the Stone is so well united with its nurse, that is, the earth, that the whole Stone is found and turned into a ferment. Just as when one makes bread, a little leaven nourishes and ferments a great deal of paste, whose whole substance is turned into a ferment, so Philosopher wants our Stone to be so fermented that it can serve as a ferment for its own multiplication.

Chapter VII.
The Cleansing of the Stone.

Next, he teaches how the Stone should be multiplied: but first he sets down the cleansing of the stone, and the separation of the parts: saying, *Separate Earth from Fire, subtle from gross, gently, with great industry.* Gently, that is little by little, not violently, but wisely and industriously, to wit, in philosophical manure or a dung heap. *Separate,* that is, dissolve: for dissolution is the separation of parts. *Earth from Fire, subtle from gross:* that is, the lees and dregs, from the fire, the air, the water, and the whole substance of the Stone, so the Stone may remain wholly without excrement.

Chapter VIII.
The Unfixed Part of the Stone must separate
from the Fixed & Raise it up.

The Stone being thus prepared, it can be multiplied. Therefore he now sets down his multiplication and speaks of the easy liquefaction or fusion of the Stone by its ability (virtue) to enter and penetrate into hard and soft bodies, saying: *It ascends from Earth to Heaven and descends again from Heaven to Earth.* Here we must note, that although our Stone is divided in the first operation into four parts, which are the four elements, nevertheless, as we have already said, there are two principal parts of it: one which ascends upward, and is called unfixed or volatile, and the other below which remains fixed and is called earth, or ferment, as has been said. But we must have a great quantity of the unfixed part, and give it to the Stone, when it is very clean and without any excrement, so often by the magistery that the whole Stone by the virtue of the spirit is carried upward, sublimating and subtlizing it. And this is it that the Philosopher says: It ascends from the earth into the heaven.

Chapter IX.
The Volatile Stone must be Fixed Again.

After all these things, this same Stone thus exalted and raised up or sublimated, must be incinerated with the Oil extracted from it in the first operation. This oil is called the "water of the Stone." It must be sublimated repeatedly until by virtue of the fermentation of the earth (which is exalted and raised up by sublimation with it) the whole stone by repetition descends again from heaven into Earth, and remains fixed and flowing. And this is what the Philosopher says: *and descends again from Heaven to Earth, acquiring the power of realities above* as it sublimates *and below* as it descends. It descends again into the earth, receiving the virtue of those above by sublimation, and of those below by descending. That is, that which is corporeal is made spiritual by sublimation and that which is spiritual is made corporeal by descension.

Chapter X.
The Usefulness of the Art & Efficacy of the Stone.

Thus you will receive the glory of the whole world. That is, by this stone thus composed you shall possess the glory of this world. *And because of this all darkness will flee from you.* That is, all poverty and sickness. *This is the power of powers,* because there is no comparison between the other powers of this world and the power of this Stone. *For it overcomes all subtle things and penetrates all solid things.* It will overcome: that is, by overcoming, it will convert living Mercury and congeal it: and it penetrates other metals, which are hard, solid, and compact bodies.

Chapter XI.
This Work Imitates the Creation of the World.

The Philosopher next gives an example of the composition of his Stone, saying: *Thus the world was created.* That is, our stone was composed in the same way as the world was created. In the beginning, the whole world and all that was in it was a confused mass and a disordered Chaos (as was said above). Later, by the workmanship of the sovereign Creator this mass was divided into the four elements, admirably separated and rectified. By means of this separation, many and diverse things were created. Likewise many different things may be made by the production and ordering of our work through the separation of the different elements from different bodies.

From this and in this way marvelous adaptations are made. That is, if you will separate the elements, there will be admirable compositions appropriate to our work by the conjunction of rectified elements in the composition of our Stone. *Of which*, that is, of which wonderful things appropriate for this, *the means*, that is, how to proceed by, *is given here.*

Chapter XII.
An Enigmatic Declaration of the Matter of the Stone.

Therefore I am called Hermes Trismegistus, that is to say: Thrice Great Mercury. After the Philosopher has taught the composition of the Stone, he shows here secretly what our Stone is made of: first naming himself so that that his disciples who will attain to this science might bear his name in continual remembrance. But then he touches on what the matter is made of by adding, *having the three parts of the philosophy of the whole world*, because all that is in the world, having matter and form, is composed of the four Elements. Hence there are an infinity of things in the world, which the Philosopher divides into three principal parts: Mineral, Vegetable, and Animal: of all of which together or separately he had the true knowledge in the work or operation of the Sun, which is the composition of the Stone. That is why he says *having the three parts of the philosophy of the whole world*, all three of which are contained in the Stone alone, namely, in the Mercury of the Philosophers.

Chapter XIII.
Why the Stone is called Perfect.

This Stone is called perfect because it contains the nature of things mineral, vegetable, and animal. That is why the Stone is called triple or triune; that is, triple and singular, having four natures, namely, the four elements, and three colors: black, white and red. It is also called a grain of corn, which if it does not die, remains without fruit: but if it does die (as is above said), that is, when, the operations mentioned above are accomplished, it brings forth much fruit. O, beloved reader, if you know the operation of the Stone, I have told you the truth: but if you do not know it, I have told you nothing. *Finished and perfect is what I have said of the work of the Sun.* Thus is fulfilled and completed what has been said of the operation of the Stone, of the three colors, and four natures, which are in only one thing, namely, Philosophers Mercury.

HERE ENDS THE COMMENTARY OF HORTULANUS,
UPON THE SMARAGDINE TABLE OF HERMES,
THE FATHER OF PHILOSOPHERS.

*

(GREEN) SOPHIA

Whether or not a universal "Great Mother" culture predated the advent of the newer historical religions, the feminine Divine is clearly present throughout the Ancient Mysteries and central in the revelations of the founding civilizations of our ongoing evolutionary moment. We find her called Inanna, Astarte, Ishtar, Isis, Maat, Hathor, Nut, Neith, Demeter, Persephone, Artemis, Athena, and Hecate... And, in the Hebrew Scriptures, Asherah, she who is Wisdom (Hokhmah), and will become Mary, Sophia, Maryam, and Fatima... The list is endless. The more one seeks, the more one finds. But this apparently riotous confusion should not be taken as evidence of any kind of polytheism. These figures—all aspects of Sophia—represent different states of one and the same primal principle, acting according to successive phases of becoming, genesis, or nature.

Green Hermeticism and alchemy, too, belong to this lineage, are under this sign. A continuous transmission of images of the Divine Feminine exists from earliest, Paleolithic times. Everywhere we find Mother Goddesses; Mother(s) of all Living Things, Mothers of Life (and Death), Virgins, and Virgins about to give birth—so-called *Virgo Parituri*—not to mention Virgins with Child. Besides being represented by such female figurations, Sophia is imaged by a Tree or a Bird: by a swallow and a dove in the case of Inanna and Isis; in the case of Aphrodite, by a goose or a swan. These very birds, which are equally emblematic among other things of the Holy Spirit, are later also frequently Hermetic or alchemical birds.

Alchemists, for instance, will refer to their "conjunctions" or "sublimations"—their sacred unions and risings—as "birds," often "Eagles." "To make the Eagle fly," for example, meant to extract light from the tomb—spirit from the letter—and bring it to consciousness in an enhanced epiphany or experience. The celebrated seventeenth-century alchemist Eireneus Philalethes (now known to be the American George Starkey), invoking Sophia (and the Holy Spirit) writes: "To bring our work to perfection, no less than seven eagles are necessary and even nine should be used. Our philosophic Mercury is the bird of Hermes, which is also called the goose, the swan, and sometimes the pheasant."

She is also associated like alchemy itself with Waters, both celestial and earthly; and also with the Tree of Life, which images not only the renewal of vegetal, plant and animal life but also of Cosmic Life and the life of the stars: "a woman clothed with the Sun, with the moon under her feet, and on her head a crown of twelve stars." (Revelations) Tombs, cave-wombs and darkness are Sophia's home from the beginning. For this reason, Mary traditionally gave birth to Jesus in a cave—and He rose from one, too. Similarly, and not unsurprisingly, many alchemical laboratories are represented as being in crypts or dark, subterranean places.

The being of Sophia thus presumes what we might call a kind of divine cosmo-biology: the divine All-Life. Moreover, the Tree of Life is also the Cosmic Tree, so that Sophia is also none other than the *axis mundi* or world axis that unites Heaven, Earth, and the Underworld. In the Christian alchemical tradition, she is spoken of in this sense as "the Mirror of the Art," which, uniting Heaven, Earth, and the Stone itself, unites all.

Her symbol is the labyrinth, which, as Fulcanelli points out is "emblematic of the whole labor of the Work." He points out that the oldest labyrinth, which was in Knossos in Crete, was called "Absolum," which is close to the term "Absolute," another name the ancient alchemists gave to their Stone.

All such mysteries flow toward us most directly through the coeval Mysteries of Demeter and Persephone at Eleusis and those of Isis and Maat in Egypt into the Judaic-Christian-Islamic world.

LADY ALCHEMY, Bas-relief on the Great Porch of Notre Dame, Paris

No wonder then that, in the Great Porch of Notre Dame in Paris, welcoming all who enter, there is a bas-relief of Lady Alchemy herself. Seated, her head touches the waves of heaven and between her knees leaning against her lap is a ladder of nine rungs—the scale philosophorum—"hieroglyph of the patience which the faithful must possess in the course of the nine successive operations of the hermetic labor." In her left hand, she holds a scepter, symbol of royal power. In her right hand, she holds two books, one open, one closed.

According to Fulcanelli's student Eugene Canseliet, the closed book represents ordinary, empty matter; the open book, the same matter after it has been penetrated by the spirit. Fulcanelli then quotes Proverbs 8 on Sophia or Wisdom.

The Lord possessed me at the beginning of his ways.
I existed before he formed any creature.
I existed from eternity, before the earth was created…

When he prepared the heavens, I was there.
When he confined the abysses within their bounds
And prescribed an inviolable law;
When he confirmed the air above the earth;
when he balanced the waters of the fountains;
when he shut up the sea within its limits
and imposed a law on the waters,
so that they should not pass their bounds;
when he laid the foundations of the earth—
I was with him and I regulated all things.
I was source of delight every day,
Playing in front of him all the time,
Playing in His inhabited world,
Finding delight with humankind.

Wisdom—Nature, the spiritual source of Nature—was thus created before heaven and earth. She was in fact the very beginning of God's creation: the first created being, the closest to Him. Present at creation, she is God's joy and delight. She is the divine presence, God's messenger in the world. She plays not only before God, but also among us, human beings in the world. She finds delight with us too.

Now, "Beginning" in its original meaning does not lie back in the sense of a chronological source, but rather "opens out." Beginning is the ever-present opening. The English word "begin" comes from old Teutonic *be-ginnan* " to cut open, to open up" and is cognate with Old English: "to gape, to yawn," as in the mouth of an abyss. The beginning, then, is an opening up of the primal, unknowable Mystery. We find her in the abyss—"the deep," "the waters"—of Genesis 1.2: "And the earth was without form and void; and darkness was on the face of the deep. And the spirit of God moved upon the face of the waters."

We have been taught that Abrahamic monotheistic story of creation rests upon *creatio ex nihilo*, creation from nothing. But the Old Testament (like the Hebrew Scriptures) does not speak of that. It speaks rather of the "waters" as the prime matter of creation. The idea of *creatio ex nihilo*, in fact, is a post-Christian invention by the so-called gnostic Basilides, who unable to fully comprehend non-duality, sought to defuse the influence of Greek philosophy and avoid any suggestion of Plato's "preexistent matter."

Wisdom, Sophia, who was at the beginning, is in reality the continuously available opening place: the primal scission that reveals the already-present divine presence. Such is the wisdom out of which all things are made. As Psalm 104.24 says: "You have made all things in wisdom." "That wisdom is the beginning, and in that beginning you have made heaven and earth," wrote Augustine, for whom this "intelligence" is "spiritual matter" of almost unbounded fluidity." For the writers of Genesis, therefore, Wisdom is the heaven of heavens, God's bride or wife, God thus being male and female.

"The Virgin Mother," Fulcanelli writes, "stripped of her symbolical veil, is none other than the personification of the primitive substance, used by the Principle, the creator of all that is, for the furtherance of his designs... Here is the very essence of things...the subject of the hermetic science of universal wisdom..." This is the spiritual vase containing all things; the burning bush, the Golden Fleece; the virgin earth...

She is also, as we noted, the "Mirror of All," Solomon tells us in his Wisdom Book:

> Like a fine mist she rises from the power of God,
> A clear effluence from the glory of the Almighty;
> So nothing defiled can enter into her by stealth.
> She is the radiance that streams from everlasting light,
> The flawless mirror of the active power of God
> And the image of his goodness.
> She is but one yet can do all things,
> Herself unchanging, she makes all things new...

"Alchemically," writes Fulcanelli, "the first matter, which the artist must chose in order to begin the work, is called the mirror of the Art." The Renaissance Hermeticist known as the Cosmopolite, likewise, speaking of Sulphur, writes: "In its kingdom there is a mirror is which the whole world is seen. Anyone looking in this mirror can see and learn the three parts of the Wisdom of the whole world..." And Basil Valentine, perhaps the greatest alchemist of the

Renaissance: "The whole body of the Vitriol must be recognized only as a Mirror of the philosophical science...It is a Mirror in which you see our Mercury, our Sun and Moon, appear and shine; by which you can show in an instant and prove to doubting Thomases the blindness of their crass ignorance."

Sophia—Nature, the Mirror—is thus simultaneously, matrix and imaginatrix, mediatrix and workshop of creation—its place and its process. She is Imagination too, the intermediary between the world of mystery and the visible world. She is the Deep In-Between. In her, incorporeal beings take body and sensuous things are "dematerialized." Through her, spiritual beings enact the evolutionary drama of the world.

She is the first image of the Godhead, its first emanation, the image of what is deepest in the Godhead. In her, the Godhead contemplates the secret of compassion—the liberation of beings by being known and loved in them. She is Sophia-Creatrix: The Androgynous Stone.

But hidden here is a mystery. The place of creation—Imagination or Wisdom, the veil between created and uncreated reality, the divine feminine creator—has another name. Sophia's other name is primordial cosmic human nature itself. That is why, as the Gnostic Valentinus taught, when the angels were creating humanity they stopped in fear when the creature they had made uttered a cry greater than its creation seemed to justify. For the angels realized that the one above had invisibly deposited in this human being a seed of itself, thereby revealing the hidden nature of the ground of all being. Jafar as-Sadik, the sixth 'Alid Imam, a famous alchemist and the teacher of Jabir, puts it thus: "The angels are peripheral, knowing only some of God's names, while the human being is central, knowing all His names." This "human" nature, concealed since the foundation of the world, was Anthropos, the cosmic archetype of the human being. The new revelation proclaimed openly that creation is creation in human nature. The world is brought forth from human nature. It fell through human nature, and through human nature in the end, when the hidden treasure will be known, it will return to God whence it came.

According to the cosmology taught in the initiatory temples of Egypt, and also practiced as the heart of their sacred science, God created all things in the mirror, the cloud, of archetypal human nature in order to be known or—in Christian terms—all in all. God's primordial divine intent has never changed. It is the true meaning of the microcosm-macrocosm analogy. The human being is not a little cosmos; the cosmos is a big human. According to this tradition, cosmic evolution is the progressive unfolding, transformation, and mutation of the seeds planted in the original human archetype.

*

DIALOGUE OF KLEOPATRA AND THE PHILOSOPHERS

Kleopatra said to the philosophers: "Consider the nature of plants and where they come from. For some come down from the mountains and grow out of the earth, and some grow up from the valleys and some come from the plains. Consider how they develop, for you must gather them up at certain seasons and days, and take them from the islands of the sea, and from the loftiest place. Consider the air ministering to them and the nourishment circling around them so that they perish not nor die. Consider the divine water which gives them drink and the air that governs them after they have been given body in a single being."

Ostanes and those with him answered Kleopatra: "A strange and terrible mystery is hidden in you. Enlighten us; cast your light upon the elements. Tell us how the highest descends to the lowest and how the lowest rises to the highest, and how that which is in the midst approaches the highest and is united with it, and what is the element that accomplishes these things. And tell us how the blessed waters visit the corpses in Hades fettered and afflicted in darkness, and how the medicine of life reaches them and rouses them as if wakened from sleep; and how the new waters, both those brought forth on the bier and those coming after the light, penetrate them at the beginning of their prostration and how a cloud supports them and how the cloud supporting the waters rises from the sea."

Then the philosophers rejoiced in what had been revealed to them.

Kleopatra said to them: "When they come, the waters awaken the bodies and the spirits that are imprisoned and weak. Again they undergo oppression and are enclosed in Hades. Yet in a little while they grow and rise up and put on different colors like the flowers in springtime and the spring itself rejoices at the beauty that they wear."

"I tell this to you who are wise: when you take plants, elements, and stones from their places, they appear to you to be mature. But they are not mature until the fire has tested them. When they are clothed in the glory and shining colors from the fire, then their hidden glory and their sought-for beauty will appear, for they will be transformed into the divine state of fusion. For they are nourished in the fire and the embryo grows little by little nourished in its mother's womb, and when the appointed month approaches is not restrained from issuing forth. Such is the procedure of this worthy art. The waves and surges one after another in Hades wound them in the tomb where they lie. When the tomb is opened they issue from Hades as a babe from the womb."

*

OUROBOROS ("TAIL-EATER") OR THE COINCIDENCE OF OPPOSITES

In the Nag Hammadi text called "Thunder (or Perfect Mind)," Sophia speaks as wife-virgin, mother-daughter, and universal midwife:

I am the first and the last
I am the honored and the scorned
I am the whore and the holy
I am the wife and the virgin
I am the mother and the daughter
(and the barren one with many sons)

I have had a great wedding
(and have not found a husband)
I am a midwife and do not give birth
I am the solace of my labor pain
I am bride and groom (and my husband has produced me)
I am the mother of my father and the sister of my husband
And he is my offspring...

Fifteen hundred years later, echoing Sophia, the legendary alchemist Basil Valentine alluded to the matter of the Work as follows:

I am the old Dragon, present everywhere on Earth. I am Father and Mother, young and old, strong and weak, living and dead, visible and invisible, hard and soft, descending into Earth and ascending into Heaven, very big and very small, very light and very heavy. The order of nature often changes in me in color, number, weight, and measure. I contain natural light. I am clear and dark. I am known and I am nothing.... (BASIL VALENTINE, *Azoth*)

Azoth, the title of Basil Valentine's work, has nothing to do with the chemical element Nitrogen (N), as Gleb Butuzov points out in "Some Traits of Hermetic Language," but rather invokes the Philosophers' goal, Alpha/Aleph Zed Omega Tau—the union of the beginning and the end. "Human beings die," wrote the Pythagorean Alcmaeon of Croton, "because they cannot join their beginning and their end." "The way up and the way down are one and the same," said Heraclitus.

In a more philosophical vein, Giordano Bruno, expounding his Hermetic philosophy in *The Expulsion of the Triumphant Beast*, writes that:

...The beginning, the middle, and the end, the birth, the growth, and the perfection of everything we see is accomplished by means of opposites, within opposites, toward opposites. Where there is opposition there is action and reaction, there is movement, diversity, multiplicity, succession, and vicissitude.

This path of opposites Samuel Taylor Coleridge, poet, philosopher, and Romantic Hermeticist, called "the universal law of polarity or essential dualism," writing "every power in nature and in spirit must evolve an opposite as the sole means and condition of its manifestation; and all opposition is a tendency to re-union."

Philosophizing, thinking, and practicing by opposites are dominant alchemical themes, thus contradicting traditional Western "Aristotelian" logic, which is based on three principles:

The principle of *identity* (that A=A, i.e., A cannot = not-A; i.e., A must have a single identity);
The principle of *non-contradiction* (that a thing cannot be and not be at the same time);
The principle of the *excluded middle*—that every proposition is either true or false.

After fifteen hundred years the German philosopher Immanuel Kant cast this logic in stone, claiming it to be "a science *a priori* of the necessary laws of thinking not, however, in respect of particular objects but all objects in general… a science therefore of the right use of understanding and reason as such, not subjectively, i.e., not according to empirical principles of how the understanding thinks, but objectively, i.e., according to *a priori* principles of how it ought to think."

Kant held the world in itself was unknowable and that all we could know was the logic or form of our own thinking. Following him, we have constructed the world according to the "logic" of our thinking—but "thinking" only as he, following Aristotle, defined it. Even today, although science is moving beyond the prison-house of non-contradiction into fuzzy, triadic, and quantum logics, most of us still see the world through Aristotelian-Kantian eyes. We see the world logically-conceptually. Before Kant, philosophers assumed concepts structured the world; after Kant, they tend to believe concepts structure thinking. As for reality, that remains unknown.

Alchemy is very different. It is not interested in concepts, but experience. It is not a metaphysic or a philosophy, but a way of being. Hence it is impossible to describe the alchemical worldview analytically, just as it is impossible to put poetry into prose without betraying it.

Alchemy's use of thinking, language, and practice are based on the coincidence of opposites: their unity or union, that is, their identity. Thinking is still the guide, but it does not "*a priori*" lead godlike to any "logical" conclusion or "answer." Hermetic thinking, as Hermetic language and laboratory practice, works through paradox and metaphor (and patience), which essentially overturn the laws of logic in that they demand the ability to hold two contrary realities simultaneously in the heart/mind as a unity.

That this is painful goes without saying. Indeed, one definition of suffering is the experience at the level of our being of contradictory truths. Such experiences, if deep enough, bring consciousness and hence thinking out of the conceptual or epistemological realm into the realm of being or creation itself. Whereas ordinary thinking and science begin with a multiplicity of parts and somehow hope to move from the details of the many to some kind of wholeness or unity, Hermeticism begins with the unity or wholeness of opposites and seeks to realize their reality in the experience of the world.

The single page of Kleopatra's *Chrysopoeia* or "Gold-making" shows that this was so from the beginning. Here we find the classic image of the Ouroboros, the serpent devouring its own tail. Inside the circle it encloses, we find inscribed the words *En to Pan*, One (is) the All.

Outside, going all the way round, we read, "One is the serpent who contains the poison according to the double sign;" and around that: "One is the all, the source of all, and the culmination of all: if the all did not contain the all, it would be nothing."

This circle, the Serpent, whose end and beginning are joined, represents both the universe and the alchemical Hermetic Work: the two are one. "One the All" asserts the identity of unity and multiplicity; and by that token, the identity of God and the world, of the Creator and Creation; and since unity is 1, and multiplicity is not-1, it also asserts by implication the identity of self and world/nature.

"I = not-I," wrote Novalis, changing it to "I = You."

What is at stake here is not a philosophical theory—it is not a matter of reducing everything to a single principle—but "an actual state brought about by the suppression of the law of opposition between I and not I and between 'inside' and 'outside.'" (Evola)

As for the "poison according to the double sign," it is that which both kills and heals. "It is a Stone and it is not a Stone; it is precious and worthless; it is unknown and known by all; it has a single name and many names ... it kills itself and gives itself life" (*Turba Philosophorum*). The double sign is therefore that of the union of opposites, beyond matter and spirit, heaven and earth. It is both itself and what overcomes itself. It is its own Father and Mother, hence androgynous, an Androgyne, both male and female, its own root.

In the words of Denis Zachaire, a Renaissance alchemist: "If we declare our matter to be spiritual that is true, and if we declare it to be corporeal we do not lie. If we call it celestial that is its true designation; and if we call it terrestrial we have spoken correctly." Thus, it is well worth meditating the identity of apparent opposites, such as the individual and all-humanity; self and other; good and evil; finite and infinite, male and female, heaven and earth, creator and creation...

*

THE QUINTESSENCE

Join the male and the female and you will find what is sought.

Marry gum with gum in true marriage.

If you do not render corporeal substances incorporeal, and incorporeal substances corporeal, and if you do not make the two bodies one, nothing of the expected will be produced.

MARIA THE JEWESS

Hermes said: Know that the secret of everything and the life of everything is water, and this water is susceptible of treatment by human beings and others, and in this water is a great secret: This is the water which becomes ferment in wheat, wine in the vine, olive oil in the olive, resin in the turpentine tree, oil in the sesame, and the different kinds of fruit in all trees.

IBN UMAIL

*

ALTERNATIVE ETYMOLOGIES

Besides the derivation from Al-Kemi, the "Black Land (Earth)," or Egypt, the word "alchemy" has been thought to evoke the name of Ham or Cham, Noah's son, who by this theory would have been the first alchemist—which also takes us back to Egypt, but with different implications.

According to legend and the Hebrew Scriptures, Noah had three sons—Ham, Shem, and Japhet—from whom, after the flood, humanity unfolded. The sons of Ham (Chus, Mizraim, Phuth, and Canaan) spread out to the "South" through "African" realms including Egypt, Canaan, Assyria, Babylon, and Phoenicia. These would then be "Hamitic" and by this token perhaps Hermetic realms. To the "East," the children of Shem dispersed as "Semites" and "Asians;" while to the "North" the children of Japhet (perhaps Indo-Europeans) were said to have populated what we now know as Europe.

"These were the three sons of Noah and of them was the whole earth overspread." (Genesis 9,19.)

If this theory has any interest, it is because, like so many others, it both points us to Egypt, confirming—what many authors have suggested—that our own epoch stands on the evolutionary spiral in direct relation to the Black Land and also suggests a relationship with Cain.

After the flood, when Noah was a husbandman and planted a vineyard, "he drank of the wine, and was drunken." Ham then saw him in his drunkenness, and told his brothers, who, approaching their father backward, their eyes averted, covered him and thus never saw him naked. But Ham saw Noah naked—when Noah realized what had happened he cursed his son because he had seen his nakedness.

Ham, then, like Cain, was cursed. He had seen what he was not supposed to see.

What is interesting here is that there is a persistent tradition that places the Hermetic tradition in such a lineage. Unfolding the story of the evolution of human freedom, Rudolf Steiner, for instance, repeatedly turns to the contrast between what he calls the paths of Cain and Abel as representing a fundamental polarity in human existence. Broadly speaking, using a Buddhist expression, we may call these two paths the path of "own power," which is the path craftsman-scientist-artist creating out of him/herself, and the path of "other power," which the creative and the receptive of the priest, open and receptive to God. As Steiner tells it, Cain, the first earthly human, was born of Eve, the First Mother of all living things, by one of the Elohim, the spirits of light. God then created Adam; and, from Adam and Eve, Abel was born. Cain, then, we may say, is divine-human, while Abel is purely human. Cain, as we know, slew Abel (with freedom comes guilt), and in his place God gave Adam and Eve, Seth. And from Cain and Seth two types or streams of human being descended. The Seth stream was gifted with the ability to receive spiritual visions. The Cain stream, however, though half-divine, forgot their divinity, and had to develop their spiritual abilities by developing their earthly forces.

In the lineage of Cain, then, we find Jabal, inventor of geometry, masonry, and architecture; Jubal, inventor of music; Tubal Cain, inventor of smith-craft and metallurgy; Naamah, inventor of weaving…and Hiram Abiff, architect of Solomon's Temple.

Taking all this metaphorically, we may say there are two human streams—one recognizes that though somehow cut off from it they contain divinity, the uncreated spark of God, and return to God through their own work, while the other believes divinity is "received" from above.

I say "metaphorically" because these are two different traditions or ways of approaching the spiritual world—rather than two different kinds of human being. There is only one kind of human being—made in the image and likeness of God and constituting the tenth hierarchy, whose mission is to recapitulate and unify them all. The "Abel" tradition or approach stresses the transcendence of divinity, available by grace to human beings who prepare their souls to receive its gifts. The "Cain" tradition, on the other hand, stresses the immanence of divinity in the human heart that makes the human a "second" God or creator on earth.

Generally speaking, this distinction is the same as the ancient Indian distinction between the Brahmans—the Priestly Stream—

and the Kshatriya or warriors—the Royal Stream. These two have always been in conflict—think of the Pope and the Holy Roman Emperor in the Middle Ages—but a little reflection or meditation will show that, as approaches, they are two sides of a single coin. Even where "own power" is emphasized, nothing happens without grace.

We may note, too, that alchemy and Hermeticism are called the "Royal Art," that is, they likewise are of what Steiner calls the "Cain" stream, another metaphor for which is "Hamitic."

In quite a different derivation, an anonymous author of an eighteenth-century manuscript claims that the word "alchemy" derives from *als*, meaning "salt" in Greek, and *chymia*, meaning "fusion." However, as Fulcanelli points out, *cheimeia* is close to and phonetically confusable with *chymeia*, which means "sap" or "secretion."

After giving these and other hypotheses, Fulcanelli gives his own opinion:

> ...We would say that phonetic cabala recognizes a close relation-ship between the Greek words *Cheimeia*, *Chymeia*, and *Cheuma*, which indicates that which *runs down, streams, flows*, and particularly indi-cates *molten metal*, the *fusion* itself as well as *any work made from molten metal*. This would be a brief and succinct definition of alchemy as a metallurgical technique. But we know on the other hand that **the name and the thing are based on** *the permutation of form by light*, **fire, or spirit**: such in any case is the true meaning indicated by the *Lan-guage of the Birds*. (Bold emphasis added)
>
> FULCANELLI, *The Dwellings of the Philosophers*

Another, simpler etymology takes "al" as "el," the Hebrew word for God, and combines with "kemia," the black "earth," to produce "God's earth," and sees in this a variant of "red earth," which is the literal Hebrew meaning of Adam, so that alchemy would be the divine science and art of being, or becoming, human.

*

MONOLOGUE

Actually, there is much foolishness around speaking and writing. True speech is pure word play. One can only wonder at the comical error people make when they think that they are speaking about things. No one knows precisely what is most distinctive about language, that it is concerned solely with itself. This is why it is so marvelous and fruitful a mystery that, when people speak simply in order to speak, they utter the most magnificent and original truths. But if they try to speak of something specific, then the capricious nature of language makes them say the most ridiculous and mistaken things.... It is with language as with mathematical formulas. These constitute a world by themselves, play only among themselves, and express nothing but their own marvelous nature. This is the reason why they are so expressive and mirror the singular interplay of things. It is only by their freedom that they are parts of nature, and only in their free movement does the world soul express itself, and make them a delicate measure and abstract plan of things. The same is true of language...Only someone with a profound feeling for language, who feels it in its application, its flow, its rhythm, its musical spirit —only those who hear its inner nature and apprehend within themselves its intimate and subtle movement... yes, only that person is a prophet...

NOVALIS

*

LANGUAGE

A plurality of names does not make a plurality of things.

HERMETIC SAYING

Alchemy can teach us much about language, without which human activity would come to nothing. But what is language? We know language is not representational: a word neither "represents" a thing nor, truly speaking, even an idea. A word is not a thing at all, and certainly not a denotative thing. It does not point to anything, not even to some other "reality." Nor is it in itself an idea or a concept. For this reason, some philosophers have preferred to call it "connotative," believing that, whenever we speak or write, a whole cloud of witnesses is present and meaning descends in tongues of flame like the Holy Spirit. In that case, we would have to say that the richer the language, the greater the cloud, and the finer the intuitive capacities required to understand the multiple means conveyed. But then, perhaps, after all, all language is a divine gift: the grace-filled fringe of a higher world we must become worthy of before we can begin to understand.

Therefore the first thing to remember when reading an alchemical text is that there is no objective world, no objective, representational language—only a living, dynamic, mobile reality. Context, experience, and function are all. Just as children playing may call the same piece of wood a plane, a boat, a bird, a soldier, but know what it is by the context and function it serves. Or they create a "private" language whose meaning they understand completely but which makes no sense to adults; so, too, alchemists use language—words, images, symbols, myths, names—to serve whatever context or function demands. Terms are therefore impossible to classify objectively. They can be understood only from within the process, which is continuously changing (mobile, dynamic) and at the level that the narrative is enacting. At the same time, any idea of separation between an inner, spiritual alchemy and an outer, material, laboratory alchemy must be resolutely laid aside. The two are one or, rather, there is only one alchemy and it is inner and outer at the same time.

As Gleb Butozov puts it: "Even superficial assessment, not one based on the arbitrary dichotomy of 'material' and 'spiritual,' shows a differentiation between two such alchemies to be conditional and, in principle, groundless, inasmuch as they represent *crossed and complementary hierarchical levels* of a sole reality. (It is sufficient to recall that the result of 'inner alchemy' is material and the result of 'external alchemy' has spiritual implications." The same is true of alchemical language. Inner work is outer work: the text and the work are one.

Alchemical language is not conceptual: in that sense, it gives us no information. It is rather injunctive: it enjoins processes that must be undergone—both in the operative and in the laboratory. If one is able to truly "do" what the text says, one realizes that understanding it is precisely analogous with what transpires in the crucible. In that sense, there is a single transformation. In the text, language itself is being subjected to the same operations as matter in the work. Language and the matter, the work and the text are one. Reading parallels the work. *Solve et coagula* is an experience of consciousness. "Little by little a kind of light emerges from the obscurity. It is as if one was in a tomb amid corpses. And gradually the tomb grows light, and the corpses revive."

Adding to the confusion, each alchemical text is singular and unique to its author's experience. Each bears witness to one person's experience of realities, not to the application of any universal theory. In fact, in a way, there is no alchemical "theory." All we have are empirical and phenomenological descriptions, but at another or "higher" level than available to unprepared consciousness and therefore available for confirmation only by those who have attained the same state as the author. Thus, such texts are an open secret for those in the game, but closed to those who are not. Alchemical language is thus notoriously obscure, and even (some would say) intentionally inaccessible.

Looking through the texts, at least those created before the Renaissance and the leap in consciousness represented by Paracelsus, we are struck first by their similarity, that is, by the apparent lack of the novelty and originality that we have come to expect of important writing. Often they just seem to shuffle hermetic-alchemical commonplaces, as it were gathering alchemical "flowers" and arranging them tastefully in hermetic bouquets. Some texts, indeed, are even called "Rosaria"—"rose gardens"—so that often it seems that the alchemist writer is just gardening with words and phrases, arranging his tropes in a fine herbaceous border. But these words and phrases must not be taken in the ordinary sense: they are not "vulgar." As the twelfth century adept, Artephius, says: "Anyone who takes the words of the Philosophers according to the ordinary signification and sound of them, having already lost Ariadne's thread, is wandering lost in the midst of the Labyrinth and as good as appointed his money to perdition."

Often therefore, though the words seem clear, their combinations seem so repetitive, ridden with contradiction, metaphor, metonymy, paradox, and wordplay, so lacking in logic and shrouded in clouds of mythological and symbolical associations, that we are tempted to conclude that the authors deliberately sought to conceal, rather than reveal, what they sought to say. But that cannot be the case because, as with all genuine esoteric texts, the authors rightly insist that they are in fact expressing what they have to say in the only, and indeed the clearest, way. As Jesus spoke in parables, not to conceal his meaning, but to reveal it in the most appropriate form, so alchemical-hermetic authors claim to communicate their meaning too in the clearest possible way.

The problem clearly is that their understanding of language is different from our own. Sometimes, it is true, some authors really don't know what they are talking about and this complicates the situation. Equally confusing is the fact that the Masters will sometimes deliberately create errors or even insert false recipes into their text. All this, however, only points us toward the reality that, in order to understand their texts, we must first learn *to think* as they do.

The errors in fact can teach us a great deal about the kind of reading that our texts require. As one master wrote: "The philosophers say he or she who has not gone wrong has not begun yet. Mistakes are the masters who teach what one must do or not do." True mistakes begin the awakening of another state of consciousness: error makes metanoia or transformation of thinking possible. And not only error, but also wordplay, puns, and multiple meanings.

Alchemists certainly feel free to play with words. After all, alchemy is an "art," which means Hermetic and alchemical writing is more like poetry than like science or philosophy. For in the best poetry sound itself is meaningful and there is never only one meaning—or a clear concept—but a cloud of meanings within and through which a vast non-conceptual experience might be had. Alchemical texts therefore abound in puns, sound play, associations that depend upon recondite etymologies and weird phonetic assonances. Some call this "argot" or slang (or Gothic Art, *Art Goth*) the "language of the birds." But such wordplay is only a beginning—

almost, as it were, by the way. Above all, we must pay heed to the instruction that the alchemists give us repeatedly: namely, "*Lege, lege, lege, labora, ora, et relege.*" Read, read, read, work, pray, and read again. In other words: consciousness, that is, *thinking*, precedes and gives rise to the text in which that thinking is entombed in words and must be resurrected into its own true light. *Lege, lege, lege* does not mean: "read, read, read" but "think, think, think... "Nowadays, we read as if the words themselves give rise to thinking: that words think. But for the hermetic-alchemist, thinking is not in words, thinking precedes words: to read is to think.

Understanding, therefore, like the realization of the work, which is a *donum dei*, a gift of god, requires a meditative reading, one that asks questions of the text. With each reading we ask a different question. Whoever grasps a word before it is spoken and begins to generate images begins to see the light of the divine Word.

*

PHOS IN THE GARDEN

...In the original hieratic language, the first human, the interpreter of all that exists and the giver of names to all corporal beings, is called Thoth. The Chaldeans, the Parthians, the Medes, and the Hebrews call this being Adam, which means "virgin earth," and "blood red earth," and "fiery red earth," and "fleshly earth."

...So, then, the first human among us is called Thoth, and among them Adam, from the language of the angels. And not only that, but with respect to the body the name they use is symbolic, composed of the four elements from the whole sphere. For the letter A of Adam's name signifies the ascendant east, and air; the letter D of Adam's name signifies the descendent west, and earth, which sinks down because of its weight; [...] and the letter M of Adam's name signifies the meridian south, and the ripening fire in the midst of these bodies, the fire belonging to the middle, the fourth planetary zone.

So, then, the Adam of flesh is called Thoth with respect to the visible outer mould, but the Human within him, the spiritual Human, has a proper name as well as a common one. The proper name no one knows for the present, for only Nikotheos, the one who cannot be found, knows it. But his common name is *Phos* [Light], and from this it follows that human beings came to be known as *"photes"* ["lights"].

When *Phos* was in the Garden, spirited along by the winds, at the instigation of Fate, they persuaded him since he was innocent and unactivated, to clothe himself with their Adam, who comes from Fate, who comes from the four elements. But *Phos*, for his innocence, did not refuse, and they began to exult thinking that they had made *Phos* their slave....

ZOSIMOS OF PANOPOLIS, *On the Letter Omega*

*

PERCEPTION AND IMAGINATION

There is a world we must recover hidden in the very act of sensible perception.

HENRY CORBIN

Knowledge differs greatly from sense perception. Sense perception takes place when that which is material has the mastery; and it uses the body as its organ, for it cannot exist apart from the body. But knowledge is incorporeal; the organ, which it uses, is the mind itself.

CORPUS HERMETICUM X

There are two ways of "perceiving." In the first, which is ordinary sense perception, the object is immediately transformed or abstracted into a representation. In the second, the perception is not abstracted or transformed but rather the act of perceiving is, as it were, allowed to germinate in the soul. As Rudolf Steiner notes, we may compare a phenomenon that we perceive to a grain of wheat, which we may either grind up, cook, and eat, or plant so that it may germinate and reproduce a thousand-fold. He remarks: "Whenever a seed of corn is processed for the purposes of nutrition, it is lifted out of the developmental pattern which is proper to it, and which ends in the formation of a new plant; but so also is a representation, whenever it is applied by the mind in producing a mental copy of a sense-perception, diverted from its proper teleological pattern."

To plant a perception in the soul is to respect its concrete specificity. It is to allow it to complete itself, to reveal its "knowledge," whereas to fix it in a representation, a "picture," is to reduce it to a mental abstraction. Rather than catching the bird in flight and flying with it, in ordinary representational perception we shoot it down and kill it. Hence we live with dead thoughts, not living realities.

True sense perception not only works to recall the inner meaning of a phenomenon to its spiritual archetype but also permits the exaltation of that phenomenon through individualized self-knowledge, which is revealed to be none other than cosmic knowledge under an individualized aspect. That is, we lovingly withhold conceptualization and the attribution of meaning and allow the perceptual image to sink uncontested within us where we dwell in and with it in unknowing warmth and reverence until our attention—now in feeling form—and the image are one. Doing so, and letting it go, remaining in pure feeling emptiness, a new meaningfulness dawns that is suprapersonal, yet individualized. In this state, we may experience a sense of being seen and feel a gaze of a being upon us. Repeating and repeating the experience more and more unfolds in what—it becomes clear—is another space, another place.

Paracelsus's great achievement was to change the meaning of science or (*scientia*) and experience (*experientia*). For him, *Experientia* is what we know for certain: it is truth. The rest is accident. What he means becomes clear when we realize that by "knowing" he means experience, which he contrasts with "experiment," the latter being "accidental." Experiment may teach the "fact" that a certain herb, Scammonea, purges, or rather that there is a virtue or knowledge in the Scammonea that teaches it how to purge, just as there is a knowledge in the pear tree that teaches it how to grow pears. Objective observation, "experiment," apprises us of the fact, *but truly experienced knowledge is union with the knowledge in the Scammonea.*

Paracelsus, perhaps, as we shall see, the father of Green Hermeticism, spoke of uniting sense perception, imagination, and intuition. Rudolf Steiner likewise speaks of three stages of cognition that he calls Imagination, Inspiration, and Intuition. Both these Hermetic Masters understood that the human being spiritually understood and realized unites the entire world—earthly, celestial, and divine. Therefore for them knowledge was not a matter of thoughts, but of uniting consciously what is within with what is without—union, identity with the object—through various "bodies"—etheric, astral, and "I."

> When you overhear from the Scammonea the knowledge that it possesses, that knowledge will be in you just as it is in the Scammonea and you have acquired the experience as well as the knowledge. (Paracelsus)

The key, then, is to bridge the distance between "inside" and "outside": to practice an intimacy where these distinctions no longer hold.

Two Arabic words, zahir and batin, indicate complementarity between outer and inner, perception and imagination. In this view, all outer (zahir) phenomena conceal (and thereby reveal to whoever has eyes to see) a hidden, inner (batin) reality. The outer, perceptual phenomenal manifestation is the place where the hidden, inner reality is disclosed. The sensory phenomenon is at the same time suprasensory. The relationship of outer and inner therefore is not allegorical, but symbolical. Appearance and reality are not separate, but symbolize each other in a mediated identity—one that we can enter. Outer is neither something imposed upon nor different from inner, but is the inner itself transposed to another, outer level or state of being. "States exist and men pass through them," wrote Blake. Phenomena (appearances) are known by being transported (metamorphosed) from one state to another—from a more hidden to a less hidden. Thereby they are made more perfect, that is, more closely approximate wholeness.

Arabic also proposes another useful set of terms: tanzil and ta'wil. Tanzil, the ordinary word for the "letter" of Revelation, means (literally) "to cause to come down." Ta'wil means, "to cause to return," i.e., to ascend or lead back. *Ta'wil* not only saves appearances by returning them to—that is, symbolizing them with—their original form, it also returns to his or her source, the person practicing it. As Henry Corbin writes: "The *ta'wil* of texts presupposes the *ta'wil* of the soul: the soul cannot restore, return the text to its truth, unless it too returns to its truth." As the Ismaili treatise *Kalami Pir* states: "[*ta'wil* is] to bring something back to its origin... Hence he who practices *ta'wil* is one who turns his speech from the outer form to the inner reality."

According to this view, such esoteric knowledge or gnosis is not only an interiorization of phenomena and a corresponding purification of the soul but also an encounter (as a being) with a being or beings. Such meetings can only take place in a world and so the Sufis called this world the *Mundus Imaginalis,* the Imaginal or "Astral" World, which is also the world of the soul and of the dead. For them, the Imagination is the realm of being where theophany—the manifestation of the divine—and gnosis (spiritual knowing) coincide. It is the place of the encounter of the human and the divine, of the *coincidence of opposites* between divine spiritual descent and human spiritual ascent. It is where human and spiritual-divine imaginations meet and pure intelligible archetypes enter knowing. It is thus a place of union, of holy reciprocity, divine, spiritual, and human love becoming one in the being of the lover, the Hermetic seeker. Love, after all, is the mode of knowledge whereby one being knows another. Such is the nature of the "cosmos" where mystical visions occur. Here spiritual realities appear, and hierohistories (like the Grail) have their truth. Here, above all, is the active mirror (or *speculum*) where spirit takes form and matter is immaterialized.

The fact is that, to attain to the world of subtle matter—to spiritualize matter—one must have an organ of cognition distinct from pure intellect or intuition and from reason and the senses. This organ is the Imagination, and the realm or world to which it corresponds—organ and realm being mutually sustaining—is the Imaginal World. We could call it the "soul" world. Not that the Imaginal World is the product of the soul; rather, the soul is the product of the *Mundus Imaginalis.* Nor is the Imaginal World a collectivity (like the "collective unconscious"); on the contrary, it is irreducibly singular and personal. Not existing outside of its activity, it is subjectivity itself. Hence one cannot say where it is. Beyond "where," it is nowhere. As "the clime to which one cannot point," it's "where" is everywhere. Unsituated, it situates all. The place of all things, it is itself in no place.

To understand this, we must realize that it is in the nature of esoteric knowledge, as it is of the Imaginal World, that, moving away from the senses (and the sense perceptible world), we arrive, by a quasi-magic topology, *outside* the world that we left, surrounding it. What was interior, hidden, invisible, suddenly becomes unhidden, environing, phenomenal. Therefore, it is said of "the world of images" that it begins at the point where the relationship interior and exterior inverts. There spiritual bodies (forms) are no longer in a world, as physical bodies are, their world is in them.

In the spiritual or heavenly world, what seemed on earth to be the microcosm is revealed to be the macrocosm. Each of us, as an angelic being, contains the whole; and that is why "behind this world there is a heaven, an earth, a sea, animals, plants, and men, all of them celestial." That is, behind, within, surrounding this world there is another world; and, we may add, another still; and another still…

Such a view is only intelligible in terms of a subject whose being is a function of its presence in these worlds, because it is as a function of this same being that these worlds are present to it. Thus the angelic form of Aristotle asks the great Sufi theosopher of light, Suhrawardi: "Is the knowledge that you have of yourself a direct perception of yourself, or do you get it from somewhere else?" In other words, is it ontological (being) knowledge, realized through the presence of oneself to oneself, or is it representational, epistemological knowledge (of objects by a knowing subject)?

Knowledge of this kind is not an abstraction or representation of external forms; it is not something added to the subject, as it were from without; rather, it is the singular, revealed knowledge of the subject's own essential being, that is, his spiritual self-identity. To say I know myself, in the sense of "The one who knows himself/herself knows his/her Lord," is equivalent to saying, I am in the presence of myself, my true I, who is a spiritual, angelic being at home in a spiritual, angelic world. Once every veil is lifted, the dawn light that the soul casts on the objects of her vision, illuminating them, so that she then knows them because they are present to her, is her own true presence.

The power to render present in this way is proportional to the degree of light, that is, of proximity to the true Light, realized by the soul. By her presence, she witnesses and casts that light, that presence; the more present, the more conscious and truer the witness, the greater the light—degrees of presence, witness, and consciousness marking ascending degrees of proximity and immateriality. Therefore, Suhrawardi prays (with all Hermeticists and alchemists):

> Cause the litany of Light to ascend,
> Cause the people of Light to triumph,
> Guide the Light towards the Light.

Suhrawardi's "precious philosophy of Light" united in a single inspiration an entire lineage of prophetic guidance—a "column of Glory"—that, beginning with Zoroaster, Hermes, and the legendary Hero-Kings of Iran, incorporated in its luminous unfolding all the "sages," including all the Hermeticists and alchemists. Such figures of world-transforming wisdom were for him the "eternal leaven" of human and cosmic history, way-stations in the progressive approach of the presence of the once and future Savior-Redeemer, Saoshyant, or Imam, whom we may call the Paraclete or Holy Spirit.

Implicit in this view is the task of the transfiguration or spiritualization of the earth called Frashkart in the Avesta by the divine fire-energy, Kvarnah. This is the "Light of Glory," the all-luminous substance, the pure luminescence that is the real nature of all created beings, as of the divinity itself. This primal energy, which is associated with fire, order, light, and even being, may also be identified not only with the Archetypal Image of the soul itself, but also with the imaginal organ that will transform the world itself into soul, that is, effect its transfiguration into the radiant body of incorruptible luminous fire that is its true nature. "May we be among those who are to bring about the Transfiguration of the Earth," runs the fundamental prayer in this tradition, echoing the Boddhisttva Vow not to seek final enlightenment until the last blade of grass is transfigured.

The Christian Desert Fathers knew of this when they spoke of "the prayer of the heart," and working "the earth of the heart," through the union of the mind and the heart in prayer. Neither mind nor heart alone, they felt, was sufficient for true prayer. Prayer of the mind was cold and inflationary and led to a kind of spiritual egotism; prayer from the heart led either to sentimentality, which is a kind of egotism of feeling, or to a kind of cosmic oceanic immersion in feeling. The true way was to unite mind and heart by a descent of the mind into the heart, so that the heart became *knowing—a sensorium* with eyes and ears, taste, touch, and smell. In the new heart, as in a deep mirror, the old monks saw that all their ideas of the world—of divine, angelic, and human natures, of animals, plants, trees, minerals, and the starry heavens—were living realities. All around them were beings, fellow players in the great drama of creation. They saw the world differently. And it *was* different. It was a new world. That is why the monks were often thought to possess the philosopher's stone. Those coming from the outside world to visit them found the world miraculously transformed. These early monks called their practice "working the earth of the heart." It is what Novalis meant when he said "We are on a mission; we are called to cultivate the earth."

Above all, Suhrawardi's essentially Hermetic prayer calls to mind Manicheanism and its "column of light." In Mani's cosmology, before the cosmos came into being, spirits of darkness sought to invade Ahura Mazda's kingdom of light, reaching the very borders of the kingdom, besieging it, and threatening to enter. What was to be done? Ahura Mazda and the kingdom of light were pure goodness and love. With what could they resist? There was no "evil" in them. Only one response was possible: to love—for the spirits of light to give themselves in love to the darkness. So with a part of their own kingdom, they embraced the darkness, merging and mixing with it at every level. The result was that Ahura Mazda's kingdom became a mixture of light and darkness. Indeed, increasingly the darkness began to predominate. Although there was a leaven, a ferment of light, in the darkness, the light seemed unable to prevail.

Thus the cosmos arose, a whirling dance, containing death, evolving into a material world, a kingdom that would ultimately destroy itself. Ahura Mazda again faced the question: What to do?

With his remaining spirits of light, He created humanity in His image and likeness and sent it down to earth, to the mixed kingdom, by love to separate the light from the darkness through its own being. Here, as Rudolf Steiner notes, "the profound thought is that the kingdom of darkness must be overcome by the kingdom of light, not by means of violence, but by love—by gentleness, mildness, and meekness—not by resisting evil but by uniting with it to redeem it. Because a part of the light enters into evil, the evil itself is overcome."

At the heart of Mani's complex vision, which includes a vibrant, imaginal, dramatic cosmology of spiritual beings, lies humanity's task as a spark of divine light lovingly to gather and redeem all light mixed in the darkness and, through love, raise the darkness into the light. Thus, as beings of light, we are given the mission to aid in the luminisation of the world of matter into love so that the Earth may become a Sun: the *terra lucida*, the Earth of Light. For the Manichean, the world as we see it is already spiritual: it is already light, but mixed with darkness. The earth, sun, and the stars—all are spiritual, are light. The task is to engage each cognition—every perception, thought, feeling, and will-impulse—and, through love, the only means available to the Good, the divine spark, separate the light from the darkness, overcoming, and transforming it through love, releasing the spark of divinity.

*

THE PHOENIX

And he took me and led me where the sun goes forth; and he showed me a chariot and four, under which burnt a fire, and in the chariot sat a man, wearing a crown of fire, and the chariot was drawn by forty angels. And behold a bird circling before the sun, about nine cubits away. And I said to the angel, "What is this bird?" And he said to me, "This is the guardian of the earth." And I said, "Lord, how is he the guardian of the earth? Teach me."

And the angel said to me, "This bird flies alongside of the sun, and spreading his wings receives its fiery rays. If he were not to receive them, neither human beings nor any other living creatures would be preserved. God appointed the bird to this task."

And the bird spread his wings, and I saw on his right wing large letters, as large as the space of a threshing-floor, and the letters were of gold. And the angel said to me, "Read them." And I read and they ran thus: "Neither earth nor heaven bring me forth, but wings of fire bring me forth." And I said, "Lord, what is this bird, and what is his name?"

And the angel said to me, "His name is called Phoenix."

And I said, "What does he eat?" And he replied, "The manna of heaven and the dew of earth."

And I said, "Does he excrete?" And he replied, "He excretes a worm, and the excrement of the worm is cinnamon, which kings and princes use. But wait and thou shalt see the glory of God."

And, while he was conversing with me, there came a sound as of a thunderclap, and the place where we stood was shaken. And I asked the angel, "My Lord, what is this sound?" And the angel said, "Even now the angels are opening the three hundred and sixty-five gates of heaven, and the light is being separated from the darkness." And a voice came which said, "Light giver, give to the world radiance."

When I heard the noise of the bird, I said, "Lord, what is this noise?" And he said, "This is the bird that awakens the cocks on earth from their slumber. For as humans speak through their mouths, so does the cock speak to those in the world in his own speech. For the sun is made ready by the angels, and then the cock crows."

(From the Greek Apocalypse of Baruch)

*

LIGHT, BODY MATTER

For the Hermeticist, according to Henri Coton-Alvart, Light exists in two states: Original Light and "optical" or "liberated" Light. The Book of Genesis perhaps alludes to these two Lights when it places the *Fiat Lux*—God's saying, "Let there be Light"—eleven verses before the creation of the Sun and the Moon.

Original Light, then, is the Light of the *Fiat Lux*, the Light of Creation that instantly fills the Abyss. Spontaneously created by God, Original Light is free, direct, unmediated, and omnipresent. It is not the result of the transformation of something else. It is the Light of the Origin: the original light. Spirit, it seeks to return to Spirit.

Optical, liberated light is secondary. It always comes from something, something into which its was previously introduced in some form or other. We know it as a form of energy: mechanical, chemical, electric, or radiant energy. These four forms of what we might call second light (in contrast to the First Light) are always dependent on some kind of "matter," which they always seek to escape, and do escape, through radiation. In fact, they seek to return to the Original Light and would do so, if some new "matter" did not interpose itself—refracting, reflecting, or absorbing it; trapping it as electrical, chemical, or mechanical energy. Original light, on the other hand, does not come from anywhere or anything. It is not the result of any transformation of any preexisting energy. Nowhere, it is everywhere.

Where then does "matter" come from? Matter—at least as we know it today— is the great mystery. All traditions speak of opposition, inertia—of forces like Satan, Ahriman—who oppose the light. We might say, as in a myth, that from the beginning—from the *Fiat Lux*—the Adversary resisted and opposed the light.

Here, it is important not to confuse "matter" and "body"—which are two entirely separate realities. Bodies can exist without matter. Matter, as we know it, is "Second Matter." It is not First Matter, which is the Abyss, also known technically as "Hyle," the Divine Water, Sophia. Plato in his *Timaeus* calls it "the receiving principle," "the receptacle and in a manner the nurse of all generation," the Mother.

First matter, the *materia prima*, this Mother, is true light: Original Light. Second Matter, in this account, is where there is no light, just empty holes, points that oppose the light. The matter we know is, in fact, nothing and nothing but opposition to the light. Original Light is neither waves nor particles like optical light, but everywhere omni-directional, like the Sun. It is diversified, varied, like the spectrum. But "matter," as we know it, is a sickness of nature, a kind of leprosy—an illusion—that the Hermeticist seeks to heal.

"Body"—in contrast to matter—is an aspect of Light: it is non-ponderable substance. Spirit is the other aspect of Light. Spirit and Light are both uncreated and created. They are "the fire or warmth of Life" (also uncreated and created). Body, for its part, is the form of life (uncreated and created). Soul is their conjunction. Form or body, again, is fourfold—elementing and elemented—and known through its qualities: heat, cold, dry, and humid.

Here the elements are important: the principles or energies we call fire, air, water, and earth. For the alchemist these are twofold: Elementing, heavenly elements; and elemented earthly elements that are contaminated, mixed, with matter—or nothing. The alchemist purifies the elements of this matter in a work of resurrection to create glorious, immaterial, light bodies. It is a work of purification. Fire is hot and dry. Air is warm and humid. Water is cold and humid. Earth is cold and dry. These clearly are convertible: Fire (hot and dry) can become air by becoming humid. Air (warm and humid) can become water by becoming cold. Water (cold and humid) can become earth by becoming dry. Earth can become Fire becoming hot.

Meditation shows, however, that there are only two primary elements: Fire and Water, Light and the Abyss—male and female—and their union.

In *The Testament of Alchemy (Morienus)*, King Khalid asks Morienus: "Tell me whether this operation is accomplished by a single principle or by several?" Morienus replies:

> In answer to your question as to whether this operation has one root or many, know that it has but one, and but one matter, and one substance of which and with which alone it is done, nor is anything added to or subtracted from it. When certain of his disciples asked

Herakleios what you have asked me, he told them how a single root grows into many things which return again to one, if they get air. Ostanes declared that the four elements, heat, wetness, cold and drying, are basically one, and that certain of these four are compounded of others, as though some were the roots of which the others were composed. The true roots are water and fire, and composed of these are earth and air...

*

A (TOO BRIEF) DIGRESSION ON CAUSALITY

> The solution of phenomena can never be derived from phenomena.
>
> COLERIDGE

True, every phenomenon seems to be connected by cause and effect to another phenomenon or group of phenomena. But cause and effect in that sense is just a concept, as Hume pointed out, inferred from the fact that two events always seem to occur together, one following the other. If we are seeking the true origin or cause of some particular phenomenon, we must look elsewhere than in the world of phenomena. A phenomenon can never be the cause of another phenomenon.

Science, for the most part, regards "reality" as a quantitative sequence in time. Cause, generally speaking, is an effect of quantity in time. But we can conceive of a world outside this frame of reference—a world of quality, the world of the present moment. Causality in that world would be simultaneous, out of time and within it. It would be vertical. Cause and effect would then be one. A cause would be a cause only at the moment it causes an effect. The effect would be the cause made visible. The effect would contain the cause: it would symbolize it.

We all know Aristotle's theory of four causes: the material cause (the matter), the formal cause (the form), the efficient cause (the agent), and the final or teleological cause (the end or purpose as cause; as the end of a dream causes the beginning. Otherwise, how would the dream know where to end?)

Today, the four causes have been reduced to one: a cause is simply what by its agency causes an effect. The sculptor is the cause of a statue, as one billiard ball hitting another is the cause of its moving. In other words, we understand by causality only one cause, the efficient cause. We no longer understand what Aristotle can have meant by the other causes and misunderstand, in fact, what he meant by the efficient cause.

Since Kant, we see things subjectively, from the human point of view: from the human perspective as subject and agent. The Greeks experienced reality differently—as coming toward the human from the gods: as soliciting human participation and cooperation. They saw reality as co-constituted and causality likewise collaborative with the gods.

To understand alchemy and Green Hermeticism, we must seek to reanimate the ancient view of causality (and technology)—of which Aristotle's "four causes" are but aspects. To do so means going beyond any idea of causality as imposition, domination, or determination.

According to Martin Heidegger (as interpreted by Richard Rojcewicz in his excellent book *Technology and the Gods*) for Aristotle: "the causes… are the conditions to which the produced thing is obliged." The causes are what help a thing along—that abet and provide the conditions, the nurture, out of which a thing comes forth. Causes do not use force, or exercise any kind of compulsion. Rather, they are what anything that comes into being is obliged to for its existence. They provide the circumstances, the context, whereby something might emerge.

Take the "efficient cause" of which Aristotle speaks as "that from which" a thing comes: "the whence of the movement," "that whence the beginning of the change emerges," "that which arouses, urges on."

To understand what this might mean, consider his examples—astonishing to us—of this kind of causality:

Counseling is this kind of cause, as a father counsels a son, and, on the whole, a maker is this kind of cause of the thing made…The sower of seeds, the doctor, the counselor, and, on the whole, the maker are all things whence the beginning of a change emerges.

We think of causality as directional, unilateral, but counseling, doctoring, and gardening are interactive. They are caring.

Here we have the difference between the ancient, Hermetic view and the modern view: nature versus force; letting be versus constraint; and aiding versus compulsion.

*

THE WORK CONSISTS ONLY IN ITSELF

Herakleios said to certain of his disciples that just as the date is brought forth by the palm, so also is the palm tree produced of that same date, and from its root grow the shoots by which it multiplies. And on this point Hermes said: consider how red is made complete by partial degrees of redness. Consider also red as a whole, and the full yellow, and partial degrees of yellowness, and yellow as a whole. And likewise full black and partial degrees of blackness as a whole. As a shoot emerges from a grain, so also do the many branches from a tree and the tree from its seed. A certain seer, who entirely renounced the world, also said things as we have spoken, namely that a human is produced of a sperm, just as of a single grain a hundred are brought forth, from which a great tree grows.... Thus also does the Great Work consist in itself, requiring nothing else. This is the proper secret of the philosophers. They moreover called it everywhere by many names, concealing it thus from all but the wise... But fools despise it and hold it of no account, ignoring what it is. This wise used many terms in the books, one being "sperm," which, when converted, becomes blood, and then is consolidated with the flesh as though part of it. Thus the process of generation proceeds by a succession of forms, until the human being is made....

MORIENUS

*

LABORATORY/ORATORY/TEMPLE/ALTAR

Two stories, one about Goethe and one about Teilhard de Chardin, tell us much about the soul mood of the hermetic-alchemist.

I.

Goethe tells us in his *Autobiography* ("Poetry and Truth") that he was about nine when he first began to forge his own, personal relation to God. It seemed to him that he could approach the "great God of Nature, Creator and Preserver of Heaven and Earth" directly only by addressing him through his works. Therefore he decided to build an altar for himself where he could serve as priest. He took his collection of natural objects—seeds, nuts, minerals, ores, bird's eggs, butterflies, and bugs—and laid them out on a beautiful, red-lacquered music stand. To create a flame to symbolize his heart's aspirations, he hit upon two "fumigating pastilles" that, ignited upon a fine porcelain saucer, would provide flame and fragrant incense simultaneously. Each morning, as the sun rose, his pre-adolescent devotion was perfect—and secret. No one knew of it. The household, which was large, saw only his collection of "curiosities" tastefully displayed. Then, one dawn, not finding the saucer to hand, the young priest placed the pastilles directly on the lacquered stand. A series of deep, scarring, black burns resulted. As Goethe puts it: "The young priest was thrown into the most extreme perplexity. It was true that the mischief could be covered up with the larger pieces of his show materials. But the spirit for new offerings was gone, and the accident might almost be considered a hint and warning of the danger there is in wishing to approach the Deity in this way."

II.

Like Goethe, Teilhard de Chardin also grew up with a passion for nature, in his case with the rocks, mountains, and wooded hills of central France, a budding geologist's paradise, a volcanic terrain where, as he puts it, one could easily fall in love with "the crimson glow… the divine, radiating from the depths of blazing matter." His first love was iron; but, realizing it rusted, he turned to a search for what truly endured and found—rocks and the Earth itself. He began a mineral and fossil collection, but through it, right from the start, what he sought was the All: the Absolute. As with Goethe, his childhood collection was his first altar. Before it, as before all subsequent altars, he stood, as he puts it, more a "votary" than a scientist. Later, as a priest, he would serve before a more conventionally religious altar. Yet, in the end, and most importantly, the Earth itself became his altar. Already during the First World War, having neither bread nor wine nor altar, he could write, "I shall spread my hands over the whole universe and take its immensity as the matter of my sacrifice…"

The perfect expression of his religion as of his science, came however in 1923 in the Ordos Desert in the "Great Bend" of the Yellow River in China, where he was collecting early human tools and other bone and fossil remains. There, too, he was without bread, wine, or altar. Instead, at dawn, he celebrated "The Mass of the World," which is also one of the great mystical texts of the twentieth century:

> Since once again Lord—though this time not in the forests of the Aisne but in the steppes of Asia—I have neither bread, nor wine, nor altar, I will raise myself beyond these symbols, to the pure majesty of the real itself; I, your priest, will make the whole earth my altar and on it will offer you all the labors and sufferings of the world.
>
> Over there, on the horizon, the sun has just touched with light the outermost fringe of the eastern sky. Once again, beneath this moving sheet of fire, the living surface of the earth wakes and trembles, and once again begins its fearful travail…
>
> Receive, O Lord, this all-embracing host which your whole creation, moved by your magnetism, offers you at this dawn of a new day…
>
> It is done.
>
> Once again the fire has penetrated the earth.
>
> Not with the sudden crash of thunderbolt, riving the mountaintop: Does the Master break down doors to enter his own home? Without earthquake or thunderclap: the flame has lit up the whole world from within. All things individually and collectively are penetrated and flooded by it, from the innermost core of the tiniest atom to the mighty sweep of the most universal laws of being…

An alchemical text, the *Sophic Hydrolith* tells us:

If anyone desires to reach this great unspeakable mystery, he or she must remember that it is not obtained by human might, but by the grace of God, and that it is not our will and desire, but only the mercy of the Most High that can bestow it upon us. For this reason, you must first of all cleanse your heart, lift it to him alone, and ask of God this gift in true, earnest, and undoubting prayer. God alone can give and bestow it… Therefore fall upon your knees. With a humble and contrite heart render God the praise, honor, and glory you owe Him because He hears your prayer. Ask Him over and over again to continue showering His grace upon you, and ask Him to grant that, after attaining to full and perfect knowledge of this profound Mystery, you may be able to use it to the glory and honor of His most Holy Name, and for the good of thy suffering fellows…

For the alchemist, then, laboratory and oratory were one. Prayer was a central aspect, often the first named, of alchemical or Hermetic practice. It was always connected to charity, indicating perhaps that prayer without love for one's fellow human beings is not prayer at all. In a sense, alchemists took on and made their own the great Benedictine adage, *Ora et Labora*—Work and Prayer—and were quite conscious of the fact that the word on which they took their stand ("laboratory") seemed to fuse the two primordial human activities of work and prayer into a single process in which the one could not occur without the other.

Prayer, for the alchemist, meant essentially (as it does primordially) trust, praise, gratitude, and lamentation: unconditional trust, without which nothing may be received; praise to the Creator for the glory, magnificence, and powers of his Work, the Universe; gratitude for the continuous gift of the Universe, its Life and Light—that is, for All that has been given and is still and ever being given; and, finally and continually, lamentation for humanity's dereliction of its appointed task as divine mediator, for its selfishness and arrogance in setting itself up as self-constituted and autonomous, for its oblivion that everything is given and its preferring itself to God and God's gifts.

It was through prayer (and the alchemical-hermetic work as an extension of prayer or prayer in action) that the alchemist, purifying

KHUNRATH'S LABORATORIUM, *Amphitheatrum sapientiae aeternae*, 1609

and midwifing his or her own rebirth could simultaneously purify and midwife the resurrection (or second birth) of Nature herself.

This is why, as Maurice Aniane has pointed out, Western Christian alchemists, practicing the primordial "sacramental" science of the sacrifice of terrestrial substances, the divine liturgy for the resurrection of inanimate matter, could liken themselves to universal priests, celebrating a universal, cosmic form of Eucharist, in which the species were no longer only bread and wine, but nature as a whole: mineral, plant, and animal. If the Spirit is everywhere, the "miracle" of transmutation—of Resurrection—is likewise omnipresent. Nature, being nothing other than the "fallen" body of God, it could through selfless human priestly action, realize its true once and future nature as the Divine Bride.

In this sense, the medieval alchemist did no more than fulfill to the letter the injunction "to preach the Word to, and heal, every creature." Preaching the word he brought the divine presence to all things, awakening them to their primordial nature as divine and medicinal, because through their divinity they were able to heal each other. "The true role of the alchemist was to celebrate analogically a mass whose species was...nature in its entirety." (Aniane)

Confirming this relationship, there is an interesting text, *An Alchemical Mass*, by the Hungarian priest and alchemist Nicholas Melchior of Szeben in Transylvania. He invokes Christ as the "blessed stone," who, for the salvation of the world, inspires the light of science and as the "divine fire" makes it possible.

Canseliet writes: "What is undeniable and gives the Church its perennial nature is that, before the sacred stone of the altar—the true builders' cornerstone—the priest, by the holy sacrifice of the Mass, offers to God the same supreme cult that the alchemist practices in constant attention before his working furnace. Both seek the same divine grace, which is indispensably necessary for human salvation and essentially gratuitous and free. Although working with different materials, both are dedicated to the secret elaboration of the physical and tangible agent of spiritual renewal."

Both seek the Universal Medicine, the living "coal," which the Seraphim took from the Divine Altar in heaven and placed on Isaiah's mouth, saying: "Lo, this hath touched your lips; and your iniquity is taken away; your sin purged." For the Eastern Church, Christ himself is the "Living Coal" (and fragments of the Eucharistic host are known as "coals), while alchemists refer to the glowing gem produced through the Great Work as the Sages' "carbuncle" (or "little coal"). Another name for the host in the Eastern Church is "Gift," which is also how the Philosopher's Stone in its ultimate perfection is also described—as *Donum dei*, gift of God. Grace. Such is the "medicine" that the alchemist prepares in order to exercise charity or pure, selfless sacrificial love for every human being, all humanity, all of God's creation. Is the alchemist, then, a physician, and a healer? Or a theurgist, who works with the gods? Or a philosopher, a lover of the wisdom of nature, who thinks as nature thinks? A scientist, who seeks above all knowledge? Or an artist, who, imitating "nature in her mode of operation," creates in imitation and praise of the only Maker? He or she is all of these.

*

FROM THE FIRST OF THE THREE VISIONS
(OR PRACTICES) OF ZOSIMOS

The composition of the waters, and the movement, the growth, and the removal and restitution of bodily nature, and the splitting off of the spirit from the body, and the fixation of the spirit on the body are not operations with natures alien one from the other, but, like the hard bodies of metals and the moist fluids of plants, are One Thing, of One Nature, acting upon itself. And in this system, of one kind but many colors, is preserved a research of all things, multiple and various, subject to lunar influence and measure of time, which regulates the cessation and growth by which the One Nature transforms itself.

Saying these things, I slept, and I saw a certain sacrificing priest standing before me and over an altar, which had the form of a bowl. And that altar had fifteen steps going up to it. Then the priest stood up and I heard a voice from above say to me, "I have completed the descent of the fifteen steps and the ascent of the steps of light. And it is the sacrificing priest who renews me, casting off the body's coarseness, and, consecrated by necessity, I have become a spirit." And when I had heard the voice of him who stood in the altar formed like a bowl, I questioned him, desiring to understand who he was. He answered me in a weak voice saying, "I am Ion, Priest of the Adytum, and I have borne an intolerable force. For in the morning someone rushed at me and dismembered me with a sword and tore me apart, according to the rigor of harmony. And, having cut off my head with the sword, he mashed my flesh with my bones and burned them in the fire of the treatment, until, my body transformed, I should learn to become a spirit." And I sustained the same intolerable force. And even as he said these things to me and I forced him to speak, it was as if his eyes turned to blood and he vomited up all his flesh. And I saw him as a mutilated image of a little man and he was tearing at his flesh and falling away.

And being afraid I awoke and considered, "Is this not the composition of the waters?" I thought that I was right and fell asleep again. And I saw the same altar in the shape of a bowl and water bubbled at the top of it, and in it were many people endlessly. And there was no one whom I might question outside of the bowl. And I went up to the altar to view the spectacle. And I saw a little man, a barber, whitened with age, and he said to me, "What are you looking at?" I answered that I wondered at the boiling water and the men who were burning but remained alive. And he answered me saying, "The spectacle which you see is at once the entrance and the exit and the process." I questioned him further, "What is the nature of the process?" He answered, "It is the place of the practice called the embalming. Men wishing to obtain virtue enter here and, fleeing the body, become spirits." I said to him, "And are you a spirit?" And he answered, saying, "Both a spirit and a guardian of spirits." As he was saying these things to me, the boiling increased and the people wailed, I saw a copper man holding a lead tablet in his hand. Looking at the tablet, he said, "I counsel all those in mortification to become calm and to each take in his hand a lead tablet and write with his own hand and that each bear his eyes upward and open his mouth until his grapes be grown." The act followed the word and the master of the house said to me, "Have you stretched your neck up and have you seen what is done?" And I said that I had and he said to me, "This man of copper whom you have seen is the sacrificial priest and the sacrifice and he who vomited out his own flesh. To him was given authority over the water and over those men in mortification."

And when I had seen these visions, I woke again and said to myself, "What is the cause of this vision? Is this not the white and yellow water, boiling, sulphurous, divine?" And I found that I understood well. And I said that it was good to speak and good to hear and good to give and good to receive and good to be poor and good to be rich. And how does Nature learn to give and to receive? The copper man gives and the water-stone receives; the thunder gives the fire that flashed from it. For all things are woven together and all things are taken apart and all things are mingled and all things combined and all things mixed and all things separated and all things are moistened and all things are dried and all things bud and all things blossom in the altar shaped like a bowl. For each, by method and by weight of the four elements, the interlacing and separation of the whole is accomplished for no bond can be made without method. The method is natural, breathing in and breathing out, keeping the orders of the method, increasing and decreasing. And all things by division and union come together in a harmony, the method not being neglected, the Nature is transformed. For the Nature, turning on itself, is changed. And the Nature is both the nature of the virtue and the bond of the world.

And, so that I need not write to you of many things, friend, build a temple of one stone, like ceruse, like alabaster, like marble of Proconnesus in appearance, having neither beginning nor end in its building. Let it have within, a pure stream of water glittering like sunlight. Notice on what side the entry to the temple is and take your sword in hand and seek the entry. For thin-mouthed is the place where the opening is and a serpent lies by it guarding the temple. First seize him in your hands and make a sacrifice of him. And having skinned him, cut his flesh from his bones, divide him, member from member, and having brought together again the members and the bones, make them a stepping stone at the entry to the temple and mount upon them and go in, and there you will find what you seek. For the priest whom you see seated in the stream gathering his color, is not a man of copper. For he has changed the color of his nature. He his become a man of silver whom, if you wish, after a little time, you will have as a man of gold…

*

VIRIDITAS

A further clue to the Hermetic mystery is given if we consider the recovery of Sophia as taught by Hildegard of Bingen (b. 1098), of whom the monk Guibert wrote that no woman since Mary had received so great a gift. Hers was the gift of vision, of being able to see in the reflection of the living light and sometimes in the living light itself. Like Mary, Hildegard was a "poor little figure of a woman," and perhaps it was this that allowed her to recognize that the humility of the feminine exalted it over every creature.

For Hildegard, Sophia, whom she calls either *Sapientia* (Wisdom) or *Caritas* (Love), is the complex reality, the cosmic glue, articulating many things we usually keep separate, such as God and nature, humanity and nature. Primarily, she is the living bond between Creator and creation, God and cosmos. But essentially she is the bond between all opposites. As such, it is by her perpetual mediation that the divine—which is the coincidence of opposites—can manifest and be known. Sophia thus lives for Hildegard in the encounter of God and creation, where God stoops to humanity/nature and humanity/nature aspires to God. As the Creator's playful companion, Sophia or Wisdom-Love makes possible not only creation itself but the incarnation of creation in time. This is the event of redemption or new creation, which, for Hildegard, is the center and cause of all, the event for which the world has been made.

For Hildegard, a woman, Mary, accomplished this new creation—the union of divinity and humanity and the earth. Thus, woman, the feminine, is the means of God's becoming all in all. And for her the feminine IS—Sophia: Wisdom-Love—is not limited just to Mary. It extends, firstly, to Jesus, the Humanity of Christ—"Jesus, our mother"—and then, by extension, to all-humanity, the earth, which is, in turn, one with the cosmos itself. Jesus, humanity, the earth, and the cosmos are feminized as Sophia, who is the place where the divine heart must come to dwell.

Humanity, potentially Sophianic, contains the universe. Hildegard writes: "O human being, look to humanity! For humanity contains in itself the heavens and the earth and all created things. It is one form within which all things are hidden." And again: "God has buckled on human beings the armor of creation so that they can know the whole world through sight, understand it through hearing, distinguish it through smell, be nourished by it through taste, dominate it thorough touch." Note here the elements: sight/fire; smell/air; taste/water; touch/earth; hearing/quintessence.

Humanity has three tasks: to work toward God; to work with God; to work with creation for God—*Opus dei, Opus alterum per alterum, Opus cum creatura*.

The human being is a unitary work—*unum opus*—body soul and spirit.

Being God's privileged creature, *opus operationis dei*, humanity is endowed with faculties. We are makers (*homo operans*), mirrors of the universe (*speculum universi*) and responsible for the salvation of the whole (*homo responsurus*).

God's plan (*praesentia dei*) was that humanity, being the center and created source of all creation, could help him in realizing the divine potentiality. This is the "work with creation" (*opus cum creatura*).

Opus cum creatura leads the cosmos in partnership with nature back to God as a bride to the altar: a simultaneous reunion of Creator and creation in a "nature that is golden"—*materia aurea*—a transformed universe, a sun.

For Hildegard: incarnation was not a simple consequence of the Fall: "When God created the world he decided in his eternal wisdom that he would become human."

Terra materia opus dei est, qui materia humana filii dei est.

From this perspective, the hearts of Jesus and Mary are one heart and also at the same time no other than the heart or center of the cosmos itself. Creating such a center in oneself by a process of radical purification and transformation made possible the indwelling of divine heart and the gift of wisdom. At its highest level, Hildegard understood that such inner work made possible the renewal of humanity's cosmogenic or Adamic function. For, once the soul was so purified that it was one with Sophia—was Wisdom and Love—the being in whom it was purified was perfected in the three realms of Sophia that are, traditionally, the perfection of the human state. Perfected in these, she became "Trismegistus"—master of the three realms. Hildegard has a marvelous antiphon that describes these realms:

O energy of Wisdom,
encompassing all
you circled circling
in the path of life
with three wings:
one flies on high
one distills from the earth,
and the third flies everywhere.

In her first vision, "On the Construction of the Universe" she writes:

I saw within the mystery of God, amid the southern winds, a beautiful image. It had a human form. Its countenance was of such beauty and radiance that I could more easily have looked at the sun than at that face. A wide golden ring encircled its head. In this ring above the head another figure appeared, like that of an elderly man… [He said] "I am the fiery life of divine essence, aflame beyond the beauty of the fields, I glisten in the waters and I burn in the sun, moon and stars. With every breeze I awaken everything to life. The air lives by turning green and being in bloom. The waters flow as if they were alive. The blazing sun lives in its light, and the moon is enkindled by the light of the sun again and again…For I am life, whole and entire—not struck from stones, not blooming out of twigs, not rooted in the human power of procreation. Rather all life has its roots in me. Reason is the root, the resounding Word blooms out of it."

Hildegard's name for this "fiery essence of life"—which for her is none other than the Holy Spirit—is *viriditas*. *Viriditas* is the greening power of God, the greening power of Sophia:

O most noble greening power,
Rooted in the sun
You, who in bright serenity
Shine in the wheel

That no earthly excellence
Comprehends:
You are enfolded
In the arms of divine ministries.
You blush like the dawn
And burn like a flame of the sun.

Viriditas is everywhere. It lives green in all things: "There are three qualities in a stone and three in a flame and three in a word. In the stone there is damp greenness, solidity to the touch, and sparkling fire..."
"There is a power in eternity and it is green."
In, with, and through this greening, healing power, humans are called to their vocations.

*

THE PRAYER OF HORTULANUS
(THE GARDENER)

Praise, honor, power, and glory to thee, O Almighty Lord God, together with your beloved son, our Lord Jesus Christ, and the Holy Ghost, the Comforter. O Holy Trinity, Who are the only one God, perfect Human, I give you thanks that, having knowledge of the transitory things of this world (and lest I should be provoked with its pleasures), through your abundant mercy you have taken me from it. But forasmuch as I have known many deceived in this art, who have not gone the right way, let it please you, O Lord my God, that by the knowledge which you have given me, I may bring my dear friends from error, so that when they shall perceive the truth, they may praise thy holy and glorious name, which is blessed for ever. Amen.

*

A GREEN HERMETIC TRADITION

Paracelsus, Goethe (and Romanticism), Rudolf Steiner (and others)

If there is a tradition of "Green Hermeticism," surely it begins, at least in the West, with Paracelsus and his followers. "Paracelsianism" is then picked up and transformed by Goethe (and other Romantics like Blake, Novalis, Coleridge, and Keats), who, already operating within the "dark, abstract night" of the new scientific paradigm, translate it into ordinary language and transform it into an alternative science and way of knowing and being. Their goal: a truly revolutionary alternative culture. Of course, they fail. By the middle of the nineteenth century, materialism has reached its apex (or nadir) and rules the day. With the turn of the twentieth century, however, and the spiritual—and occult—revival more or less associated with Spiritualism, H.P. Blavatsky, and the origins of the "New Age," Rudolf Steiner recovers the whole tradition—consciously reaching back to the Mystery Centers—in a new way for contemporary consciousness. He provides a method (called "spiritual science" or Anthroposophy) whereby any person can begin to realize the truths of the tradition for themselves in an appropriate way. Using this method himself, he unfolds a dynamic and wholly Hermetic cosmology. Applying the insights realized by his method to our present situation—his aim was always to heal and to serve the Earth and humanity—he lays the foundation for new "Green Hermetic" arts and sciences: biodynamic (alchemical) agriculture, anthroposophical (alchemical-Paracelsian) medicine, and much else. Steiner is not of course alone in this venture. Many others—like Fulcanelli, Edward Bach, Schwaller de Lubicz, Henri Coton Alvart, Alexander von Bernus, Manfred Julius—also brought the Hermetic tradition into the twentieth century, though not always (it must be said) with the explicit intention of healing humanity and the Earth. Gurdjieff, too, could be mentioned in this context; as could the Surrealists and certain postmodern philosophers. On a broader scale, but without the explicit connection to Hermeticism, the evolutionary and cosmological implications of the work of Teilhard de Chardin, Hazrat Inayat-Khan, Henry Corbin, Sri Aurobindo (and the Mother) also have great contributions to make to any future Green Hermetic synthesis. In all, it is a glorious company.

"The Luther of Medicine" "the German Hermes," Paracelsus (1493-1541)—also called "Elias Artista," the herald of the new Messianic age, because he knew all nature's secrets and prophesied a new age of peace and justice for all—marks the first "modern," "Green" approach to Hermeticism. Christened Philip Theophrastus Bombast von Hohenheim, he took other names (Aureolus, for instance) as his life unfolded and the situation warranted. "Paracelsus" itself does not appear as one these until 1536/37. Nevertheless, despite appearances, "Paracelsus" was humble by origin, nature and destiny. As he wrote:

> I cannot boast of any rhetoric or subtleties. I speak the language of my birth and country, for I am from Einsiedeln, of Swiss nationality and let no one find fault with me for my rough speech. My language must not be judged by my language, but by my art and experience, which I offer the whole world, and which I hope will be useful to the whole world.

His other defining characteristics are love and compassion ("the highest ground of medicine is love;" "Compassion is the true physician's teacher"), radical individualism ("Let no one belong to another who can belong to himself"), and reliance on experience—"experiences." Each moment, each country, each season, each plant, each patient is a new experience, each is different, and each must be experienced—united with—in its particularity. Paracelsus thus vaunts experience over all other authority and, on the basis of experience, espouses and promotes the interdependence of radical religious and intellectual freedom, freedom of the will, pacifism, and the unity of humanity and the Earth. Always on the side of the poor and the oppressed, all that he did was out of love for the suffering of creatures and the Earth, and the goal of all his work was to hasten the great redemption or healing.

His father, Wilhelm von Hohenheim, was the illegitimate son of a German Knight of the Order of St. John, whose illegitimacy made life difficult in his homeland. A gentle, pious learned man with a good working knowledge of botany, medicine, alchemy and theology, he settled in Einsiedeln, Switzerland, in the shadow of the Abbey housing the famous Black Virgin, Our Lady of the Dark Forest, still a place of pilgrimage today. He was his son's first teacher initiating him into the medicinal mysteries of the plant world. From the beginning, small and frail, Paracelsus found strength, companionship, and continual inspiration in the mountains, meadows, fields, and streams surrounding his birthplace. "From early childhood," too, he writes, the transmutation of metals occupied his mind.

When he was nine, the Swabian War broke out, his mother died (perhaps a suicide) and father and son left Einsiedeln for Villach in Carinthia (Austria). Here his father would teach in the mining school, owned by the celebrated Fuggers of Augsburg, the wealthiest merchants in the Empire, alchemical patrons, and the first modern bankers. Amid the mountains of Carinthia, which "are like a strong box which when opened with a key reveals great treasure," vast amounts of metals were mined and smelted— lead, iron, tin, copper, silver, gold, mercury, and others. Surrounded by smelters and laboratories, Paracelsus went to the local Benedictine schools, where he met and began to study with the first of many alchemists, Bishop Erhart, who worked for the Fuggers.

In 1507, at the age of fourteen, young Theophrastus (as he was known) left for university and the world. From then on, he would wander incessantly in search of experience. His teachers, as he says, included profound experts in "adepta Philosophia" and related arts, including the famous Johannes Trithemius of Sponheim. But he says he learned more down in the mines and from old country women. At the same time, he seems to have been very well read. He aimed at an encyclopedic understanding that he called "pansophia": all-wisdom. He was familiar with Hermeticism, Neo-Platonism, magic, and Kabbalah, as well as Sufism and Latin, in which he wrote his theological treatises. At once contemplative and a man of action, his aim was always on the truth.

He spent much time at many universities: Tübingen, Heidelberg, Mainz, Treves, Freiburg, and Cologne in Germany. But "at all the German universities," he concluded, "you cannot learn as much as you can at the Frankfurt fair." He sought knowledge and experience wherever he could find it:

Wherever I went I eagerly investigated and sought the tested and reliable arts of medicine. I went not only to doctors, but also to barbers, bath-keepers, learned physicians, women, and magicians who pursue the art of healing; I went to alchemists, to monasteries, to noble and common folk, to the experts and the simple.

From Germany, in pursuit of what was officially known as "medical education," he went first to Vienna in Austria, thence back to Wittenberg in Germany, thence to Ferrara in Italy, and Basel in Switzerland. But wherever he went, he found the curriculum based not upon experience but upon the ancients: above all, Aristotle, Galen, and Avicenna. Paracelsus rejected their approach as theoretical, fantastic, and false.

I found that the medicine, which I had learned, was faulty, and that those who had written about it neither knew nor understood it. They all tried to teach what they did not know. They are vainglorious babblers... and there is not more in them than in a worm-eaten coffin. So I had to look for a different approach.

In Basel, one St. John's Tide, after lecturing in German rather than Latin, he tossed the sacred texts of the Masters into the student bonfire—"so that all this misery should go up in the air in smoke."

Then he was off again on further wanderings. He seems to have covered thousands of miles. Britain, Ireland, Spain, North Africa, Sicily, Greece, Turkey, and Syria; Russia, Poland, Lithuania, Croatia, Slovenia, Denmark, Holland—even Jerusalem by way of Malta, and Rhodes: he was sighted in all of these. But his motive was clear. He felt authorized:

The arts are not all confined within one's fatherland, but they are distributed over the whole world. They are not in one person or in one place. Rather, they must be gathered together, sought out and captured, where they are...Art pursues no one, but must be pursued. Therefore I have the authority and reason to seek her, not she me. If one would go to God, one must go, but he says: "Come..." Since this is so, we must go after what we want.... The way for anyone who would see and experience something is that he go after the same and competently inquire, and when things go best, move on to further experiences.

He believed that nature was the best teacher and he continually searched her out, believing that experience is knowledge: that to know was to live the knowledge innate in nature—which one cannot do from books, but only from nature, which is experience:

What is nature? Experience. Experience comes from Almighty God; this and no other must be the origin of the physician. For we are not our own schoolmasters: the one who shows us the force of nature is the one who describes the ground for us.

Otherwise stated:

From experience the physician receives his help, and upon it rests his skill. He must have rich knowledge based on experience, for he is born blind, and book knowledge never made a single physician. For this purpose, he needs not human but divine things, and therefore he should not treat truth lightheartedly. He does not act for himself but for God and God bestows his grace upon him so that he may come to the assistance of his fellow human beings in their needs.

In other words:

Whoever would explore nature must tread her books with his feet. Holy Scripture is explored through its letters, but nature is explored from country to country... This is the code of nature and thus must her leaves be turned.

Wherever he went, as he went, books, tractates poured forth: Theology, astrology, alchemy, and medicine.

His philosophy was based on the correspondences, analogies, and affinities between the macrocosm and microcosm. "Everything is the product of one universal creative effort," he wrote. "The Macrocosm and the human being (the Microcosm) are one. They are one constellation, one influence, one breath, one harmony, one time, one metal, one fruit."

His method was imagination and intuition. Since the human being as microcosm unites the entire world, earthly, celestial, and divine, knowledge is not a matter of reason, but of uniting what is within with what is without.

This is not achieved by the brain, but by what he calls the astral body: "The astral body teaches man." Through this "star" body, we communicate with the astra, not so much the star, as the virtue or function essential to it and, by this means, the great works of nature are revealed. Paracelsus is a new kind of naturalist. He wants to explore how nature works from within nature herself, experienced as the visible reflection of the invisible work of God. The invisible virtues—Arcana, Magnalia—that he seeks to discover are thus direct emanations from God. As such, they are uncreated: original Light. They are supernatural. They are not from the stars. The stars only "cook" them. They are uncreated—divine—signs in creation. And "Who would not grasp the hub of nature whence these signs come?"

Our task is only to seek, to knock, and to find. Research into natural phenomena is a religious duty. It is outside and beyond specific religions.

> The Light of Nature is like crumbs from the table of the Lord for all to grasp and it behooves us not to give in but to pick up the crumbs as long as they fall.

Simplicity is the key here. Attend to imitate nature inwardly in her ways. Go everywhere. Travel with open eyes. This is the path of true self-knowledge, which comes from "the greater world," not from within: " The concordance that makes us whole, from which we derive knowledge of the world, hence of ourselves—these two are one thing, not two. I put this to the test of experience."

Precisely because we are one with God and his creation, we can collaborate with God in the healing of creation. Through the star in us we can bring that star's work into our healing. We can activate the correspondences, analogies, and affinities. Disease and remedy both come from the disharmony of these.

> The remedy should be prepared in the star and it should become a star. For the stars on high make sick and kill and also make whole and healthy.

You should not say: Melissa is a herb for the womb, marjoram a herb for the head—thus the ignorant talk. Their action lives in Venus and Luna; if you want it heaven must be propitious.

Time, likewise, derives from the stars and is qualitative. It is not conceivable outside actual processes taking place. Everything manifests its own time, has its own moment. Time is becoming: it is biological. Each being has its own time, its own life. There are thus many times; and healing must take account of them.

As for the elements, Paracelsus argued against them, yet used them. However, they were not fundamental. Fundamental for him were the three principles: *Sulphur, Mercury, and Salt*. The elements are only the matrices. They are not physical, but dynamic, qualitative. They are the mothers. But the fundamental principles—combustibility, vaporability, and fixability—determine what happens.

If wood is burnt: the flame, its Sulphur; the smoke, its Mercury; the ash, its Salt. Each object and each condition thus has its own Sulphur, Mercury, and Salt.

In addition, each thing has its own *Archeus*, or life—its own vector of specificity, of perfection. The Archeus is the individualizing principle in the matrix. What works in the Archeus, in the individualized life, Paracelsus calls Vulcan (Greek Hephaestus, Egyptian Ptah), who is the fire immanent in the matrices. Vulcan draws on the "prime matter," the Yliaster: the all-potential. The Yliaster, Unconditioned Life, is without individual life, which is what the Archeus gives it.

"The Archeus directs everything to its essential nature." It is thus a kind of spiritual DNA. As a principle, it resides in the stomach. It makes sure that whatever we eat becomes us. It is the principle of digestion: it turns bread into blood.

The Archeus acts by Imagination, which is a celestial state and a seminal force and has its source in the stars, the astral body—the star in us. Everywhere, acting through the Imagination, the Archeus leaves signs that we might read: in "the horns of a stag, the petals of the plant, the rings of the tree."

Confusing as all this sounds, some clarity appears when we learn that, for Paracelsus, medicine has four pillars: Philosophy, Astronomy, Alchemy, and Virtue.

In the first pillar, Philosophy, is knowledge of earth and water; the second pillar, Astronomy, together with Astrology, has a complete knowledge of the two elements air and fire; the third pillar, Alchemy, is knowledge of the experiment and preparation of the four elements mentioned; and the fourth pillar, Virtue, should remain with the physician until death, for this completes and preserves the other three pillars.

Paracelsus's worldview is thus, in the largest sense, holistic and ecological. It encompasses the Earth and the Heavens (and, as ground, the Divine) as a single, living, and evolving physical, psychic, spiritual—and, ultimately, divine—organism, whose "biology" is alchemical: the whole is God's crucible in the alchemical work of which humanity, as microcosm and "little god" is called to collaborate. What makes this and that on which all depends possible is the transformation of the co-worker, whose path is that of "virtue"— in one word, of love: that is, the selfless dedication to serve, to sacrifice, to heal. Only love in this sense makes experience, true knowledge, possible.

Goethe, the great opponent of Cartesian-Newtonian mechanico-materialism, did not come to his scientific views unaided. He was, as R. D. Gray showed in his *Goethe the Alchemist* "profoundly influenced throughout his life by the religious and philosophical beliefs he derived from his early study of alchemy." Goethe's science in essence was alchemical and Hermetic.

In his time, Goethe was not alone in his interests, though he alone by his genius made a science out of them. The study of alchemy was still widespread. Many people had alchemical laboratories. Alchemical language and philosophy, deriving from Paracelsus, Jacob Boehme, and Gottfried Arnold, had become part of the then dominant spiritual revival called Pietism. Indeed, it was a Pietist friend of his mother's, Katerina von Klettenburg, who introduced Goethe to alchemy when he was nineteen. He was deathly sick with a tumor in his neck, which could have been fatal.

As Goethe describes Katerina, she was an extraordinary woman: "a beautiful soul," that is to say, serene, graceful, patient, accepting of life's vicissitudes, intelligent, intuitive, imaginative, and above all a moral and religious genius. In their meeting, one genius discovered another. "She found in me," Goethe writes, "What she needed, a lively young creature, striving after an unknown happiness, who, although he could not think himself an extraordinary sinner, yet found himself in no comfortable condition, and was perfectly healthy neither in body nor in soul."

Katerina provided medical assistance in both body and soul. She found him a doctor, Dr. Metz, who prescribed, in addition to the conventional remedies of the time, some "mysterious medicines prepared by himself of which no one could speak, since physicians were strictly prohibited from making up their own prescriptions." These medicines included "certain powders" as well as a "powerful salt"—"a universal medicine." To encourage their efficaciousness, Dr. Metz further recommended "certain chemical-alchemical books to his patients…to excite and strengthen their faith," and to encourage them to attain the practice of making the medicines for themselves.

Thus, as Goethe convalesced he and Fraulein von Klettenberg began an intensive study of certain texts: above all, Paracelsus, Basil Valentine, Eirenaeus Philalethes (George Starkey), Georg von Welling's *Opus Mago-Cabbalisticum et Theosophicum*, Van Helmont, and the *Aurea Catena Homeri* (The Golden Chain of Homer).

At the same time, Goethe began laboratory work.

Goethe's alchemical work continued intensely for the next few years. He continued to study alchemical and Rosicrucian authors. Two years later, he still claimed "chemistry" was his "secret love." As he wrote to his mentor E.T. Langer: "I am trying surreptitiously to acquire some small literary knowledge of *the great books*, which the learned mob half marvels at, half ridicules, because it does not understand them; but whose secrets the wise man of sensitive feeling delights to fathom. Dear Langer, it is truly a great joy when one is young and has perceived the insufficiency of the greater part of learning, to come across such treasures. Oh, it is a long chain indeed from the *Emerald Tablet of Hermes Trismegistus…*" For a time, his alchemical studies occupied Goethe completely. In fact, until he met the cultural genius Herder and turned to more "acceptable" studies, they dominated him almost obsessively. As he writes, "My mystical-religious chemical pursuits led me into shadowy regions, and I was ignorant for the most part of what had been going on in the literary world at large for some years past."

It was these studies that determined Goethe's worldview and especially his science, which is alchemy translated. His "mystical-religious chemical pursuits" provided the ground for his phenomenological, participant, anti-materialist, living approach to nature and natural processes—an approach that differed fundamentally from ordinary, "value-free," quasi-objective science in that the *raison d'être* was clearly *to heal: to serve humanity.* Many alchemical texts, in fact, were explicitly "medical" in orientation. Unfolding an alternative science, they also provided a theoretical and practical model for an approach to medicine.

Goethe, although he lived in the age of Kant, claimed never to have thought about thinking. In his essay "The Influence of the New Philosophy," he wrote:

> As vegetation demonstrated its method to me step by step, I could not possibly go astray, and by letting vegetation tell its own story, I necessarily became acquainted with its ways and means of developing to completion the most obscure phenomena.
>
> In my study of physics, I gained the conviction that one's highest duty in observing phenomena is to trace accurately every condition under which a phenomenon makes its appearance.
>
> Kant's *Critique of Pure Reason* had long since appeared, but it lay completely beyond my orbit. Nevertheless, I was present at many a discussion of it, and with some attentiveness I could notice continually reappearing the old question: How much do we, and how much does the outside world, contribute to our intellectual existence? I myself had never separated the two, and when I did philosophize about subjects in my own way, I did so with unconscious naïveté, in the belief that I actually saw my views before my very eyes....

This is the Olympian Goethe, very crafty, and not at all naïve. It is not that he does not understand Kant, but that on most fundamental issues he stands opposed to him. Kant attributed all we know of nature to the forms of knowing of the human mind. But Goethe, following his Hermetic masters, considered everything, including the human mind and its forms of knowing, as aspects of nature. For Goethe human knowing was nature's knowing raised into self-consciousness of humanity. He was, as he said, "always unwilling to see the rights of nature infringed upon." He was her great defender. For him nothing was to be torn out of the interconnected totality. Art and beauty were not apart from nature, or in any way opposed to it, but rather a higher expression of nature. The same "laws" should operate in art as operate in nature, laws that are in their essence "divine." In 1811 he wrote:

> My mode of world conception—purely felt, deeply-seated, inborn and practiced daily as it were—had taught me inviolably to see *God in Nature, Nature in God,* and this to such an extent that this world view formed the basis of my entire existence.

The scientist was thus a priest and his laboratory, nature, was his altar and liturgy. And the study of nature was the way humanity could both raise nature into human consciousness and transform itself into a whole and healthy vehicle for the creative activity upon which both humanity and nature rest.

What was his method? He tells Eckermann:

> All our efforts should be in the direction of eavesdropping on the methods of Nature herself, so that we may prevent her from becoming obstinate over enforced prescriptions, and yet not be deterred from our purpose by her arbitrary behavior."

Elsewhere he speaks of restoring "to the intellect its old privilege of taking a direct view of nature" that, by the same stroke, will both restore to nature her own freedom and also free the intellect from the prison cell of logic. Goethe's thinking was "objectively active," never "divorced from objects," by which he means phenomena. At the same time, "subject" and "object" "interpenetrate." "What is seeing without thinking?" he asks, and, we may add: What is thinking without seeing? For, if observing is thinking, thinking is also a way of seeing.

Human and world were one for Goethe, who believed:

> We know ourselves only insofar as we know the world, becoming aware of it only within ourselves, and of ourselves only within it. Each new subject that is well observed opens up within us a new organ of thought.

"Make an organ of yourself," he said. Goethe is a phenomenologist and his path lies through the lived experience of phenomena. His method trains perception to see things as they are. He sought the principles whereby the multiplicity of nature could be experienced as a unity. We can see him working at this in his *Italian Journey*, when he asks himself: "How far will my scientific and general knowledge take me? Can I learn to look at things with clear, fresh eyes? How much can I take in at a single glance? Can the grooves of old mental habits be effaced? This is what I am trying to discover." A year later in Rome, we have evidence that the practice has born fruit. He writes: "My eye is becoming better trained than I would have believed possible."

He calls the principles he is seeking the *Ur Phenomena*, the Primal Phenomena: they are the irreducible functions or activities through which nature creates and through which humanity must understand. They are direct traces of Divinity and of one nature with consciousness or mind. Eckermann reports:

> We then spoke of the high significance of the primal phenomenon, behind which we believe the Deity may directly be discerned. "I ask not," said Goethe, "whether this highest Being has Reason and Understanding, but I feel He is Reason and Understanding itself. Therewith are all creatures penetrated; and man has so much of it that he can recognize parts of the Highest."

Paradoxes abound here, chief of which is that the Primitive Phenomenon is an "idea," which Goethe claims to be able to "see." The most famous evidence of this is the well-known exchange between Goethe and Schiller following a lecture on plants; the two agreed that the lecturer's way of observing nature was not to be admired and that another method must exist. Goethe described the exchange:

> The conversation lured me in. I gave a spirited explanation of my metamorphosis of plants with graphic pen sketches of a symbolic plant. He listened and looked with great interest, with unerring comprehension, but when I had ended he shook his head, saying, "That is not an empirical experience, it is an idea." I was taken aback and somewhat irritated, for the disparity in our viewpoints was here sharply delineated.... The old antipathy was astir. Controlling

myself, I replied, "How splendid that I have ideas without knowing
it, and can see them before my very eyes."

What did Goethe sketch? What did he see? As far as one can
gather, the Archetypal Plant is of the nature of a leaf principle, the
set of relations defining a leaf. *The Metamorphosis of Plants* shows that
every plant, from seed to seed, unfolds through seven varying
embodiments of leaf—into which process, polarity and ascension
enter. Yet Goethe went looking for the Archetypal Plant. He seeks
it throughout his Italian journey, apparently in the hope of finding
it. He calls it an *En kai Pan*, a one-in-all, a principle of unity in multiplicity.

> While walking in the Public Gardens of Palermo, it came to me in a
> flash that in the organ of the plant which we are accustomed to call
> the *leaf* lies the true Proteus who can hide or reveal himself in all
> vegetal forms. From first to last, the plant is nothing but leaf, which
> is so inseparable from the future germ that one cannot think of the
> one without the other.
>
> Anyone who has had the experience of being confronted by an
> idea, pregnant with possibilities ... will know that it creates a tumult
> and enthusiasm in the mind.

Since he can recognize when a flower is a flower, there must be a
principle of "flower-ness" by which he does so. Goethe seeks this
universal flower in phenomena.

The Archetypal Phenomenon is at once a thought and a perception, an idea and a sensation. It is a fusion of thought and nature,
concept and percept, in a timeless unity, to which the only appropriate human response is wonder. To try to look beyond the Archetypal Phenomenon, Goethe says, is childish. It is like trying to look
behind a mirror.

Here is a paradox. Goethe's method was aimed at living in the
present moment so as to fuse timeless and temporal in a single perception. Archetypal Phenomena seem to have been such eternal
percepts. Goethe was extremely sensitive, naturally, to the difficulty. It is not clear he ever overcame it. In a piece called "Reserva-
tions and Surrender," he writes that we feel God is operative in
nature, nature in God, *"from eternity to eternity."* Intuition, observation,

contemplation, he goes on, lead us closer to the mysteries; then, "we encounter a characteristic difficulty—one of which we are not always conscious—namely, that a definite chasm appears to be fixed between idea and experience." And he continues:

> Our efforts to bridge this chasm are forever in vain, but nevertheless we strive eternally to overcome this hiatus with reason, intellect, imagination, faith, emotion, or if we are capable of nothing better—with folly.
>
> By honest persistent effort we finally discover that the philosopher might probably be right who asserts that no idea can completely coincide with experience, nevertheless admitting that idea and experience are analogous, indeed must be so.
>
> In all scientific research the difficulty of uniting idea and experience appears to be a great obstacle, for an idea is independent of time and place, but research must be restricted within them. Therefore, in an idea, the simultaneous and the successive are intimately bound up together, whereas in an experience they are always separated. Our attempt to imagine an operation of nature as both successive and simultaneous, as we must in an idea, seems to drive us to the verge of insanity. The intellect cannot picture united what the senses present to it separately, and thus the duel between the perceived and the ideated remains forever unsolved.

Whether or not Goethe ever solved his quandary, it was the intention of his method to do so. That he did is indicated in that his method bore fruit—in his theory of plant metamorphosis, in his color theory, etc. We know that Goethe began his career with an intense and committed practical as well as speculative study of alchemy in deeply religious and pietistic circles. We know too that though he ceased his overt study of alchemy, he continued to employ alchemical principles and ideas. Therefore his science can be seen as "hermetic." At the same time, he looked upon himself as a spiritual pilgrim, whose life was to be a continual process of rebirth through renunciation, purification, and devotion. His aim, as he writes to Herder, was "the divesting of all personal will," the achieving of a timeless center, the realization of spiritual androgyny. Yet he says that idea and experience will never coincide in the center. Only art and action can effect a synthesis.

What was nature to Goethe? We have heard him speaking of it "scientifically" and philosophically, but something has been lacking—the other central aspect of Goethe, the "Eternal Feminine." The young Goethe wrote nature and love poems; the old Goethe ended his *Faust*, upon which he worked fifty years, among rocky mountain gorges, "at the holy shrine of love." The whole is an invocation to the "glow of love's pure empire ... immortal love's core." Love it is whose powers enfold the struggling inner life of human beings. Pure pilgrim souls rise, aided by love's powers, until they come to the Heavenly Queen. She sanctions "what in humans may move feelings tender and austere," which lifts them to her presence.

> Virgin, pure in heavenly sheen,
> Mother, enthroned above,
> Highest birth, our chosen Queen
> Godhead's peer eternal.

The souls rise toward her. She is invoked as "the visage of salvation." Through her gaze the pilgrims arise in "glad regeneration." Then the "mystical chorus" ends the play with its enigmatic coda:

> All things transitory
> But as symbols are sent
> Insufficiency
> Here becomes event.
> The inexpressible,
> Here it is seen,
> Here it is done;
> The Eternal Feminine
> Lures to perfection.

All this comes together in Rudolf Steiner. Explicitly Goethean and Paracelsian, alchemical and Hermetic, Steiner encapsulates and confirms, on the basis of his own experience and research, the reality of the "Green Hermetic" worldview, going back to the most ancient Mystery Centers.

His language, however, is his own, created on the one hand by his experience and on the other by the contexts—Western philosophical, Theosophical, Western occult, and Christian esoteric—which he represented and through which he taught. To unfold his theory of knowledge, his vast evolutionary spiritual cosmology, his profound spiritual anthropology and Christology, his spiritual understanding of the Earth and the Heavens, humanity and the gods, would be impossible here.

While nearly all that Steiner accomplished has value for anyone on a "Green Hermetic" (which is also to say, in this context) Rosicrucian path, some guidance is needed to find one's way through the six thousand lectures and forty plus books. The beginning is clear: Steiner begins as an epistemologist-philosopher and an interpreter of Goethe and the Western mystical tradition. The early works are thus an accessible, ordinary language introduction to the precincts of Hermeticism. Once he begins his work as a Theosophical (or Anthroposophical) teacher, however, it is harder to find one's way. The basic cosmology (*An Outline of Esoteric Science*) establishes the "big picture." The works dealing with spiritual beings and nature and elemental spirits in relation to humanity and the Earth then begin to fill it out. The works on science provide a counterpoint. Against this background—and the background of Green Hermeticism generally—the works dealing specifically with biodynamic agriculture and medicine begin to show what a "Green" Hermeticism would look like. Biodynamic agriculture, which arose in 1924, in the last year of Steiner's life, in a set of lectures given in response to the concerns of a group of farmers, gardeners, veterinarians, and others concerned with the new dangers threatening the fertility, vitality, and health of the Earth, clearly and practically demonstrates it.

Biodynamics, "the spiritual foundations for the renewal of agriculture," as Steiner conceived it, has two functions. On the one hand, it seeks to heal and enhance the vitality of the Earth, already dying, and now sickened and weakened by the now all-too-familiar onslaught of pollution, pesticides, etc.; on the other, it seeks to provide food, whose life forces are sufficiently enhanced to provide the nourishment and inner strength human beings require in order to maintain their spiritual orientation—so as to be able to aid the waning nature forces—in a technologically advanced world.

Consider the Biodynamic farm or vineyard. It is, first of all, viewed essentially as an extension of the garden: a place of nurture and caring, contemplation and meditation, whose scale is human. Second, it is created and treated as an "organism," a self-sustaining, ecological, complex whole. It is a living being, as the Earth herself is a living being. It is also both a "little cosmos," a microcosm of the solar system and the larger universe," participating in its cosmic Life; and, at the same time, unique and individual. In this view, each piece of land, each ecology—like every patient—is different and requires its own concrete approach. As a "cosmos," it is also, by definition, diversified, whatever its function is intended to be. Thus, every Biodynamic farm or garden organism contains plants (vegetables), crops, flowers, and animals. The animals, when not primary, provide manure for compost, as well as their "astral" presence. Compost, viewed as a kind of alchemical crucible, is, of course, of first importance: it is the most obvious approach to enhancing soil quality. But many other practices are equally important: planting and working by the moon, planets, and stars as they weave and cycle through the seasons; the rotation of crops; a deep understanding of the living contours and "spiritual sheaths" of the landscape, including its history and the memories inscribed with it; and to work with the elemental and nature spirits and the "etheric formative forces"—the alchemical elementing elements (fire, air, earth, and water) as formative "etheric" powers. But what perhaps best distinguishes Biodynamics from any other form of agriculture or horticulture is its use of alchemically produced homeopathic Preparations. There are nine of these, six of which are known collectively as the "compost preparations."

The first two are spray preparations, made in a cow horn. In one, cow manure is packed into a cow horn and buried during the winter months, while the cosmos works upon it. In the second, ground silica is placed in the horn and it is buried during the summer months.

The first of the compost preparations is a yarrow preparation: the blossoms are taken and sewed inside a stag's bladder, which is then hung in the summer sun and buried for the winter. The second uses chamomile blossoms, stuffed into a bovine intestine, and again buried for the winter months. In the third, stinging nettles are buried in moss for a winter and a summer. In the fourth, oak bark is stuffed into the skull (still containing the meninges) of a domestic animal and buried in swampy conditions for the winter. Next, the dandelion preparation takes blossoms, sews them into a sack made from a bovine mesentery or peritoneum membrane and buried for the winter. The last preparation involves the juice of a valerian plant, extracted and allowed to ferment. The ninth preparation is simply a horsetail tea.

All these preparations, except the last, are administered homeopathically: small amounts are mixed rhythmically with water in a complex series of clockwise and counterclockwise stirrings. The cosmic importance of rhythm, cyclical-helical movement, which is one of the alchemical mysteries, goes without saying.

However odd these preparations sound, one thing above all should be noted: they work. Green Hermeticism works! Many of the best, most prestigious vineyards, for instance, are now biodynamic, which is not surprising, since viticulture is one of the few forms of agriculture which depend on quality not quantity: in other words, you cannot make a better wine than the grape you start with will permit.

Suffice it to say, then, that anyone interested in Green Hermeticism should at least look at the works by Rudolf Steiner listed in the bibliography.

*

To human beings the stars once spoke
Whose growing muteness is world destiny.
Awareness of the silence can pain earthly humans.
But what human beings speak in the stars'
unspeaking can ripen for human spirits.
Becoming aware of it can become strength for them.
RUDOLF STEINER

*

DEW

By wisdom the Lord founded the earth;
by understanding, he established the heavens;
by knowledge the deeps broke forth,
and the clouds drop down dew.

PROVERBS 3:13-20

To renew herself and bring all the seeds in the earth's womb into
the movement of growth proper to vegetation, Nature impregnates
the air surrounding the Earth with a mobile, fermenting Spirit,
which comes from her Father. This Spirit is the subtle nitre that
assures the fecundity of the Earth, whose Soul it is, which the Cosmopolite calls the 'saltpetre of the Philosophers.'

LIMOJON DE ST. DIDIER

The cover image, taken from the celebrated *Mutus Liber* or "Mute
Book" (it has no words, only images), depicts alchemists gathering
dew, "the blossom of heaven" (*flos coeli*) in spring when cosmic conditions are most propitious for undertaking alchemical work.

Dew is clearly a special substance in our tradition. One interpretation of "F. R.C." or "Fraternity of the Rose Cross" is even *Fratres
Roris Coctis*, "Frères de la Rosée Cuite," —"Brothers of the Cooked
Dew." In the same spirit of Hermetic cabala, I.N.R.I (*Jesus Nazarenus
Rex Judorum*, Jesus of Nazareth King of the Jews) was been turned to
read *Ignis Nitrium Roris Invenitur:* "by fire the nitre and the dew are
found." Rudolf Steiner, for his part, after alluding to the rose-dew
connections, points out that dew in German is Tau, phonetically
the same as Tau Cross or Ankh, the Egyptian symbol of Life and
the Tao of Taoism that cannot be named.

Above all in springtime, in the couple of months following the
Equinox, the dews, celestial waters, descending from heaven (rather
than rising from the Earth as in Autumn)—as well as to a lesser
extent the fertile spring rains—were held to contain properties associated with the *Spiritus Mundi*, the Spirit of the World, that last echo
of the original Light. It was then that the air was believed to hold a
tincture of "the invisible substance of Life," shaped by the Sun and
Moon, which incarnates as the dews (rain) descends in the "nitre" as
"the salt of the dew," whence it must be extracted, a process known

as the "Labors of Hercules." As Chaucer famously puts it in the opening of the Canterbury Tales:

> When April with his showers sweet with fruit
> The drought of March has pierced unto the root
> And bathed each vein with liquor that has power
> To generate therein and sire the flower;
> When Zephyr also has with his sweet breath,
> Quickened again, in every field and heath,
> The tender shoots and buds, and the young sun
> Into the Ram one half his course has run,
> And many little birds make melody that sleep
> Through all the night with open eye
> (So Nature pricks them on to ramp and rage)-
> Then do folk long to go on pilgrimage...

There is an astonishing little text, written under the pseudonym "Cyliani" (or Silenus, the foster father, woodland deity, and companion of Dionysius) at the beginning of the nineteenth century, called *Hermes Unveiled.* Cyliani tells how for thirty-seven years, he strove to accomplish the Great Work, struggling year after year in vain, misfortune besetting him on every side. Then, one day, walking in the country, he sat himself down to ponder his fate beside a stout oak tree. Falling asleep, he began to dream a dream in which the tree suddenly cracked open and "a nymph, an image of beauty," emerged from it. Her clothes were so light-filled they seemed transparent. Introducing herself she said:

> My essence is celestial—you could even consider me an efflux of the Pole Star. My power is such that I animate all things. I am the astral spirit. I give life to all that breathes and grows. I know all.

After opening with a cosmological prologue, the nymph turns to the "labors of Hercules" to be undertaken by any alchemical pilgrim. She enjoins Cyliani to "think of the dew of May, how she becomes indispensable as a vehicle and the principle of all things." Then, after various processes (or labors) have been described, she gives a kind of summation:

Consider well Nature's toils. Within the bowels of the earth she has formed the metals, but something more is necessary—their quintessence. See where she draws the quintessence from out of things. But this is only at the surface of the earth, within those realms that live or grow; thus follow Nature little by little. Consider also how she operates in the vegetable realm, for it is not at all a mineral that you wish to create. See her moistening with dew or rain the seed entrusted to the earth, drying it with the help of the celestial fire, and reiterating thusly until the embryo is formed, developed, budded, and flowered, and has attained its multiplicative virtue, and finally to the maturity of its fruit. It is very simple! Dissolve and coagulate, that is all, and take care that you attend to the fire other than that of the heavens.

Thus, step-by-step, the salt of the "dew" must be concentrated (and extracted).

An enigmatic, somewhat hard-to-follow text by De Saulx, a doctor from Versailles, dated 1727, and entitled "New Discoveries concerning Health and Illnesses," gives another approach:

At the spring equinox, gather dew with a linen cloth that you must squeeze when it becomes wet until you have half a bucketful; then fill the remainder of the bucket with rainwater. Filter this water first through clay, then a second time immediately through very coarse paper. Place this water in well-sealed flasks for the month of May.

For the month of May, you must have a concave, conical glass vessel, ending in a point at the bottom, with a saucer of the same glass capable of holding as much as the vessel.

May being over, the next morning, take your vessel and expose it at your window for a half-hour before the sun rises; and with great astonishment and satisfaction you will witness a marvelous effect: your vessel will be refilled with a red, highly odorous liqueur. The vessel can overflow into the saucer; but take care to withdraw your liqueur before the sunrise, which will remove it faster than it gave it. The Philosophers calls this liqueur "the soul of the world," which forms minerals, vegetables, and animals. This is the liqueur that one use in alchemical operations, for with it one must fill two thirds of the capacity of the Philosophical Egg before putting it into the oven.

Contradicting De Saulx, other authors speak of exposing one's dew to evaporation in the sunlight until the very last moment when all that is left in one's vessel is a tiny drop of gelatinous substance, which, if one doesn't catch it, will disappear. This gelatinous, greeny substance, sometimes called "nostoc," may sometimes be seen appearing suddenly (and just as suddenly disappearing) in the garden as the sun begins to burn the dew away...

*

V.I.T.R.I.O.L

VISITA INTERIORA TERRAE RECTIFICANDO INVENIES OCCULTUM LAPIDEM

(Visit the Interior of the Earth and Rectifying You will Find the Hidden Stone)

*

Musaeum Hermeticum, Frankfurt edition, 1749

SOURCES

Goethe's "Nature" may be found in *Goethe's Scientific Studies* (ed. Miller); on the web at www.nature.com/nature/about/first/aphorisms.html; in German in *Goethe Anschauendes Denken* (Frankfurt: Insel Verlag, 1981). Multiple version of The Emerald Tablet may be found on the Alchemy Website, www.levity.com/alchemy, which also contains an early English version of Hortulanus' Commentary, for which see also: *La Table d'Émeraude de Hermés Trisimègiste, suivie d'une explication par Hortulain* (Paris: La Table d'Émeraude, n.d). Versions of "The Dialogue of Kleopatra and the Philosophers" may be found in Jack Lindsay, *The Origins of Alchemy in Greco-Roman Egypt* and *The Alchemy Reader* (Linden), also in the Journal *Ambix*. Novalis' "Monologue" may be found in Margaret Stoljar, *Novalis Philosophical Writings* (Albany: SUNY Press, 1997) "Phos in the Garden" may be found in *Zosimos of Panopolis on the Letter Omega* (ed. and trans. Howard M. Jackson) (Missoula: SBL, 1978) "The Phoenix" (in French) may be found in Claude d'Ygé, *Anthologie de la Poésie Hermétique*, Paris: Dervy, 1976. "The Work Consists only in itself" in Stavenhagen, Lee (ed), *A Testament of Alchemy, Being the Revelations of Morienus to Khalid ibn Yazid* (Hanover: University Press of New England, 1974) "The Visions of Zozimos" in Richard Grossinger (ed) *Io* "Alchemy Issue" (Cape Elizabeth: 1973)

from Plate 8 of the MUTUS LIBER, [Altus], 1677

5

The Manufacturing and Use of Planetary Tinctures

KEVIN TOWNLEY

THE WHOLE CONCEPT of the planetary tincture comes to us from the related teachings and spagyric practices of Paracelsus (1493-1541). Over the past five hundred years there have been many schools and students dedicated to his teachings. Perhaps the most interesting and useful application of his teachings used today are those related to his work in spagyrics, a unique method of preparation of plant medicines. Paracelsus had many other preparations from the vegetable and metallic kingdoms; however our focus here will be on the plant kingdom.

WHAT IS SPAGYRICS?

The term "spagyrics" was coined by our brother Paracelsus. The term indicates the process of separating and recombining the three principles, in our case, of a plant. After separating the three principles from all foreign matter, we proceed to purify them. Following the purification process the three principles are recombined in one vessel thus completing a preparation of a spiritual medicine. This type of product is called a spagyric preparation.

THE THREE PRINCIPLES

A principal is something that is irreducible and therefore a primary existent. In the spagyric practice a principle is a component of a living conscious existent. In alchemy and spagyrics all things that exist are considered to have some type of manifested life and consciousness no matter how latent that life or consciousness may appear to the observer. Life and consciousness are two of the principles worked upon in the spagyric process. Life and consciousness are contained within a form and the form constitutes the third principle, the body.

In alchemy or in our case spagyrics the three principles are called mercury, sulfur and salt. The mercury deals with some aspect of life, the sulfur with the principle of consciousness, and the salt with the form or vessel that contains the life and consciousness.

In the plant kingdom the three principles can be found accordingly: the spirit is contained in the alcohol, the consciousness aspect in the essential oils, and the salt, which makes up the inorganic compounds and some subtle organic salts, constitutes the body of the plant.

None of these principles are readily visible to the observer while the plant is connected to the earth. However, through the spagyric art, they can be separated through the process of fermentation and/or extraction, followed by the incineration of the plant matter. After extraction and separation from the rest of the matter, the three principles can be purified and then reunited, thus creating a true spagyric product.

In the plant kingdom we have several different types of preparations. Our main focus here is upon the planetary elixirs. However there is a list given here for the student of the healing arts to investigate. Some of the other types of products produced from the plant kingdom are: infusions, fomentations, decoctions, tinctures, elixirs, and plant stones.

The infusion is basically a cup of tea while the decoction is generally the boiling down of a plant product to make a syrup or tonic. The fomentation is used externally as a poultice, while the tincture is usually an alcohol extraction. The plant stone is a very difficult process, which is produced from the purified three principles. In that case, the process is taken in another direction than that of the elixir. Our attention will now be upon the planetary elixir.

THE ELIXIR

The elixir is one of the first major evolutions in the preparation of a plant medicine. It is made through the spagyric process, separating, purifying, and recombining the three principles of the plant. When this process is complete the operator has made an elixir according to the spagyric definition.

There are a couple of methods available to the practitioner in the making of an elixir. The most simple of these processes is the extraction of the plant spirit and sulfur through the maceration of the plant in alcohol. The alcohol used should be close to absolute or 95-97 percent pure. The traditionally preferred type of alcohol is grape alcohol. Many practitioners today use grain or sugar alcohol. The traditional remedies, however, call for a grape alcohol. Once the extraction is complete, the liquor is decanted from the plant matter and the plant matter is incinerated.

The process of incineration destroys most of the organic matter and leaves the inorganic matter behind. The desirable matter for the spagyrist to recover is the plant salts.

Following the incineration process the ash is placed in a vessel containing recently boiled water where the salt compounds are dissolved. Following a period of about an hour of maceration of the ash in hot water, the liquid is strained, removing any large particles and then filtered separating the salts from the ash. This process leaves a tincted liquid that usually has an amber or golden color. The water is then allowed to evaporate causing the crystallization process to begin. After several cycles of crystallization, dissolving, filtering and re-crystallization the salts will become larger and more translucent. When the salts are satisfactorily pure they are added to the liquor for the purification of the sulfurs.

During the process of the alcohol extraction of the oils and spirit, the operator finds that the tincture is usually a dark green, largely due to the high content of chlorophyll. Sometimes the tincture is of a different color, depending on the plant; however there is usually a heavy somewhat opaque color that needs to be purified if the tincture is to become an elixir.

The method of purifying the essential oils or sulfurs is through the medium of the salt. After the purification of the salt, the salt is added to the liquor and left to stand for one philosophical month, which is a period of 40 days. The liquid containing the salt is occasionally shaken during this period. Following the cohabitation period the salt is found to absorb much of the heavy green oils. The liquor is slowly decanted from the salts separating the salts from the liquor. After the salt is separated from the liquor, it is then placed in a vessel to be calcined, burning away the non-essential oils from the salts. This process is repeated until the dark green oils have been removed from the tincture leaving a translucent or clear liquid. Once this process is completed the tincture becomes an elixir.

THE PLANETARY ELIXIR

The planetary elixirs are a very highly developed plant medicine. The application of these medicines is employed for the benefit of the entire being as intimated by the purification of the three principles of the spirit, soul and body. The planetary elixir is unique relative to other preparations. The premise behind the use of the planetary elixir is based upon the doctrine that every plant is ruled by a particular planet. The planets referred to here are the seven planets known to the ancients, as represented on the Tree of Life. These planets are, Saturn, Jupiter, Mars, the Sun, Venus, Mercury and the Moon.

Although there are ten spheres on the Tree of Life, it is the lower spheres that bear the planetary signatures that relate to the planetary ruler of each plant. The lowest sphere is related to the earth and therefore does not fit into the planetary signatures used in the practice of planetary elixirs. The counting is from the second to the last sphere to the upper left sphere, which is attributed to Saturn.

THE TREE OF LIFE

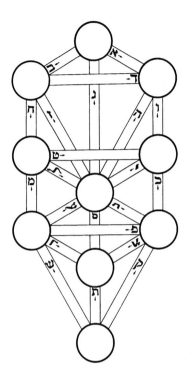

    The Tree of Life is a pictorial glyph that consists of ten spheres that are arranged in a particular geometrical pattern representing the decent of divine energies manifested as life, consciousness, and form. These energies and forces represent the descent and ascent of a Divine influence and flame. The Divine influence descends as water from the most abstract ontological planes all the way down to the most concrete or physical plane of existence. The Divine flame ascends from a condition of total involvement of spirit in matter, with all the gains of experience. The flame ascends back to its source via the same spheres and paths used in the process of descent, only in a reversed manner.

    The ten spheres represent the graded stages of the involutionary descent and evolutionary ascent of the creative powers until completing the involutionary and evolutionary cycle during a particular period of activity.

With the attributions of planet to plant we can now look further into the philosophy relative to the use of the planetary elixir. Since each plant is ruled by one of the seven sacred planets, and spheres on the Tree of Life, we can further say that the particular plant holds and expresses some aspect of that planet within its intrinsic nature. We can experience the relationship of the planet and plant in the fragrance, color, and healing properties of the plant. We find in the study of astro-biology that certain parts of the human body are likewise attributed either to a sign of the zodiac or a planet. Thus we find that certain organs of the human body have a relationship to the seven planets. The medicinal quality of a plant that is ruled by the same planet as a particular organ in the human body tends to be a strong remedy for that part of the body.

Since there are different ontological planes of existence and bodies of the human constitution we find that the planetary elixir acts as a medium of expressing planetary consciousness to the various parts of the human constitution, be it physical, astral/etheric, or mental/manasic.

The three principles of life, consciousness, and form, operate as corollaries for the three lower ontological planes mentioned above. Since the plants transmit the qualities of planets it follows that the proper preparation of the spagyric products, properly taken with right motive and right timing, can cause the individual participating in the use of planetary elixirs to:

a. assist in healing the physical body

b. assist in vitalizing the contact between the physical body and the astral/etheric body

c. assist in removing the veil of illusion that exists between the lower mental and higher mental planes thus establishing a greater contact between personality and soul and eventually spirit.

With the basic premise being laid for the use of the planetary elixirs we can bring our attention to the actual use of the elixir as it relates to the sphere on the Tree of Life.

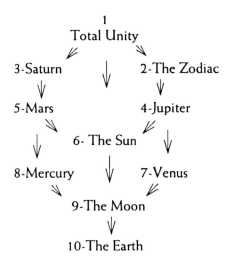

1
Total Unity

3-Saturn   2-The Zodiac

5-Mars   4-Jupiter

6- The Sun

8-Mercury   7-Venus

9-The Moon

10-The Earth

THE PRACTICE

The actual practice and use of the planetary elixirs is very specific. Although the practitioner is at liberty to use them in any manner he or she wishes it is best to begin with the traditional approach and develop one's creative approach as experience is gained. In order to maintain an accurate record of the preparation, from harvesting through completion of the product, and the actual use of the elixir, it is advised that the student use a lab notebook or journal. It is also advised to keep within this journal, as best you can, a record of the dreams experienced during a period of practice.

After the seven planetary elixirs are made, then comes the time of practice. Each day of the week is attributed to a planet: Monday-Moon day, Tuesday-Mars day, Wednesday-Mercury day, Thursday-Jupiter day, Friday-Venus day, Saturday-Saturn day and Sunday-the day of the Sun.

When taking the planetary elixirs one should attune oneself with the elixir attributed to the planetary day of the week. When taking the elixir on the proper planetary day of the week one is aligning oneself with the consciousness of the planet contained within the elixir and the vibratory energies of the planet as it expresses itself during that particular planetary day.

There are several approaches to the practice of planetary elixirs; however I will give only one here. It is recommended that a particular period of the day, preferably upon rising in the morning, be dedicated to this practice. The student goes through a process of alignment with the soul, as best as one knows how. It is often the case that anyone who would take on this work will already have a developed spiritual practice. It is also helpful to have an image of the Tree of Life and focus on the Planetary Sphere which is attributed to the planetary day. There are other useful symbols that can be used in order to assist in activating one's consciousness.

The daily routine of focusing on a planetary sphere of the Tree of Life, the ingesting of a dropper full of elixir and meditating on the planet of the day must be attended to for a prolonged period of time, preferably a year. Everything about this practice is a method of attunement. From the harvesting of the plant, to the preparation of the elixir, to the actual process of ingestion and meditation, all is designed to instill upon the consciousness of the practitioner a sense of the interdependent nature of reality within the context of our solar system and thus within the life of the One within which we live and move and have our being.

HOW TO OBTAIN A SPAGYRIC ELIXIR

It is often the case, in the busy modern western world, that we find it difficult to participate in the practice outlined here because of our inability to manufacture our own elixirs. The problem usually stems from lack of time or the proper space to make the products. For the most part there have been little to no planetary elixir products available for those who, given their situation, are unable to produce their own. Recently at the *Abode of the Message*, through *Suluk Academy*, a group of dedicated students/practitioners has been preparing these products for those who might otherwise be excluded from participating in these practices. I earnestly suggest that those who lack the time to prepare their own products investigate what is available through this group.

It is my sincere hope that this little effort here may support and inspire those who wish to participate in this Green Hermetic Practice.

Bibliography

The field of alchemy and Hermeticism is vast. Each seeker must make his or her own way among the texts. Some are essential, some peripheral, and some are even fraudulent. Laying down a path is part of the process. The titles listed here are only a beginning. Start with whatever you are drawn to, and follow your heart. (Christopher Bamford)

CORPUS HERMETICUM:

Ed. Brian P. Copenhaver, *Hermetica* (Cambridge: Cambridge University Press, 1992)

Ed. Walter Scott, *Hermetica* (Four Volumes) (Boston: Shambhala, 1985)

Ed. Mead, G.R.S., *Thrice-Great Hermes* (Three Volumes) (London: John. M. Watkins, 1964)

Albertus Frater, *The Alchemist of the Rocky Mountains* (Salt Lake City: Paracelsus Research Society, 1976)

Albertus, Frater, *Alchemist's Handbook* (York Beach: Weiser, 1989)

Allen. Paul M. (ed), *A Christian Rosenkreutz Anthology* (Blauvelt: Rudolf Steiner Publications, 1968)

Atwood, M.A., *Hermetic Philosophy and Alchemy: A Suggestive Inquiry into the Hermetic Mystery* (New York: Julian Press, 1960)

Barbault, Armand, *Gold of a Thousand Mornings* (London: Neville Spearman, 1975)

Boehme, Jacob, *The Signature of All Things* (Cambridge: James Clarke, 1969)

Bortoft, Henri, *The Wholeness of Nature: Goethe's Way Toward a Science of Conscious Participation in Nature* (Hudson, NY: Lindisfarne Books, 1996)

Burckhart, Titus, *Alchemy* (Louisville: Fons Vitae, 1997)

Cattiaux, Louis, *The Message Rediscovered* (Barcelona: Beya Editions, 2005)

Cockren, Archibald, *Alchemy Rediscovered and Restored* (Mokelumne Hill: Health Research, 1963

Corbin, Henry, *Spiritual Body and Celestial Earth* (Princeton: Princeton University Press, 1977)

Cotnoir, Brian, *Alchemy: The Weiser Concise Guide* (San Francisco: Weiser, 2006)

Coton-Alvart, Henry, *Les Deux Lumières* (Paris: Dervy, 1996)

Coudert, Alison, *Alchemy: The Philosopher's Stone* (Boulder: Shambhala, 1980)

Culpepper, Nicholas, *Culpepper's Complete Herbal* (New York, etc: W. Foulsham, n.d.)

Cyliani, *Hermes Unveiled* (Sequim: Holmes Publishing, 2005)

Eberly, John, *Al-Kimia: The Mystical Islamic Essence of the Sacred Art of Alchemy* (Hillsdale, NY: Sophia Perennis, 2004)

Evola, Julius, *The Hermetic Tradition* (Rochester: Inner Traditions, 1995)

Faivre, Antoine, *The Eternal Hermes* (Grand Rapids: Phanes Press. 1995)

Flamel, Nicholas (ed. Laurinda Dixon), *His Exposition of the Hieroglyphical Figures* (Garland: New York, 1994)

Fowden, Garth, *The Egyptian Hermes* (Cambridge: Cambridge University Press, 1986)

Fulcanelli, *The Dwellings of the Philosophers* (Boulder: Archive Press, 1999)

Fulcanelli, *The Mystery of the Cathedrals* (London: Neville Spearman, 1971)

(Godwin, Joscelyn, tr.), *The Chemical Wedding of Christian Rosenkreutz* (Grand Rapids: Phanes, 1991)

Goethe, Johann Wolfgang (ed. Miller, D.), *Goethe: Scientific Studies* (Princeton: Princeton University Press, 1995)

Goethe, Johann Wolfgang (ed. Mueller, B.) *Goethe's Botanical Writings* (Honolulu: University of Hawaii Press, 1952)

Helmond, Johannes, *Alchemy Unveiled* (Salt Lake City: Merkur Publishing, 1991)

Jung, C.J. *Alchemical Studies* (Princeton: Bollingen 1967)

Jung, C. J., *Psychology and Alchemy* (Princeton: Bollingen, 1968)

Junius, Manfred, *The Practical Book of Plant Alchemy* (Rochester: Healing Arts Press, 1993)

Kevran, Louis J., *Biological Transmutations* (Binghamton: Swan House, 1972)

Kingsley, Peter, *Ancient Philosophy, Mystery, and Magic: Empedocles and the Pythagorean Tradition* (Oxford: Clarendon Press, 1995)

Kingsley, Peter, *In the Dark Places of Wisdom* (Inverness, CA: Golden Sufi Center, 1999)

Klossowski de Rola, Stanislas, *The Golden Game: Alchemical Engravings of the Seventeenth Century* (New York: George Braziller, 1988)

Klossowski de Rola, Stanislas, *The Secret Art of Alchemy* (London: Thames and Hudson, 1973)

La Croix-Haute, Henri, *Propos sur "Les deux Lumières" suivis de Fragments de Hermetisme* (Grenoble: Mercure Dauphinoise, 2001)

Lapidus, *In Pursuit of Gold: Alchemy Today in Theory and Practice* (New York: Weiser, 1976)

Lehrs, Ernst, *Man or Matter* (London: Rudolf Steiner Press, 1985)

Linden, Stanley. J., *The Alchemy Reader* (Cambridge: Cambridge University Press, 2003)

Lindsay, Jack, *The Origins of Alchemy in Greco-Roman Egypt* (London: Frederick Muller, 1970)

Lory, Pierre, *Alchimie et mystique en terre d'Islam* (Paris: Verdier, 1989)

Lory, Pierre (ed), *Dix Traités d'alchimie de Jabir ibn Hayyan* (Paris: Sindbad, 1983)

Maier, Michael (trans. Joscelyn Godwin), *Atalanta Fugiens* (Grand Rapids, MI: Phanes Press, 1989)

Newman, William, *The Gehennical Fire: The Lives of George Starkey, an American Alchemist in the Scientific Revolution* (Harvard: Harvard University Press, 1994)

Novalis, *The Novices at Sais* (New York: Archipelago, 2005)

Pagel, Walter, *Joan Baptista Van Helmont: Reformer of Science and Medicine* (Cambridge: Cambridge University Press, 1982)

Pagel, Walter, *Paracelsus: An Introduction to Philosophical Medicine in the Era of the Renaissance.* (S. Karger: Basel and New York, 1958)

Paracelsus: *Essential Readings* (Berkeley: North Atlantic Books, 2003)

Paracelsus, *Four Treatises* (Baltimore: Johns Hopkins University Press, 1996)

Paracelsus (ed A.E. Waite) *The Hermetic and Alchemical Writings of Paracelsus* (Berkeley: Shambhala, 1976)

Patai, Raphael, *The Jewish Alchemists* (Princeton: Princeton University Press, 1994)

Pelikan, Wilhelm, *The Secrets of Metals* (Great Barrington: SteinerBooks, 2006)

Pernety, Antoine Jospeh, *The Great Art* (York Beach: Weiser, 2000)

Philalethes, Eireneius, *Alchemical Works* (Boulder: Cinnabar, 1994)

Redgrove, H. Stanley, *Alchemy, Ancient and Modern* (East Ardsley: E.P. Publishing, 1973)

Schwaller de Lubicz, R.A., *Esoterism and Symbol* (Rochester, Vermont: Inner Traditions, 1985)

Schwaller de Lubicz, R.A., *Sacred Science* (Rochester, Vermont: Inner Traditions, 1982)

Schwaller de Lubicz, R.A., *The Egyptian Miracle* (Rochester, Vermont: Inner Traditions, 1985)

Schwaller de Lubicz, R.A., *Nature Word* (Rochester, Vermont: Inner Traditions, 1982)

Stavenhagen, Lee (ed), *A Testament of Alchemy, Being the Revelations of Morienus to Khalid ibn Yazid* (Hanover: University Press of New England, 1974)

Szydlo Zbigniew, *Water Which Does Not Wet Hands: The Alchemy of Michael Sendivogius* (Warsaw: Polish Academy of Sciences, 1994)

Steiner, Rudolf, *Alchemy: Selections* (London: Sophia Books, 2001)

Steiner, Rudolf, *The Cycle of the Year as the Breathing Process of the Earth* (Hudson, NY: Anthroposophic Press, 1984)

Steiner, Rudolf, *Harmony of the Creative Word: The Human Being and the Elemental, Animal, Plant, and Mineral Kingdoms* (London: Rudolf Steiner Press, 2001)

Steiner, Rudolf, *Introducing Anthroposophical Medicine* (Hudson, NY: Anthroposophic Press, 1999)

Steiner, Rudolf, *Nature's Open Secret: Introductions to Goethe's Scientific Writings* (Hudson NY: Anthroposophic Press, 1999)

Steiner, Rudolf, *An Outline of Esoteric Science* (Hudson: Anthroposophic Press, 1997)

Steiner, Rudolf, *Spiritual Foundations for the Renewal of Agriculture* [Agriculture Course] (Kimberton: Biodynamic Association, 1993)

Steiner, Rudolf (ed. Hugh Courtney), *What is Biodynamics?* (Great Barrington: SteinerBooks, 2005)

Steiner, Rudolf, *Spiritual Beings in the Heavenly Bodies and the Kingdoms of Nature* (Hudson: Anthroposophic Press, 1992)

Trinick, John, *The Fire-Tried Stone* (Stuart and Watkins: London, 1967)

Valentinus, Basil, *The Triumphal Chariot of Alchemy* (London: Vincent Stuart, 1962)

Von Franz, Marie Louise (ed), *Aurora Consurgens: A Document Attributed to Thomas Aquinas on the Problem of the Opposites in Alchemy* (New York: Pantheon/Bollingen, 1966)

Waite, A.E. (ed), *The Hermetic Museum* (London: Watkins, 1973)

Waite, A.E. (ed), *The Turba Philosophorum* (London: Stuart and Watkins, 1970)

Yates, Frances, *Giordano Bruno and the Hermetic Tradition* (Chicago: University of Chicago Press, 1993)

SEE ALSO (ANYTHING BY):

Jacob Boehme
Nicolas Flamel
Basil Valentine
Bernard Trevisanus
Limojin de St. Didier
Henri Coton-Alvart
Eugene Canseliet

About the authors

PIR ZIA INAYAT-KHAN is the spiritual leader of the Sufi Order International, a mystical and ecumenical fellowship rooted in the visionary legacy of his grandfather, Hazrat Pir-o-Murshid Inayat-Khan. Pir Zia is also the President of the Suluk Academy and Executive Editor of Elixir magazine. Pir Zia holds a Doctoral degree in Religion from Duke University and is a recipient of the U Thant Peace Award. He has had a longstanding interest in Hermeticism and "Romantic science."

PETER LAMBORN WILSON is a poet-scholar of Sufism and Western Hermeticism and a well-known radical-anarchist social thinker. He is the author, among others, of *Sacred Drift: Essays on the Margins of Islam* and *Escape from the Nineteenth Century*.

CHRISTOPHER BAMFORD, editor of SteinerBooks and Lindisfarne Books, is a writer and scholar of Western esotericism, esoteric Christianity, and Anthroposophy. He is the author of, most recently, *An Endless Trace: The Passionate Pursuit of Wisdom in the West*.

KEVIN TOWNLEY is an esotericist and practicing alchemist and spagyrist (and former President of the Philosophers of Nature). He is the author of *The Cube of Space*.

"Let Nature be thy guide..."
ATLANTA FUGIENS, M. Maier, Oppenheim, 1618

Printed in the United States
77501LV00003B/193-210